M000279374

"Writing a theology of ministry is far more difficult than it seems, for it must bring worlds together that remain stubbornly separate . . . The task is made all the more difficult because of the subject matter itself, which is as peculiar as the gospel. This is the point Webster makes so thoroughly and insightfully. As a pastor, preacher, and theologian, he has done the work to write this book. It is his masterpiece. It will set the standard for how we understand ministry as learning to live in biblical tensions."

—Gerald L. Sittser,
Professor of Theology, Whitworth University

"Now, after a long immersion in pastoral ministry, supplemented with reflective periods of teaching, Webster has mined for us a rich vein of pastoral theology . . . The theme of tension in ministry is the note we need sounded in this 'add water and stir' culture. The layers of resources in these pages will open the reader to a whole world, the depth of which is exactly what the church today desperately needs."

—Jim Singleton,
Associate Professor of Pastoral Leadership and Evangelism, Gordon-Conwell
Theological Seminary

Living in Tension—A Theology of Ministry

Living in Tension
A Theology of Ministry

—VOLUME 2—

The Practice of Ministry:
Faithfulness to the End

DOUGLAS D. WEBSTER

CASCADE *Books* · Eugene, Oregon

LIVING IN TENSION
A Theology of Ministry

Copyright © 2012 Douglas D. Webster. All rights reserved. Except for brief quotations in critical publications or reviews, no part of this book may be reproduced in any manner without prior written permission from the publisher. Write: Permissions, Wipf and Stock Publishers, 199 W. 8th Ave., Suite 3, Eugene, OR 97401.

Cascade Books
An Imprint of Wipf and Stock Publishers
199 W. 8th Ave., Suite 3
Eugene, OR 97401

www.wipfandstock.com

ISBN 13: 978-1-63032-150-8

Cataloging-in-Publication data:

Webster, Douglas D.

Living in tension — a theology of ministry : the practice of ministry / Douglas D. Webster.

x + 226 p. ; 23 cm. — Includes bibliographical references.

Living in Tension, Volume 2

ISBN 13: 978-1-63032-150-8

1. Pastoral Theology. 2. Clergy—Office. 3. Laity—Reformed Church. I. Title.

BV4011 .W33 2012

Manufactured in the U.S.A.

For my Beeson Students

Contents

Introduction

Originality signifies a return to origins.[1]

LIVING IN TENSION FOLLOWS the prophet Jeremiah's prescription, "Stand at the crossroads and look; ask for the ancient paths, ask where the good way is, and walk in it."[2] The Bible is our primary source for shaping the message and method of our ministry. We are looking for "the truth that is in Jesus" to inspire and shape the meaning of discipleship and the mission of the church.[3] For many of us it takes a long time to begin to feel proficient in the whole counsel of God. After twenty years of pastoral ministry, I feel called to take what I have learned and work out a theology of ministry that applies to pastor and congregation alike. In volume one, we explore four important themes: the priesthood of all believers, the call of God, personal spiritual formation, and leadership.

To pursue the ancient paths generates plenty of tension. We run up against deeply ingrained habits that make practicing the Jesus Way difficult. These negative tensions obscure the truth of the priesthood of all believers and the call of God. The notion persists that some believers are more called than others. The church has been slow to grasp the common New Testament truth that all believers are called to salvation, service, sacrifice and simplicity. Religious habits and outside pressures have blinded us to some obvious truths that the early church accepted as foundational. In this work, we seek to recover these truths by engaging in a personal and practical study of God's Word. In volume two we examine the public impact of the priestly ministry in and through the body of Christ. Faith in Christ seeks a deeper understanding of how to interface with culture,

1. Steiner, *Errata: An Examined Life*, 32.
2. Jer 6:16.
3. Eph 4:21.

embrace the truth, preach the Word, and submit to one another in humility and grace. Instead of promoting cheap grace, we want to practice costly disciple-making. We seek to be resilient saints, living out our own passion narrative for Christ and his kingdom.

Negative tensions are the result of disobedience, ignorance, and resistance to the will of God. Positive tensions arise from obedience, biblical integrity, faithfulness to the will of God, and authentic discipleship. It is impossible for those who take up their cross daily and follow Jesus to live tension-free lives. A church that ignores negative tensions and avoids positive tensions is a church that may be either slowly dying or stunningly popular. Numbers prove very little. What counts is faithfulness to the Word of God. Healthy churches thrive on positive tension and minimize negative tension. This requires discernment, humility and courage. Living in tension distinguishes the followers of Jesus from the admirers of Jesus— from being almost Christians to being altogether Christians.

The strategy behind this two-volume work is to blur the distinction between pastoral theology and a theology of ministry. I am convinced that the Bible overcomes the clergy/laity divide in a way that strengthens the authority of the pastor and empowers the priesthood of all believers. Not only have the old hierarchical patterns and ecclesiastical structures gotten in the way of a faithful and effective theology of ministry, but so have the new trends of mega-church charisma and generational tribalism. The originality and vitality that we long for is found neither in preserving extra-biblical traditions nor in embracing non-biblical trends.

1

Christ *for* Culture

The priestly ministry of the body of Christ moves us into the world on a mission. We are in the world, but not of the world. Each and every believer is called to a holy vocation and together we are called to be a faithful presence in the world. We are ambassadors for Christ, called not to conform to the world, but to be transformed by the renewing of our minds, so that we will be able "to test and approve what God's will is—his good, pleasing and perfect will." The nature of ministry forged out of the personal tensions we have explored leads all believers to the priestly and sacrificial practice of ministry. Together we face the culture tension.

I READ H. RICHARD Niebuhr's *Christ and Culture* in college for a course taught by the late Bob Webber. I bought my used copy of Niebuhr's classic from a freshman co-ed who had taken the course the previous semester. She tried to sell me her book for more than the retail value, because, as she explained, her marginal notes made it more valuable. Forty years later I am still struggling with the Christ and culture issue and the girl who sold me the book became my wife.

The Enduring Problem

Niebuhr's dense prose and Bob Webber's enlightening course introduced me to "the enduring problem" of how the followers of Jesus Christ are to relate to culture.[1] Niebuhr observed that Jesus' cultural critics concluded that Jesus ignored culture. Niebuhr cites the famous historian Edward

1. Niebuhr, *Christ and Culture*, 1.

Gibbon, who laid much of the blame for the decline and fall of the Roman Empire on Christians. According to Gibbon, Christians were "animated by a contempt for present existence and by confidence in immortality." Rome was bound to reject the followers of Christ, because the followers of Christ claimed "the exclusive possession of divine knowledge" and disdained "every form of worship except its own as impious and idolatrous."[2]

Christians are a strange paradox. They are out to win the respect of outsiders and show compassion for the needy. They are commanded to love their enemies and pray for their persecutors. They are tolerant in matters of spirit, but intolerant in matters of truth. When it comes to the exclusive truth claim of Christ or abortion rights or same sex marriages, there's not much give. To the dismay of their cultural critics they hold to principles in God's Word that the world finds offensive.

They love the Buddhist, the Moslem, and the atheist, but they believe people who reject Christ's redemption will be judged by God. The Christian's humility, in so far as it is a humility derived from Jesus, is different from any other kind of humility. Niebuhr calls it a kind of "proud humility and humble pride" because "the humility of Christ is not the moderation of keeping one's exact place in the scale of being, but rather that of absolute dependence on God and absolute trust in Him, with the consequent ability to remove mountains. The secret of the meekness and the gentleness of Christ lies in his relation to God."[3]

Jesus challenged Christians to be in the world but not of the world.[4] The Body of Christ was not meant to be sequestered from the world. Escape does not appear to be an option and building megachurches that function as self-contained communities is probably not the best idea either. Jesus intended for us to live in the neighborhood, befriending and serving. God wants the church entering into culture, building, painting, policing, teaching, healing, inventing, and farming. Christians were meant to inhabit culture and contribute to the good of a pluralistic society. The New Testament church is like Joseph in Pharaoh's Egypt and Daniel in Nebuchadnezzar's Babylon. We pray and work for the prosperity of the city and we seek to be salt and light in a fallen world.

Tim Keller of Redeemer Presbyterian Church of Manhattan sees the Book of Jonah as a special Christ *for* culture biblical text. Three times the Lord God called Jonah to go to the great city of Nineveh. Keller weighs the

2. Ibid., 5, 7.
3. Ibid., 27.
4. See John 17:13–19.

significance of God's love and concern for a large, important and strategic city of 120,000 people who cannot discern right from wrong. God called Jonah out of a safe, comfortable, homogenous religious culture to bring the message of God to a big, unjust, violent, pagan city. But Jonah's initial response, according to Keller, is typical of the city-disdaining, city-phobic, hypocritically righteous who go outside the city to condemn the city. Keller believes that the reason we know that Jonah was such a disobedient jerk was because *he told us.*

Jonah changed and was so joyfully secure in his newfound missionary love for the city that he could share how resistant he was to the love of God. Whether Jonah changed or not—we must change and embrace the mission of God. Christ's disciples do not confuse the human city with God's eternal city of love and truth. Following the wisdom of Augustine, Tim Keller emphasizes that the best way to love the city is not to mistake it for the city of God, because if we do we cannot love the city the way Jesus did. We must recognize its shortcomings and minister to its true needs. The best citizens of the city ought to be those who belong to the city of God.

Niebuhr outlined five answers to the Christ and culture problem. Each of his categories is a generalization that has been hotly debated and his theology has been questioned, but taken together his five types stimulate a conversation about how Christians are to live and work in culture.

1. *Christ against culture* emphasizes the moral and spiritual difference between the church and the world. 1 John 2:15 is a key verse for this type: "Do not love the world or anything in the world. If you love the world, love for the Father is not in you." Niebuhr identified Tertullian, with his rigorous morality and his sharp rejection of the claims of culture, as an illustration of this view.

2. *Christ of culture* stresses the compatibility between the church and the world. Christians who are representatives of this view feel no great tension between the church and the world. The Spirit of Christ and the spirit of the times seem to merge. The culture defines their view of Christ and Christ defines their view of culture. "Christ is identified with what men conceive to be their finest ideals, their noblest institutions, and their best philosophy."[5]

3. *Christ above culture* seeks a meaningful interaction between the radical claims of Christ and the good of culture. Niebuhr points to

---

5. Niebuhr, *Christ and Culture*, 103.

Clement of Alexandria and Thomas Aquinas as examples of this type. In Christ, they found the key for raising the standards of culture and God's grace and wisdom were manifest in society's best philosophy and in its noblest institutions. The church was the supreme institution over all other institutions and functioned as the guardian of culture.

4. *Christ and culture in paradox* sees the tension between the church and the world as either God-ordained or God-condoned. This both-and or dualist approach stresses the depravity of humanity. The church and the culture are both corrupted by evil and there is no way of ridding either one of sin and degradation on this side of eternity. Yet both the church and culture are ordained by God. Niebuhr used Luther to illustrate this deeply theological and pragmatic view. His understanding of the two kingdoms epitomized the paradox: "God's kingdom is a kingdom of grace and mercy . . . but the kingdom of the world is a kingdom of wrath and severity." Niebuhr offers a perspective on the Reformer: "Luther affirmed the life in culture as the sphere in which Christ could and ought to be followed; and more than any other he discerned that the rules to be followed in the cultural life were independent of Christian or church law."[6]

5. *Christ the transformer of culture* shares the dualist perspective on Christ the Redeemer and humanity's depravity, but the conversionist has a more positive and hopeful attitude toward culture than the dualist. Three factors contribute to this outlook: the goodness of creation, the fact that human beings, although fallen, are made in God's image, and the conviction that God is working out his purposes in history. Jesus' conversation with the woman at the well captures this hope. Christ has the power to transform fallen human beings and fallen human institutions to bring glory to his name. Evangelicals can readily identify with the power of the gospel of Jesus Christ to transform fallen human beings into salt and light disciples, but Niebuhr reinterpreted the meaning of conversion and transformation in a way that went beyond and contradicted the Bible on salvation and judgment.

Niebuhr applied his conversionist perspective to culture as a whole rather than to the individual. Within human history he envisioned an evolution or transformation of all humankind through the new beginning

6. Ibid., 174.

inaugurated by Jesus Christ. Instead of the final judgment and God's separation of humanity into two types: the saved and the lost, those who are in Christ and those who have rejected Christ, those destined for heaven and eternal life and those destined for hell and eternal damnation, Niebuhr saw the eschatological sequence of salvation, judgment, and the consummation of the end of the age compressed within temporal history. He held that all of culture and humanity will be transformed by the grace of Christ. In Niebuhr's vision the transformist church "busied itself with making America a better place in which to live . . . without providing any discriminating modes for discerning how Christians should see the good or the bad in 'culture.'" This led William Willimon and Stanley Hauerwas to conclude, "We have come to believe that few books have been a greater hindrance to an accurate assessment of our situation than *Christ and Culture*."[7]

Niebuhr acknowledged that his favorite text for the conversionist type, the Gospel of John, did not fully cooperate with his proposed universalism. He admits that "its universalistic note is accompanied by a particularist tendency." The Christian life "seems to be possible only to the few" and the Fourth Gospel "draws a sharp division between the Church of Christ and the outlying world."[8] Don Carson argues that since Niebuhr fails "to integrate all the non-negotiables of biblical theology," evangelicals "cannot adopt Niebuhr's 'pure' form of the conversionist model."[9]

In spite of Niebuhr's flawed theological assumptions, his typology helped me to grasp the complexity of the Christ and culture issue. To be in the world but not of the world is not so easily done. We may take pride in our conservative theology and our staunch moral stand but be down-right worldly in our neglect of the poor and in our greedy ambition for wealth. Our doctrinal stance may be conservative, but our devotion to sports and material success may be idolatrous. We may never miss a Sunday worship service, but we spend the rest of the week living for self. In the name of patriotism we may wrap the cross in the American flag. We may celebrate Christmas with traditional piety and give ourselves to materialistic idolatry.

How much easier it would be to simply write the culture off and wash our hands of the whole mess and go about being nice to our friends and living the Christian good life. Or how much easier it would be to simply

---

7. Hauerwas and Willimon, *Resident Aliens*, 40.

8. Niebuhr, *Christ and Culture*, 204–205.

9. Carson, *Christ and Culture Revisited*, 59.

equate the expectations of our suburban culture with God's will, rather than to wrestle with what the Bible teaches and our responsibility to a very needy world. Ironically, many conservative churches reflect their worldliness in how they go about evangelism and church growth. In the name of winning souls they think like Madison Avenue and act like Wal-Mart. The Christ and culture tension is complex and has a huge impact on our theology of ministry.

Don Carson's critique of Niebuhr's typology is helpful:

> We will be wiser if we refrain from distinguishing discrete patterns or paradigms or models of the relations between Christ and culture, and think instead of wise integration. . . . Culture frequently ignores Christ and Christians; sometimes culture explicitly contradicts Christ and Christians; sometimes culture persecutes Christ and Christians; on occasion culture very selectively approves and disapproves Christ and Christians. And the responses of Christians correspondingly adapt (sometimes wisely, sometimes unwisely) to such varying cultural stances.[10]

Not one of Niebuhr's types is sufficient in itself to encompass the comprehensiveness of the whole counsel of God on this issue. When it comes to shoes, one size does not fit all, and neither does any one of Niebuhr's categories fit all the ways Christ expects us to relate to culture. The biblical canon embraces a variety of valid ways for the followers of the risen Christ to relate to culture. This canonical approach necessitates a holistic understanding of Christ and culture. Instead of accentuating a negative and contradictory tension between various biblical texts, we seek to understand a particular text along the trajectory of salvation history and the culmination of God's revelation. Joshua was commanded by God to enter the promised land and annihilate its Canaanite inhabitants, but Jesus, his name's sake, declared, "For God so loved the world that he gave his one and only Son . . ." Jesus said, "Do not resist an evil person . . . Love your enemies and pray for those who persecute you, that you may be children of your Father in heaven."[11] These two approaches to culture are radically different, but consistent within God's redemptive plan and provision for humankind.

There are plenty of variables that influence how believers engage culture. We consider three of these variables below:

10. Carson, *Christ and Culture Revisited*, 62, 64.
11. John 3:16; Matt 5:39, 44.

1. *Where we stand on the salvation timeline makes a difference.* In an effort to preserve the identity of the people of God, the Israelites were instructed to form their own culture. Through diet, clothing, language, ritual, and the law, God separated out a people for himself. The purpose of this apparent "Christ against culture" position was to preserve the identity of Yahweh's people so that they might fulfill their God-given purpose. God chose to make a great nation out of an enslaved people. He redeemed them from bondage and set them apart to be a holy people. Yahweh honored the promise he made to Abraham, "I will make you into a great nation and I will bless you . . . and all peoples on earth will be blessed through you."[12] God chose one nation among the nations to deliver the message that Yahweh was the God of all creation and the Lord of history. Israel's integrity and survival as the people of God depended upon obeying God's specific command to destroy the nations that occupied the Promised Land. Under no circumstance was Israel to accommodate herself to the surrounding cultures. These idolatrous and degenerate cultures were a serious threat to her relationship to the Lord and the message of Moses made this clear.

> Make no treaty with them, and show them no mercy. Do not intermarry with them. Do not give your daughters to their sons or take their daughters for your sons, for they will turn your sons away from following me to serve other gods, and the Lord's anger will burn against you and will quickly destroy you. This is what you are to do to them: Break down their altars, smash their sacred stones, cut down their Asherah poles and burn their idols in the fire. For you are a people holy to the LORD your God. The LORD your God has chosen you out of all the peoples on the face of the earth to be his people, his treasured possession.[13]

Israel and the church were *set apart* and *set above* for the holy purpose of revealing the one and only God to all the nations, but their respective strategies are polar opposites.[14] The church is commanded to "go and make disciples of all nations, baptizing them in the name of the Father and of the Son and of the Holy Spirit, and teaching them to obey everything I have commanded you."[15] Joshua's conquest strategy was necessary in his day and Jesus' great commission strategy is necessary in our day.

12. Gen 12:2–3.
13. Deut 7:2–6.
14. 1 Pet 2:9.
15. Matt 28:19–20.

The power of the cross, which refuses to rely on violence and coercion, replaces political and military aggression.

2. *Where God places us and how God intends to use us makes a difference.* In the Book of Kings, two stories and two different strategies converge. The prophet Elijah was called of God to confront Ahab king of Israel and Obadiah was called of God to be Ahab's chief of staff. Both were devout believers in the Lord and both played strategic roles. Elijah stood on the outside declaring judgment and Obadiah served on the inside saving one hundred of the Lord's prophets from Jezebel's rampage. When the fiery wilderness prophet and the diplomatic insider met they had trouble understanding one another. Neither may have appreciated the other's predicament and both might have felt alone.[16] After the victory on Mount Carmel, Elijah fled to Horeb and complained to God, "I have been very zealous for the Lord God Almighty . . . I am the only one left, and now they are trying to kill me too."

But Elijah overstated his situation. He wasn't alone. The Lord God said, "Yet I reserve seven thousand in Israel—all whose knees have not bowed down to Baal and whose mouths have not kissed him."[17] Obadiah was like Joseph in Egypt and Daniel in Babylon, serving God behind enemy lines. Elijah reminds us of Isaiah, Jeremiah and Amos, calling down judgment. Both groups are devout believers and necessary in God's kingdom strategy. Their basic Christ and culture stance is forged in the furnace of hostility and on the anvil of God's call.

3. *Where culture's opposition to the gospel is most immediate makes a difference.* There are many dimensions to fallen human culture (politics, education, religion, the arts, work, family, sports, etc.) and each of these dimensions may require a different response. Jesus strongly opposed the religious leaders of his day—the decent, honorable, and upstanding people of his culture. But he warmly received the overtly immoral people of his day—the prostitutes, the greedy tax collectors, and other known sinners. Jesus never lectured explicitly against Rome's political oppression or environmental pollution or homosexual immorality or slavery. In the foreground of his ministry was the announcement of the good news of salvation. His presence embodied the coming kingdom of God and his signs and sermons pointed to his pivotal and personal role as the Son of Man, the Anointed One.

16. 1 Kgs 17–18.
17. 1 Kgs 19:14–18.

The religious leaders were up in arms over his message and Jesus took them on. They opposed his authoritative teaching and condemned his self-understanding as blasphemous. Undoubtedly the scribes and Pharisees thought Jesus was against culture—their culture, but the tax collectors must have been pleased that Jesus recognized them as part of his culture, even though they knew from Jesus' teaching that he did not condone swindling and greed. As Jesus said, "It is not the healthy who need a doctor, but the sick. I have not come to call the righteous, but sinners."[18]

Jesus told his followers to be as wise as serpents and as harmless as doves. He modeled this strategy when the Pharisees and Herodians set a trap and tried to trick him into speaking against Rome. The exchange between Jesus and his enemies illustrates the positive tension between conviction and strategic thinking. A full and transparent disclosure of Jesus' perspective on Rome would have ended his ministry right there and then. Suppose Jesus had said, "Caesar is a despicable and oppressive ruler, whose reign of terror and evil will be condemned by the Lord God, who will one day raise up his Anointed One, King of kings and Lord of lords, to rule and reign with justice and righteousness." Don Carson asks,

> Shall we tell Christians in southern Sudan to adopt a different paradigm of Christ-and-culture relations than Christians in Washington, D. C., and vice versa? Shall we tell them that the Bible sets forth several discrete patterns, and they can choose the pattern that seems best to them? Or do we seek to work out a more comprehensive vision, a canon-stipulated vision, of what such relations should be (recognizing, of course, how imperfect all syntheses are), while insisting that the outworking of that comprehensive vision is sufficiently rich and flexible to warrant appropriate diversity in outworking in these two very different cultural contexts?[19]

When Jesus said, "Give back to Caesar what is Caesar's, and to God what is God's," he was underscoring the tension between respect for God-ordained civil authority and obedience for God's all-encompassing authority.[20] The coin stamped with Caesar's image symbolized the power of the civil authority. Christians should pay their taxes. But the authority of the state and the authority of God are not two parallel authorities that deserve equal respect. Jesus made that clear when he said to Pilate, "You

18. Mark 2:17
19. Carson, *Christ and Culture Revisited*, 43.
20. Matt 22:21; Mark 12:17; Luke 20:25.

would have no power over me if it were not given to you from above."[21] The authority of the state is subsumed under God's authority and deserves support and compliance only up to a point. Of course, that point may lead all the way to the cross. When Jesus was arrested, he asked a rhetorical question with an obvious answer, "Am I leading a rebellion, that you have to come with swords and clubs?"[22] He rejected rebellion for the sake of redemption, which proved to be far more revolutionary than anyone ever imagined.

Jesus' whole ministry was politically subversive from its inception down to the present. Herod's massacre of innocents greeted his birth and in the decades following his resurrection countless Christians died because they would not bend the knee to Caesar. True Christians make good citizens. They are dependable, law-abiding, trustworthy, and hard working, but invariably the culture wants some kind of loyalty oath that the Christian is not willing to give because of his or her devotion to the Lord Jesus. In a variety of ways, the culture at large finds it infuriating that the followers of Jesus actually believe that "Salvation is found in no one else, for there is no other name given under heaven by which we must be saved."[23]

The best way to phrase this comprehensive and integrative approach to Christ-and-culture may be to use the little, yet flexible, preposition "for." Christ *for* culture includes what Christ opposes in our sinful, broken and fallen human culture, not for the sake of opposition, but for the sake of redemption and reconciliation. Christ *for* culture underscores the love and compassion that Christ and his followers demonstrate on behalf of culture. "Greater love has no one than this: to lay down one's life for one's friends."[24] If Christ is *for* culture, who can be against it? The ultimate victory of the risen Lord Jesus Christ is assured, having conquered sin and death and overcome the devil and his forces. No one has the power to raise culture up and transform its members but Christ alone. Christ is *for* culture, as Creator, Savior, reigning Lord, and coming King.

What are the implications of Christ for culture in the local church? At Central Presbyterian Church in Manhattan, where I serve as a pastor, we offer the following description to our new members. This statement has been adapted from membership materials by City Church, in San

21. John 19:11.
22. Luke 22:52.
23. Acts 4:12
24. John 15:13

Francisco, and Redeemer Presbyterian Church, in New York City. The statement underscores the Christ *for* culture theme:

The gospel is the center of all that we do.

The gospel is God's explosive power that changes everything. We preach the gospel to believers and unbelievers with great hope and confidence. We are motivated out of grace not guilt.

The gospel makes us a church for personal transformation

Religion makes nice people; the gospel makes new people. Religion reforms from the outside; the gospel transforms from inside. Religion says: "If you live a good life, God will love you," leading to a combination of pride and despair. The gospel says, "Not one of us is good. In fact, we are far worse than we think, but through Jesus Christ we are far more loved than we ever dared dream." Because we are "in Christ," we are given a new identity, a new Father, and a new family. Because "Christ is in us," we have new wisdom, new love, and new power, new motivation, a new way of living.

The gospel makes us a church for community

The body of Christ is a chosen people, a priesthood of believers, a temple of living stones, a holy nation, and the family of God. The church is a community, a household of faith, rather than a collection of individuals. Jesus came to create a new community, empowered by the gospel. In Christ and in community, we devote ourselves to one another with increasing vulnerability, because the gospel frees us from hiding our faults.

The gospel makes us a church for non-Christians

Jesus creates a community that is open to others. Non-Christians are expected, welcomed, and respected, with all their questions, objections, struggles, and doubts. The gospel enables us to overcome our apathy (because of gospel joy), our pride (because of gospel grace), and our fear (because of gospel love). We seek friendship, not conflict. We realize that unbelievers will be "looking on and listening in" to the conversation and conduct of the household of faith. We embrace the call to love our neighbors daily. The gospel shapes a community where Christians say, "This is the place to bring my non-Christian friends. This is what they need to hear, and how they need to hear it."

The gospel makes us a church for New York City

We partner with the people of New York City to serve the physical and spiritual needs of our area. We encourage Christians to learn from the city, to accept and love its people, to invest their resources back into the city, and strive for excellence in all we do.

The gospel makes us a church for mission

The gospel is dynamic, always spreading, always reaching out. The advance of the kingdom of God inspires and empowers compassion to see neighborhoods, and other cities reached with the unique message of the gospel. The church is the primary agent of God's kingdom; supporting, planting and revitalizing other churches is a high priority. By proliferating churches centered on the gospel, we can play a significant role in healing and mending a broken world and testifying to our hope of Jesus' return when he will set all things right.

The gospel makes us a church for the poor, marginalized, and oppressed

The gospel shows compassion to the poor and seeks justice. In the Spirit, the gospel of the Kingdom of God works for the healing of the world's woundedness. We long for an environment in which the gospel is understood and people are discovering the joy of living out their commitment to the gospel. We seek to live into the priorities and passions of the kingdom of God. To bear witness (evangelism) and to show love (social action) are the distinct and inseparable holy actions of the body of Christ. For Christ and his kingdom, the community sacrifices for the individual—it does not sacrifice the individual for the community.

On this side of eternity we live with an on-going unresolved *positive* tension—to live for Christ in a culture that is often hostile or indifferent to the only one who can bring true transformation and hope to the world. Don Carson describes the nature of this tension:

> We await the return of Jesus Christ, the arrival of the new heaven and the new earth, the dawning of the resurrection, the glory of perfection, the beauty of holiness. Until that day, we are a people in tension. On the one hand we belong to the broader culture in which we find ourselves; on the other, we belong to the culture of the consummated kingdom of God, which has dawned among us. Our true city is the new Jerusalem, even while we still belong to Paris or Budapest or New York. And while we await the consummation, we gratefully and joyfully confess that God of all is our God, and that we have been called to give him glory, acknowledge his reign, and bear witness to his salvation. By the proclamation of the gospel, we anticipate the conversion of men and women from every language and people and nation.[25]

The Cultural Captivity of the Church

This positive tension becomes a negative tension when Christians are beguiled or seduced or awed by culture. When Christians settle for manning the "Lost and Found" department in the mall of spiritual options, they lose their vision for worship, mission, and the everlasting hope. "Instead of being in the world but not of it, we easily become of the world but not in it."[26]

The account below, from a friend, is sadly typical of what many young Christians are experiencing in the church.

> I attended a "hip" church in the Bay area. I didn't miss a Sunday. It was great entertainment. It was fun. And it was easy. There was no suggestion that being a Christian would require any effort on my part. Show up on Sunday, watch the show, and off you go. I'm sure that if I had tried, I could have found the message of the Cross, the true requirements needed to follow Jesus' message, and the reality of the Christian life, had I tried. But it wasn't obvious. It was a drop-in-and-be-entertained-for-an-hour-so-you can-say-you-are-Born-Again church.
>
> I attended that church at a critical point in my life; at a time when I would be asked to make many serious decisions about life. I bear full responsibility for choosing that church, but it was the worst possible place for me. I got the message that all

25. Carson, *Christ & Culture Revisited*, 64–65.
26. Horton, "How the Kingdom Comes," 46.

life was to be easy and entertaining, including the center of my life, my faith. As you might guess, almost every decision I made was based on a fast-food convenience store quick-fix, get-rich and above all *feel good all the time* mentality. Fifteen years ago I found myself in a non-marriage, making lots of money, addicted to alcohol, and miserable because of all those quick-fix decisions.

It's wonderful that no matter what mistakes we make Jesus forgives us and is waiting for us! No matter how many wrong turns we take, God is waiting for us. I realize now how far I had drifted from the ten-year-old boy who accepted Jesus as his savior. I don't like the word "Born Again" because it reminds me of the fast-fix life style that got me where I was. I returned to God and I began to make decisions based on what Jesus would have me do. The changes have been remarkable. The un-wife is gone, the money is gone, the alcohol is gone, and above all the misery is gone. It has been replaced by joy. Joy was something that was gone from my life; it is back.

My friend had to be converted from Christianity to Christ! His church was so much like the world that a totally secular environment might have been less confusing for him. Compare the above description to a moving second-century description of Christian life attributed to Diognetus:

Christians are distinguished from other people neither by country, nor language, nor the customs which they observe . . . Following the customs of the natives in respect to clothing, food, and the rest of their ordinary conduct, they display to us their wonderful and confessedly striking (paradoxical) method of life. They dwell in their own countries, but simply as sojourners. As citizens they share in all things with others, and yet endure all things as if foreigners. Every foreign land is to them as their native country, and every land of their birth as a land of strangers. They marry, as do all; they beget children; but they do not destroy their offspring. They have a common table, but not a common bed. They are in the flesh, but they do not live after the flesh. They pass their days on earth, but they are citizens of heaven. They obey the prescribed laws, and at the same time surpass the laws by their lives. They love all people, and are persecuted by all. They are unknown and condemned . . . They are poor, yet make many rich . . . they are dishonored, and yet in their very dishonor are glorified. They are evil spoken of, and yet are justified; they are reviled and bless; they are insulted, and repay the insult with honor; they do good, yet are punished as evil doers . . .

Diognetus sums it up this way:

> . . .What the soul is in the body . . . Christians are in the world. The soul is dispersed through all the members of the body, and Christians are scattered through all the cities of the world. The soul dwells in the body, yet it is not of the body; and Christians dwell in the world, yet are not of the world . . . The flesh hates the soul . . . the world also hates Christians: the soul loves the flesh that hates it, Christians likewise love those that hate them. The soul is imprisoned in the body, yet preserves ("keeps together") that very body, and Christians are confined in the world as in prison, and yet they are the preservers of the world . . ."[27]

Mainline Protestants and market-driven evangelicals are struggling with evangelism in a post-Christian culture. It has become increasingly more difficult to draw the line between church and culture and to offer the gospel of Jesus Christ in a distinctive voice. Our evangelism sounds either like spiritualized political correctness or Christianized self-help. We have been secularized, on the one hand by pluralism and on the other by pragmatism. Mainliners seek cultural respectability and church marketers seek popularity. Cultural forces shape our identity; arts and education for mainline Protestants and entertainment and the marketplace for evangelicalism. We have become secularized by the culture we are trying to reach with the gospel.

In pastoral ministry I have experienced both extremes. My prevailing culture has been the church, and I can testify to its need for evangelization. The very things we take pride in exhibit our cultural captivity. Mainline Protestantism offers a politicized ethic influenced by secular culture, while market-driven evangelical Protestantism offers a psychologized gospel influenced by consumer-oriented felt needs.

The postmodern world has demanded from the church a reason for its existence, and the church has answered with reasons intended more to impress than to transform. On the one hand we are for diversity and pluralism, tolerance and acceptance. On the other hand we are for personal peace and prosperity, fun and fulfillment. Jesus helps us cope with stress and equips us for success. In commending ourselves after this fashion we hope to give the world a reason for thinking we have a place in the postmodern age.

27. Quoted in White, *Christian Ethics*, 20.

For all their differences, liberal Protestants and popular evangelicals are more alike than they realize. Both poles of the Protestant continuum are in significant ways being evangelized by the world rather than evangelizing the world. For some mainline churches evangelism is defined by the goal of their concert committee: "to provide spiritual uplift and cultural enrichment." "Outreach" translates into making a name for ourselves in the community.

The Christ and culture tension is also evident in the market-driven evangelical church, where the quest for relevance and success seems to hold people's attention. I was on the staff of a church that experienced phenomenal growth under its founding pastor. Within a few years the church audience numbered in the thousands, with a highly trained professional staff, full-service programming and expansion plans for the future. The major factor in this formula for success was a slightly irreverent, very entertaining, thirty-something pastor who preached acceptance and love in Christ. Everything he did from start to finish was high-energy. The sermon was a fast-flowing stream of consciousness. He pumped the audience up, gave them a boost, made them laugh and cry. Whenever he sensed he was coming on too strong, making a truth too definite, a conviction too strict, he interjected a joke. He had a gift for connecting with people.

Inspired by his phenomenal popularity and the growth of the church, the pastor envisioned a new expansion plan, one church on two sites. This vision would allow him to reach audiences at two separate locations as he shuttled between worship services and sites. The core group at the original site could not imagine life without the preacher and the preacher could not imagine staying in a sanctuary that held only 900 people. This new site held the promise of a megachurch: thirty-eight acres of prime real estate at the crossroads of two interstate highways, situated next to the largest residential real estate development in the country. It was the modern equivalent to the ancient cathedral on the city square: excellent accessibility, plenty of room for parking, with a great view and high visibility.

However, unknown to anyone else in the church, the pastor who had generated both the numerical growth and the vision was talking to a pastoral search committee from a much larger church. They were already in the process of planning a major building program to service their Sunday-morning audience of 5,000. For a time the preacher kept his options open, secretly candidating for a call to the larger church and promoting the vision for a megachurch. Whether the resistance to his one-church-two-site vision was too much for him or the call of a bigger church too attractive, he chose the new church over the new vision.

In both the mainline church and the market-driven church, Christians seem to accommodate and compete on the culture's terms. In 1850, Søren Kierkegaard identified this capitulation to culture as Christianity without Christ. He argued that this phenomenon occurs when the church no longer distinguishes between people who admire Jesus and those who follow Jesus. Christianity without Christ raises anxiety over our problems without genuine repentance and the message of the cross. It promotes individual empowerment without teaching self-denial and the way of the cross. Christ-less Christianity redefines faith as a private, hidden inwardness instead of a total life commitment to Jesus Christ. Evangelism seeks to entertain people, rather than convict them of their sin and draw them to Christ. Missions aims to convince the world that the church is relevant and helpful. Ethics is based on the spirit of the times and cultural respectability. Christianity without Christ substitutes the rich young ruler for the cross-bearing disciple.

Admirers or Followers?

In cultural Christianity, the crucified and risen Christ is replaced by an heroic Jesus or an iconic tradition. He is a figment of the admirer's imagination. Kierkegaard acknowledged that it was easy to blur the distinction between admiration and obedience and mistake an admirer for a follower. Jesus may be celebrated as the answer for every question, the slogan for every praise, and the solution for every problem, but admirers don't know Jesus. Everything is in the name of Jesus, but no one is willing to become like Jesus. Admiration replaces discipleship. Jesus is a symbol for success, an icon for living, but no one imitates his life. Everyone assumes that they already know what they need to know about Jesus. Over-familiarity shrouds the spirituality, purity, and passion of Jesus in mystery. The admirer's eyes are blinded to the meaning of Jesus. Instead of the crucified Lord, who calls us to take up our cross and follow him, their fantasy Jesus presides over their vision of success. An almost Christian is not an altogether Christian.

Nevertheless, Kierkegaard also believed that the life of Jesus "from beginning to end, was calculated only to procure *followers*, and calculated to make *admirers* impossible."[28]

28. Kierkegaard, *Training in Christianity*, 232.

His life was *the Truth*, which constitutes precisely the relationship in which admiration is untruth . . . But when *the truth*, true
to itself in being the truth, little by little, more and more definitely, unfolds itself as the truth, the moment comes when no
admirer can hold out with it, a moment when it shakes admirers
from it as the storm shakes the worm-eaten fruit from the tree.[29]

If the truth of Jesus is calculated to make admirers impossible then
the truth must be obscured because we have many admirers and few
followers. The distinction between an admirer and a follower of Jesus
is important and deserves our attention. Consider three characteristics
of the admirer that may help us see how inadequate admiration is as a
response to Jesus.

Admirers are consumers. Admirers enjoy the object of admiration for
their own sake. Their admiration is based on their personal satisfaction.
When their felt needs are met, whether those needs are real or imagined,
tangible or intangible, the admiring crowd offers its devotion. Admiration
is based on the law of supply and demand. As Jesus said. "You are looking
for me . . . because you ate the loaves and had your fill."[30] We admire art-
ists and musicians because they please our senses and make us feel more
alive. We admire people who achieve great things because they merit *our*
recognition. In the competitive game of life we enter into the arena of success vicariously through admiration. Admirers are *consumers*, satisfying
their own felt needs through the success of the object of their admiration.

The church that entertains the admirers of Jesus and caters to their
felt-needs inevitably attracts a host of self-absorbed weaklings who have
no intention of changing their egocentric ways. They use their many
weaknesses to lobby the church into paying attention to them. They tend
to be narcissistic, hungry for attention, eager to have their opinion heard
and absorbed in their own story. They benefit from the clergy/laity divide,
because they want pastors to feel responsible for them. They want the selfish freedom to impose on the pastor the obligation of their neediness and
weakness. Even the way these weak believers intone the word "pastor,"
triggers a warning in experienced pastors.

What better place to try to satisfy their insatiable needs than the
church where they feel people are supposed to pay attention to them? Such
weaklings have withdrawn from the world and retreated to the church.
They have done this without confronting their sin or turning to Christ for

29. Ibid., 239.
30. John 6:26.

transformation. Frequently they have left a trail of relational destruction in their path, but they have no intention of setting things right. When they attempt to serve others they are usually more trouble than they're worth, because they serve according to their whim and preference, always expecting to receive high praise for their efforts. Christ did not call his followers to this kind of weakness. This is the sin-nursing, blame-casting weakness that Christ came to overcome.

Admirers are critics. The admirer sits in judgment and critiques the object of her admiration, even though she knows she has no competence to judge other than the fact that she is an admirer. Spectators with no particular athletic talent feel perfectly free to judge the performance of an Olympian. Admiration alone seems to give people the right to criticize. Sports fans feel it is their inalienable right to judge their beloved home team. Then again, we may feel we have an eye for art even though we cannot draw a good circle. That doesn't stop us, though, from being an art critic, since we flatter ourselves as admirers of good art. We may have an ear for music but we've never been able to play an instrument or carry a tune. That doesn't stop us from offering our critical review. We are connoisseurs of fine taste but the best we can cook is macaroni and cheese. Admirers meet no qualifications except the price of admission, and by virtue of being spectators, ticket holders, and pew sitters, they believe they have the right to evaluate. An admiring crowd freely evaluates the object of their admiration because they feel entitled to their opinion. They can easily conclude as Jesus' admirers' did after his "Bread of Life" message, "This is a hard teaching. Who can accept it?"[31] The rich, young ruler, must have been an admirer of Jesus, but he reserved the right to draw the line between admiration and discipleship.[32] Admirers are *critics*, offering their assessment from a safe distance.

Admirers are carefree. Admirers bear no other responsibility to the object of their admiration other than their admiration. The object of their admiration has no claim on them. The appreciative audience and the boisterous fans remain at a safe distance from the object of admiration. The greater the fame and popularity of the one admired, the less the individual admirer is known by them. There is no personal responsibility and commitment, let alone meaningful exchange between the admirer and the one being admired. A signed autograph and a front row seat are the best that can be expected. Admirers can switch the object of their admiration

31. John 6:60.
32. Matt 19:16–22.

with little effort. The performer is only as good as the last performance. It is not clear whether the throng that greeted Jesus waving palm branches and shouting "Hosanna!" became the crowd that shouted "Crucify him! Crucify him!" But what is clear is that at the cross Jesus had no admirers. Admirers can come and go as they please. They are *carefree*, because the object of their admiration has no claim on them.

The difference between Christianity without Christ, and Christianity with Christ, is the difference between admiring Jesus and following Jesus. Disciples are called to become like Jesus. They understand that following Jesus is not optional. It is a prerequisite for living the normal Christian life. We are not talking about an advanced level of spirituality or a higher order of commitment, but basic New Testament Christianity. If Jesus "offered up prayers and petitions with loud cries and tears to the one who could save him from death, and he was heard because of his reverent submission," then his followers can expect to experience along the path of obedience their own dark night of the soul. Jesus "learned obedience from what he suffered" and we cannot expect anything less.[33] As Jesus said, "A student is not above his teacher, nor a servant above his master. It is enough for the student to be like his teacher, and the servant like his master."[34]

If the author of salvation was made perfect through suffering, why do modern Christians believe that they will be made perfect through success? Admiration is the highest possible goal when Jesus is accepted *minus his life of suffering*—when the scandal of the cross is ignored and when he is treated like a great teacher and moral man. Admiration is the best that can be hoped for when the apostle Paul's admonition is forgotten. "Your attitude should be the same as that of Christ Jesus: who, being in very nature God, did not consider equality with God something to be grasped, but made himself nothing, taking the very nature of a servant, being made in human likeness. And being found in appearance as a man, he humbled himself and became obedient to death—even death on a cross!"[35] Søren Kierkegaard held that the desire to admire instead of imitate was not the invention of bad people; "no, it is the flabby invention of what one may call the better sort of [people], but weak people for all that, in their effort to hold themselves aloof."[36] Instead of working out their salvation with fear and trembling, admirers choose the features of Christianity that they

33. Heb 5:7.
34. Matt 10:24.
35. Phil 2:5–8.
36. Kierkegaard, *Training in Christianity*, 237.

like best, such as inspirational services and programs that will meet their needs. Successful churches cater to this spirit of admiration and attract large numbers of admirers, but are they growing disciples? In its Christ-less admiration, cultural Christianity may be all for culture, but it is not for culture as Christ is for culture. Cultural Christianity may either reflect or react against culture, but its relationship to culture is not informed, inspired, or empowered by the crucified and risen Lord Jesus Christ.

Law and Gospel

The only way Jesus' followers can be *for* culture is by the redeeming grace of Christ.[37] The comfort people need is not a pat on the back or an affirming nod of approval. While a smile and a hug are nice and may brighten our day, the human soul longs for a deeper comfort. The comfort Jesus promises to those who mourn for their sin is much deeper than either the approval of our friends and loved ones or a personal sense of self-satisfaction.

Over the course of a year I met several times for lunch with a self-professed agnostic who was seriously considering the claims of Christ. His friends at work gave him *Mere Christianity* by C. S. Lewis, *Born Again* by Chuck Colson, and Philip Yancey's *The Jesus I Never Knew*. He attended church with his wife and followed the Sunday morning message as closely as anyone in the congregation. When we met, our conversations centered not so much on intellectual issues of faith and reason as on ethical concerns of faith and practice. He claimed that the biggest hurdle he had to overcome was his wife, a believer. She had faithfully attended church for years and felt the problems in their marriage were rooted in the fact that he was not a Christian.

In our first meeting, he asked me, "Do you believe it is right for my teenage daughter to invite her boyfriend home to spend the night in the

---

37. Karl Barth describes our dependence on the Law and Gospel beautifully: "In God alone is their faithfulness, and faith is the trust that we may hold to Him, to His promise and to His guidance. To hold to God is to rely on the fact that God is there for me, and to live in this certainty. This is the promise God gives: I am there for you. But this promise at once means guidance too. I am not left to my waywardness and my own ideas; but I have His commandment, to which I may hold in everything, in my entire earthly existence. The Creed is always at the same time the gospel, God's glad tidings to man, the message of Immanuel, God with us, to us; and as such it is necessarily also the law. Gospel and law are not to be separated; they are one, in such a way that the gospel is the primary thing, that the glad tidings are first in the field and, as such, include the law." *Dogmatics in Outline*, 19.

same bed?" Before I could answer he said, "My wife does. She believes Jesus desires intimacy in relationships, so it's okay for my daughter to sleep with her boyfriend. I'm sorry, but I think that's wrong!" The longer we talked, the more apparent it became that, at least from his perspective, his wife had used "the love of Jesus" to condone their daughter's sinful behavior. He may have been using the situation as an excuse for not becoming a Christian, but I think he was honestly struggling with what it meant to follow Jesus. He could not accept the unconditional love of Jesus as an excuse for immorality.[38]

In the course of one year we had three nationally known communicators visit our church in San Diego. All three gave essentially the same message. They defined grace as God's acceptance of broken people and each speaker gave a series of stories of despised and destitute people, who were victims of abuse, addiction, and abandonment. Often they had been rejected by religious conservatives, but in the end they were rescued by the love and grace of Christ. The positive aspects of God's acceptance were stressed, but nothing was said regarding the changes that the grace of Christ makes in our lives. No one implied that the same grace that saves is the grace that sanctifies. If Paul's words to Titus had been quoted it would have helped underscore the meaning of grace:

> For the grace of God has appeared that offers salvation to all people. It teaches us to say "No" to ungodliness and worldly passions, and to live self-controlled, upright and godly lives in this present age, while we wait for the blessed hope—the appearing of the glory of our great God and Savior, Jesus Christ, who gave himself for us to redeem us from all wickedness and

---

38. Unknowingly, some Christians favor the views of Marcion, a second-century theologian who tried to divorce the Old Testament from the New Testament. Marcion believed that the God of the Old Testament was vindictive and judgmental. He claimed that the God of the Jews performed evil acts and was self-contradictory. According to Marcion, Jesus was not the fulfillment of Old Testament messianic prophecies but a revelation of the God of love. Marcion's ancient heretical thesis is still popular today as self-styled "enlightened" Christians distance themselves from the commands of God's Word. It is almost as if many modern Christians wished that the malicious rumors spread by the Pharisees about Jesus were true. It would be a relief for them to find that Jesus rendered the Old Testament commands obsolete. They would find it easier to believe that Jesus liberated people from the allegedly pre-scientific, anachronistic commands of the Bible than to think that Jesus lined up with the Law and the Prophets. They confuse Jesus' resistance to the scribes and religious leaders with opposition to the moral order of the Old Testament.

to purify for himself a people that are his very own, eager to do what is good.[39]

The danger we ought to fear is unwittingly distorting the gospel by emphasizing grace at the expense of the law. H. Richard Niebuhr described liberalism, "as consisting in a God without wrath bringing people without sin into a kingdom without judgment through a Christ without a cross."[40] If we equate grace with acceptance and law with legalism we fall into that danger.

Dietrich Bonhoeffer warned that the very grace of Christ, which is so essential for healing, is often used as a poison. Repeated exposure to the Word of God may render the hearer impenitent and callous. "One hears and yet does not hear. One receives and yet is not helped. God's forgiveness is not accepted but the person learns how to deal with himself gracefully. Forgiveness is taken into one's own hands." When a person lives in "unrecognized and undisclosed sin," "the word of grace becomes a poison." Bonhoeffer concluded that "countless Christians hear the word of grace only in this way. For them it has become a sleeping pill. The person is cheated out of a salutary life in awe of God."[41] Such a place is far from the throne of grace. Kierkegaard expressed his longing this way: "that I might learn not only to take refuge in grace, but to take refuge in such a way as to make use of grace."[42]

John Wesley saw the vital connection between Law and Gospel. In 1751 Wesley defended his conviction that people needed a mix of gospel and law. He wrote:

> I mean by preaching the gospel, preaching the love of God to sinners, preaching the life, death, resurrection, and intercession of Christ, with all the blessings which, in consequence thereof, are freely given to true believers. By preaching the law, I mean, explaining and enforcing the commands of Christ, briefly comprised in the Sermon on the Mount.
>
> I think, the right method of preaching is this: At our first beginning to preach in any place, after a general declaration of the love of God to sinners, and his willingness that they should be saved, to preach the law, in the strongest, the closest, the most

39. Titus 2:11–14.
40. Niebuhr, *The Kingdom of God in America*, 191–192.
41. Bonhoeffer, *Spiritual Care*, 31.
42. Kiekegaard, *Training in Christianity*, 7.

> searching manner possible; only intermixing the gospel here
> and there, and showing it, as it were, afar off.[43]

Without a true conviction of our great need, Wesley believed that we would deal with our sin too casually. To be convinced of one's own sin was a prerequisite for a true personal application of the gospel. There was no question in his mind as to the importance of theology over therapy, redemption over affirmation.

Bonhoeffer, Kierkegaard, and Wesley emphasize the importance of recognizing our sin and our need for repentance. All good theology builds on this conviction. The great Reformer Martin Luther used a graphic figure to depict our responsibility in the death of Christ. He said we carry around the nails of Christ's cross in our pocket. We cringe at the very thought of the crucifixion; we hardly feel responsible for spikes driven through the hands and feet of Jesus. But that is what our sins did. He "was wounded for our transgressions, crushed for our iniquities; upon him was the punishment that made us whole, and by his bruises we are healed."[44] We prefer the role of victim; it is shocking to find out that we are not the crucified, but the crucifiers.

I have never met anyone who mourned more painfully and in greater agony than David Conner. The lines on his face seemed frozen and contorted in a cry of pain. His eyes, swollen and red, filled with an endless supply of tears. He shivered as if he was cold. I believe David grieved as deeply as anyone could grieve. And when I visited him in prison, even his faint smile seemed to hurt. David was in prison because he killed a mother and child on a two-lane road in Indiana. The tragic accident occurred on a Saturday afternoon and David had been drinking. He was impatient and annoyed at a motorcyclist who had passed him on a curve. He sped up to pass and lost control on the next curve. He hit the oncoming car head-on. The mother and child died instantly.

It was as if in a split second David entered hell itself. Every evil thing that he had ever done was now discharged, dumped, deposited in his despairing soul. How could a human being do what he had done? He went from an ordinary husband, okay father, and average worker to the very personification of evil. Overnight he became an object of hate in our small town, strongly condemned by the victim's family. And who could blame them? Two white crosses marked the spot on the highway where the accident occurred. Yet through this ordeal David reminded me of myself, of

43. Wesley, "Letter on Preaching Christ," 486.

44. Isa 53:5.

my own sin and moral culpability. He was not alone in his need. There was a glaring obviousness about his evil, but it did not obscure my own. David honestly mourned what he had done. He tried to understand his actions, but he did not excuse them. He was filled with remorse and repentance. Did Jesus have David in mind when he said, "Come to me, all you that are weary and are carrying heavy burdens, and I will give you rest?"[45] Yes indeed. Was the second Beatitude intended for David—"Blessed are those who mourn, for they will be comforted?"[46] Most certainly.

Whether there is an empty six-pack in the trunk or some leftover crucifixion spikes in our pockets, we all need to repent and turn to Christ for forgiveness. For only then can we begin to experience the comfort we need. It was not easy for David to mourn the way he did, but anything less would have been self-defeating. Only the forgiveness and comfort of Christ's grace was powerful enough to turn David's mourning into rejoicing and make him a husband and father again. David's conversion from Christendom Christian to faithful follower of the Lord Jesus was deep and long-lasting. His transformation was real and radically changed his belief, behavior, and belonging. It has now been over two decades since the tragic accident. David still lives in that Indiana town and serves as an elder in his church.

Bilingual Saints

Tension over *culture* is the fault line between the emerging church and the traditional church. "The new emerging voices," writes Pastor Jim Belcher, "often reacting against their culturally narrow fundamentalist upbringing, blame the traditional church for being sectarian, having no desire to reach people in postmodern culture, being uninterested in the biblical call to be creative in the arts and having sold out to Christendom (the church-state political alignment)." Belcher continues, "The traditional church fires back that the emerging church has succumbed to the worst forms of syncretism, becoming indistinguishable from the postmodern world they say they want to reach. They have assimilated, become worldly and lost their ability to be salt. The world has squeezed the emerging church into its mold."[47]

These charges and counter-chargers are not limited to the emerging church and the traditional church but echo through the centuries as the

45. Matt 11:28.
46. Matt 5:4.
47. Belcher, *Deep Church*, 183–184.

church has struggled with how best to be in the world but not of the world. Belcher's solution for overcoming the polarizing dangers of assimilation and syncreticism, negativity and complicity, focuses on recovering a comprehensive Christian worldview. True "resident aliens" need to become bilingual. They need a working knowledge of two languages: the common-grace language that engages culture with the conviction that all people are image-bearers of God. They are people for whom Christ died and beneficiaries of the Great Commandment and the Great Commission. They also need to know the kingdom of God language that evangelizes culture with the gospel of Jesus Christ and edifies the counter-cultural community of the Body of Christ.

There may be no more succinct description of what it means to be Christ-like "resident aliens" than Jeremiah's letter to the Babylonian exiles. Jeremiah sent an open letter to the first wave of exiles in 594 BC to challenge them to accept the hard work ahead and to warn them against delusional alternatives. He told them to live into the future by obeying God today. The will of God was simple and plain: "Build houses and settle down; plant gardens and eat what they produce. Marry and have sons and daughters; find wives for your sons and give your daughters in marriage, so that they too may have sons and daughters. Increase in number there; do not decrease."[48] Ordinary life was meant to be the proving ground of faithfulness. Trust in Yahweh was to be worked out in community through work, marriage, and parenting.

This spiritual direction recalls the apostle Paul's exhortation to the church, when he wrote, "We hear that some among you are idle. They are not busy; they are busybodies. Such people we command and urge in the Lord Jesus Christ, to settle down and earn the bread they eat. And as for you, brothers and sisters, never tire of doing what is right."[49] The exile afforded a new opportunity for the chosen people of God to discover all over again what it meant to live faithfully and obediently. The stranglehold of false spirituality, self-indulgent materialism and sexual promiscuity, that had squeezed the life out of Jerusalem, had been broken in Babylon of all places. They were given a fresh opportunity to live for God in a foreign land. God's plan for them, as it is for us, was to live in the world but not of the world. If we seek first Christ's kingdom and his righteousness, God will take care of the future.[50]

48. Jer 29:5
49. 2 Thess 3:11–13.
50. Matt 6:33.

26

"For I know the plans I have for you," declares the Lord, "plans to prosper you and not to harm you, plans to give you hope and a future. Then you will call upon me and come and pray to me, and I will listen to you. You will seek me and find me when you seek me with all your heart. I will be found by you," declares the Lord, "and will bring you back from captivity. I will gather you from all the nations and places where I have banished you," declares the Lord, "and will bring you back to the place from which I carried you into exile."[51]

University of Virginia sociologist James Davison Hunter advises today's Christian in the spirit of Jeremiah's letter to the exiles. We are mandated to reflect God's intentions in creation. We live in a fallen world, knowing that Christ's life, death, and resurrection have fundamentally altered our relationship to the powers. Hunter writes,

> What this means is that faithful Christian witness is fated to exist in the tension between the historical and the transcendent; between the social realities that press on human existence and the spiritual and ethical requirements of the gospel; between the morality of the society in which Christian believers live and the will of God. These oppositions are a fact of existence for the church and each Christian believer and they pull in conflicting directions—one toward the necessities of survival and the other toward the perfect will of God. There is no place of equilibrium between these oppositions and no satisfying resolutions. In this world, the church can never be in repose. The tension is not lessened by the fact that there are unavoidable ambiguities that inhere in the application of biblical promises, values, and ideals to everyday life. Nor is it lessened by the fact that the love required of the Christian is unlivable, except in flawed approximation.[52]

In the Spirit, the ancient prophet and the modern sociologist are asking the people of God to acknowledge three fundamental realities:

> (1) the inherent and endlessly complex intermingling of Christian practice and worldly power, (2) the inescapable tensions that are present for the church operating faithfully in the world, and (3) to acknowledge the unavoidable failure that awaits even the most faithful Christians who seek to obediently witness to

---

51. Jer 29:11–14.
52. Hunter, *To Change The World*, 183.

the good news of Christ's kingdom does not mean that they accept things as they are.[53]

Living in this tension requires the free and daily exercise of the spiritual disciplines. Jeremiah emphasizes a prayerful work ethic, the necessity
of discernment, and life-long devotion.

God's plan challenges us to pray and work for the good of others. The
prophet who was told by the Lord at various times *not* to pray for his own
people wrote to the exiles on behalf of the Lord saying, "Seek the peace
and prosperity of the city to which I have carried you into exile. Pray to the
Lord for it, because if it prospers, you too will prosper."[54] This is remarkable counsel because it was given to a people who were far more inclined
to hate their captors than pray for them. Normally, oppressed people define their identity in opposition to the culture that exploits them, but in
this case, Jeremiah exhorted them to do what Jesus told his disciples to do,
"love your enemies and pray for those who persecute you."[55] They were to
love their neighbors as themselves.[56] Jeremiah's counsel, given about 600
years before Christ, gave the people of God a hint of the gospel ethic to
come. The apostle Peter wrote, "Slaves, submit yourselves to your master
with all respect, not only to those who are good and considerate, but also
to those who are harsh. For it is commendable if a person bears up under
the pain of unjust suffering because he is conscious of God."[57]

*God's plan resists deception, especially the strong tendency to deceive
ourselves.* In his letter, Jeremiah issued an emphatic warning, "'Yes, this
is what the Lord Almighty, the God of Israel, says: 'Do not let the prophets and diviners among you deceive you. Do not listen to the dreams you
encourage them to have. They are prophesying lies to you in my name. I
have not sent them,' declares the Lord."[58] Jeremiah knew that the redemptive plan of God would come under attack by leaders who thought they
were doing God and the people a favor. In the name of popular spirituality, religious pluralism, civil religion, and national pride, self-designated
prophets in Jerusalem and Babylon predicted a short exile and a quick
return to the homeland. They insisted on an upbeat, pragmatic message
that they thought would encourage the people, but Jeremiah insisted on

53. Ibid., 184.
54. Jer 29:7.
55. Matt 5:44.
56. Matt 22:39.
57. 1 Pet 2:18–19.
58. Jer 29:8–9.

seeing the captivity for what it was and enduring it by God's grace. The false prophets were preaching independence from Babylon and Jeremiah was preaching dependence upon God. To express Jeremiah's thought in the apostle Paul's words, Jeremiah warned them against gathering around them "a great number of teachers to say what their itching ears want to hear."[59] Jeremiah knew that when we take ourselves and our culture as the basic and authoritative text for making decisions and living life we are bound to fail. The temptation to exegete our hopes and dreams, as a primary sacred text with a little biblical terminology and spiritualized self-help thrown in, is always a recipe for failure.

God's plan is fulfilled in an abiding, intimate relationship with God. The sign of knowing God's plan is not material wealth or career success or the perfect family, but an authentic, whole-hearted communion with God.[60] Jesus used the imagery of the vine and the branches to describe what it meant to know God's will: "I am the vine; you are the branches. If you remain in me and I in you, you will bear much fruit; apart from me you can do nothing."[61] The apostle Paul described knowing God's plan this way, "I consider everything a loss compared to the surpassing greatness of knowing Christ Jesus my Lord, for whose sake I have lost all things . . . I want to know Christ and the power of his resurrection and the fellowship of sharing in his sufferings, becoming like him in his death, and so, somehow, to attain to the resurrection from the dead."[62]

Christians living in exile need to be bilingual saints, fluent in the language of common grace and in the language of the kingdom of God. They work for the good of Babylon and advance the kingdom of God.

59. 2 Tim 4:2–3.
60. Jer 29:12–14.
61. John 15:5.
62. Phil 3:8-11.

2

All Truth Is God's Truth

The importance of the Christian mind and the significance of the Spirit's teaching gifts are fundamental to a theology of ministry. The church can ill afford an anti-intellectual bias. We are called to understand the fullness of the wisdom of God in every sphere of life. In Christ we have an understanding of the truth that corresponds to the priesthood of all believers and a sacramental view of life. The truth-tension quickens and enlivens the Christian mind.

I FIRST HEARD THE phrase, "all truth is God's truth" from philosophy professor Art Holmes at Wheaton College. It struck me as an instant rebuke to my narrow-minded religious conservatism. It attacked the "Bible alone" mentality, that tried to make life easy by refusing to think seriously about science, philosophy, history, economics, and political theory. We so easily forget that the apostle Paul's goal was that we "may have the full riches of complete understanding, in order that [we] may know the mystery of God, namely, Christ, in whom are hidden all the treasures of wisdom and knowledge."[1]

Holmes drew out the significance of Paul's declaration. Truth, by its very nature, is accessible and intelligible to thinking people. Christians do not have an inside track on comprehending truth. They have to use their minds. All truth, and especially the gospel, is not hidden in gnostic secrets. It is a mystery revealed by God in Christ. The truth of Christ centers all knowledge: "For in him all things were created: things in heaven and on earth, visible and invisible, whether thrones or powers or rulers or

1. Col 2:2–3.

authorities; all things have been created through him and for him. He is before all things, and in him all things hold together."[2] xz

The phrase "all truth is God's truth" gave me a line that summed up my father's philosophy. My dad was a mathematician and I remember him stressing to my brother and me that there were not two classes of Christians, one spiritual and the other secular. He countered the vocational hierarchy that placed mathematicians below ministers and missionaries. When I became a Bible major in college he encouraged me, but he would have been just as encouraging if I had gone into hospital administration. He believed in holy vocations and that every believer was called to salvation, service, sacrifice, and simplicity. In Christ all things hold together. Truth is everywhere. God designed it that way.

Art Holmes was convincing and convicting because he demonstrated the Bible's concern for every aspect of life. The Bible is not a science textbook, nor does it lay out economic theories, but the Bible does embrace science and economics as significant endeavors rooted in God's plan and purpose. From the creation mandate to the great commission and from Mosaic legislation to John's Logos concept, Christians are challenged to focus on truth. We are to comprehend truth's universality and recognize the ultimate unity of all truth in God. Holmes reasoned persuasively that the Christian faith must not be seen "as a private affair of the heart without reference to the larger scope of human knowledge and cultural affairs. Such a faith is too small to match the understanding which the early church had of the message of Scripture. God is creator and lord of all; Jesus Christ reaffirms this by becoming incarnate to redeem life. For the Christian, then, all of life matters and all of thought."[3]

Ordinary life is the arena of discipleship. "In God's eyes there is no division between the secular and the sacred. All spheres of life belong to him. 'Let a man sanctify the Lord God in his heart,' writes spiritual writer, A. W. Tozer, 'and he can therefore do no common act. All he does is good and acceptable to God through Jesus Christ. For such a [person] living itself will be sacramental and the whole world a sanctuary.'"[4]

2. Col 1:16–17.

3. Holmes, *All Truth is God's Truth*, 14.

4. Sittser, *Water from a Deep Well*, 206.

The Christian Mind

In the late seventies, as I was trying to wrap my mind around the fact that "all truth is God's truth," I read Harry Blamires' classic, *The Christian Mind*. Blamires left no doubt as to the state of the Christian mind. He lamented the demise of the thinking Christian and the church's "abdication of intellectual authority" which he claimed led to "the modern Christian's easy descent into mental secularism."[5] His critique was unequivocal, "We have too readily equated getting into the world with getting out of theology. The result has been that we have stopped thinking christianly." Christianity has been "emasculated of its intellectual relevance," convictions are looked upon as a "personal possession," and we have been reduced to encountering one another on the shallow level of gossip and small talk.[6]

As Christian thinking shrinks, secular thinking about Christian matters expands. The Christian preacher thinks Christianly about Sunday's sermon but thinks secularly about hiring a worship leader, administrating the building fund, or negotiating his salary. For an hour a week we think Christianly, although even that time may be debatable, and the rest of the time we think just like the world. In many cases, Christians have grown so accustomed to secular thinking that they are not even aware that it is secular. For example, the Christian who claims practicing homosexuality is a sin, but refuses to take that stand publicly because it may turn people off, is thinking secularly. It has become so common for us to "treat worldly possessions as status symbols rather than as serviceable goods" that we hardly see the contradiction.[7] We don't even bother to think Christianly about war, politics, advertising, sports, business, education, marriage, and divorce.

Blamires' emphasis on the difference between thinking Christianly and thinking secularly is rooted in the radical distinction made by the apostle Paul in his Corinthian correspondence. Paul asked, "Where are the wise? Where is the teacher of the law? Where is the philosopher of this age? Has not God made foolish the wisdom of the world?"[8] The followers of Jesus do not expect the message of the cross to impress the social and cultural elite. Then and now, the intelligentsia reject the metanarrative of salvation history and the revelational epistemology of the

5. Blamires, *The Christian Mind*, 4.

6. Ibid., 38, 16, 40, 13.

7. Ibid., 29.

8. 1 Cor 1:20.

Christian mind. But the apostle's critique of social status was never an argument against thinking Christianly. Christians may not be "wise by human standards" nor influential in the eyes of the world, but the apostle Paul does not use this fact to disparage the importance of the mind. On the contrary, Paul said, "God chose the foolish things of the world to shame the wise."[9] In Christ, the mind realizes its true significance, not as a capacity for self-advancement and self-expression, but as a gift to be developed and disciplined for the sake of the truth—all God's truth. The importance of the mind is a positive tension challenging all believers to a rigorous engagement and rethinking of all of life in accord with the person and work of Christ.

Of particular interest to me as a young teacher was Blamires' distinction between the scholar and the thinker:

> The scholar evades decisiveness; he hesitates to praise or condemn; he balances conclusion against competing conclusion so as to cancel out conclusiveness; he is tentative, skeptical, uncommitted. The thinker hates indecision and confusion; he firmly distinguishes right from wrong, good from evil; he is at home in a world of clearly demarcated categories and proven conclusions; he is dogmatic and committed; he works towards decisive action.[10]

Blamires referred to the scholar in a pejorative way. He had in mind the proud, self-reliant academician. What we need, he claimed, was more thinkers and fewer academics. "The thinker challenges current prejudices. He disturbs the complacent. He obstructs the busy pragmatists. He questions the very foundations of all about him, and in so doing throws doubt upon aims, motives, and purposes which those who are running affairs have neither the time nor patience to investigate. The thinker is a nuisance."[11]

Scholarship as a necessary intellectual enterprise was encouraged by Blamires, but the dark side of scholarship as a self-serving, career-enhancing, ego performance was exposed. One way to tell whether you are a scholar or thinker is to ask whether you are pleased or resentful when someone expresses a truth that you hold dear. Blamires was critical of a scholar who cornered truth as his or her very own intellectual property. As if they had proprietary rights to their discovery and that the world was in

9. 1 Cor 1:26–27.

10. Blamires, *The Christian Mind,* 51.

11. Ibid., 50.

their debt for a good idea. Thinkers, on the other hand, rejoice when others express the truth that they have understood and embraced. They never think to themselves, "That's my idea and you stole it." In Blamires' critique scholars are competitive. They want credit for their good ideas. Thinkers are cooperative. They want the fellowship of fellow thinkers.

In 1675, German Pietist Philip Jacob Spener argued for "pure simplicity" not "human sophistry" in his classic work *Pia Desideria*. He lamented the negative influence of scholastic theology: "Thus we learn much that we often wish we had not learned."[12] Stuffing minds with theology, to use his image, fed human inquisitiveness but not the soul. A steady diet of "subtleties unknown to the Scriptures" had its origin in scholars who "desire to exhibit their sagacity and their superiority over others, to have a greater reputation, and to derive benefit therefrom in the world."[13] "It is certain," declared Spener, that a person "who fervently loves God, although adorned with limited gifts, will be more useful to the church of God with his meager talent and academic achievement than a vain and worldly fool with double doctor's degrees who is very clever but has not been taught by God."[14]

Competitive scholarship has its roots in a broken and fallen, sin-twisted academic world. Cooperative thinking has its roots in a home environment that celebrates learning, honors understanding, and encourages reflection. Obviously, the home environment is fallen and sin-twisted, too, but where parents read to their children and encourage their children to think and explore, learning has a chance to take root in a non-competitive environment. The academy can be a war-zone of conflicting self-interest, crushing the relational dynamic essential for true learning. Competitive scholarship tends to be highly individualistic and isolationist.

Blamires describes six marks of the Christian mind. Each mark highlights an aspect of the truth-tension:

1. *Its Supernatural Orientation*: a mind that cultivates the eternal perspective, that believes in the fact of Heaven and the fact of Hell, that understands that all of creation, all of history, all of humankind is under the sovereign control of the triune God. One of the places that I am most aware of the supernatural orientation of the Christian mind is at funerals. I sense a strange collision of perspectives cutting right

12. Spener, *Pia Desideria*, 54–55.
13. Ibid., 56.
14. Ibid., 108.

through the sanctuary, between those who believe death ends all and those who believe in eternal life.

2. *Its Awareness of Evil*: a mind that understands the pervasive and pernicious presence of evil, that is alert to the tragic extent of human depravity and resists evil in all of its manifestations within fallen creation. The Christian mind "assumes that the powers of evil will exploit every possible occasion" and in the name of morality seek to blur concepts and twist values.[15] The Christian mind is also sensitive to the extent to which evil pervades our own judgments. The tragedy of this world is not primarily social or political, but personal. Evil begins with me. The prophet Jeremiah wrote, "The heart is deceitful above all things and beyond cure" and Isaiah likened our righteous acts to "filthy rags."[16] British author G. K. Chesterton was asked to write a magazine article on the subject "What's Wrong with the Universe?" He responded to the editor's request with two words, "I am."

3. *Its Conception of Truth*: a mind that is transformed by the revelation of God, that is founded on doctrines of Divine Creation, the Incarnation, the Redemption, the work of the Holy Spirit, and that accepts as a description of fact, the Virgin Birth, the efficacy of Christ's atoning sacrifice, and life everlasting. The truth of the gospel is an audacious truth that must "be defended for the right reason."[17] We must not beguile unbelievers into thinking that Christianity is good because it builds self-esteem, strengthens marriages, offers comfort, and leads to success. "We have to insist that the Christian Faith is something solider, harder and tougher than even Christians like to think. Christianity is not a nice comforting story that we make up as we go along, accommodating the demands of a harsh reality with the solace of a cherished reverie. It is not a cosy day-dream manufactured by each person more or less to suit his own taste. It is a matter of hard fact." Blamires continues, "We Christians appreciate its hardness just as much as those outside the Church. We are as fully aware of its difficulties as the outsiders are. We know that, in a sense, Christianity leaves us with an awful lot to swallow . . . We must outdo the unbelievers in agreeing with them on that subject."[18]

15. Blamires, *The Christian Mind*, 102.
16. Jer 17:9; Isa 64:6.
17. Blamires, *The Christian Mind*, 120.
18. Ibid.

4. *Its Acceptance of Authority*: a mind that submits to the God-given nature of truth, revelation, and the church, that finds its freedom in surrender to the will of God, and that leads "to that state of personal inadequacy, human dependence, utter lowliness and lostness, which brings the Christian to his knees and throws him into the hands of our Lord."[19] The secular mind that is "trying to hold the Christian Faith in its grip" cannot understand this humility. It invariably leads "to a case-hardened self-satisfaction of the pharisaical kind" which refuses to accept the truth of a crucified and risen Jesus Christ.[20] People who ask, "Can the Church survive?" have no idea what they are asking. The survival of the world is in question, but not the church. "The Church can never be destroyed. It cannot even be gravely damaged. It cannot be decimated numerically: too many of the Church's members are already beyond the barrier of death; too much of the Church is already safe home."[21]

5. *Its Concern for the Person*: a mind that values the human person in light of the Incarnate One, that holds to the sacredness of the human personality, and that seeks to preserve the person against all forms of dehumanization. Blamires identified various forms of dehumanization that the Christian ought to be committed to "pointing the finger of condemnation" at including "servitude to the machine," "the eerie loneliness of personal solitude in the midst of the crowded urban civilization," the exalted status attributed to the user of "mechanical gadgets," behavior modification, transactional relationships, and target-market evangelism.

6. *Its Sacramental Cast*: a mind that is focused on "life's positive richnesses," that is life-affirming, rather than life-rejecting, and that revels in the beauty, truth, and love derived from the Divine Nature.[22]

Blamires describes the Christian mind's positive view of life:

> A living Christian mind would elucidate for the young a finely articulated Christian sacramentalism which would make sense of, and give value to, the adolescent's cravings towards the grandeur of natural scenery, towards the potent emotionalism of music and art, and towards the opposite sex. A living Christian

19. Ibid., 146.
20. Ibid.
21. Ibid., 152.
22. Ibid., 173.

mind will not be content to refer to these things only in cold abstract terms which annihilate wonder and transmute them into bloodless modes of experience, unrecognizable as the stuff of passion and exaltation. Nor will the Christian mind allow these richnesses of life to be vaguely identified with sins of the flesh, or even with a life of the body which it is the Christian's duty to transcend.[23]

This brief sketch of Blamires' description of the Christian mind is meant to convey a sense of the fullness and richness of a Christian worldview. Blamires' contrast between the self-promoting scholarly specialist and the breadth and depth of the Christian thinker recalls the contrast between the genius and the apostle drawn by Søren Kierkegaard. To praise the apostle Paul for his brilliance or eloquence is to miss the heart of his message. Paul was not a genius that we should celebrate his clever and creative rendition of some new idea. He was not a man ahead of his time with a high I.Q. Paul was an apostle, called and appointed by God, to proclaim the revelation of God. His authority resided in his calling from God and in the message given to him by God to proclaim. His voice was heard, not because he was a great speaker, but because he was submissive to the revelation of God.

Kierkegaard complained that "the pernicious thing" about Christian discourse in his day was that "the whole train of thought [was] *affected*."[24] Preachers relied on their own ingenuity and profundity as if the truth depended on their abilities and powers, instead of relying on the authority of the Word of God. A person is a genius by virtue of his or her extraordinary abilities, personal uniqueness, and self-sufficiency. An apostle is one who is called of God, submissive to God, and compelled by God to be faithful. Kierkegaard compared the leisurely life of the scholar, who is "momentarily clever, and afterwards a publisher and editor of the uncertainties of his cleverness," to the faithful life of the follower of Christ, who lives purposefully and obediently under the authority of God.[25] In relationship to the truth, Kierkegaard contended that the former is blasphemous, the latter beautiful.

---

23. Ibid., 175.
24. Kierkegaard, *Of the Difference Between A Genius and an Apostle*, 103.
25. Ibid., 106.

Training in Truth

This all encompassing and uniquely Christian view of truth is reflected in John Wesley's address to pastors in 1756, in which he explored the qualifications for pastoral ministry. What was both impressive and unsettling about Wesley's comprehensive description of the pastor was his extraordinary expectations of what was required to correctly handle the word of truth.[26] Pastors need to have "a good understanding, a clear apprehension, a sound judgment, and a capacity for reasoning with some closeness."[27] Wesley asked, "Can a fool cope with all the people that know not God and with all the spirits of darkness?" Wesley expected pastors to be intellectually gifted, blessed with a good mind coupled with "some liveliness and readiness of thought" and "a good memory," so that they would not be "ever learning, and never able to come to the knowledge of the truth."

Given the pastor's natural ability to think, reason, remember and articulate, Wesley proceeded to describe the necessary "acquired endowments." He identified ten competencies: (1) All pastors should have a thorough understanding of their ministry responsibilities; (2) a comprehensive knowledge of the Scriptures right down to "the literal meaning of every word, verse, and chapter;"(3) a knowledge of the original languages; (4) a knowledge of history, "of ancient customs, of chronology and geography;" (5) a knowledge of the sciences, along with logic, philosophy, and mathematics; (6) a knowledge of the early church fathers; (7) a practical knowledge of humanity, including anthropology, sociology, and psychology; (8) "an eminent share of common sense;" (9) a knowledge of cultural custom and good manners; and (10) a knowledge of effective communication.[28]

Wesley's list of competencies was consistent with the principle that all truth is God's truth and was based on the need to cultivate a Christian mind. The breadth and depth of knowledge Wesley required of a pastor is enough to make the modern seminarian question his realism. But Wesley was only half way through his list of qualifications! In addition to these natural and acquired endowments, he insisted on a clear demonstration of the grace of God. Truth was a matter of the mind and the heart. Intellectual preparation needed to be complemented by a focus of affection. Apart from a full measure of the grace of God, energizing and guiding "the whole intention, affection, and practice of a Minister of Christ" how could

26. 2 Tim 2:15.

27. Wesley, "An Address to Clergy," 481.

28. Ibid., 482–85.

anyone undertake this ministry? Without a passion to see others come to Christ and grow in Christ, a person would have to be "a madman of the highest order" to become a pastor.[29] Wesley's truth-focused criterion of ministry stands out in comparison to the contemporary competencies for pastoral ministry that accentuate church management over worship and spiritual formation. Wesley contended that it was not in the truth's best interest to lower the intellectual and spiritual qualifications of the pastor.

In his address to clergy he called for pastors to examine themselves, because too many of them were "dull," "heavy," boring, and "shallow," with "no life, no spirit, no readiness of thought."[30] Wesley came down hard on the pastors of his day. They were intellectually and spiritually incompetent. His criticism was bold. Who would have the gumption to point out to a pastor that his poor preaching may be due to his genetic makeup? In many ways we are more attuned to genetics than Wesley was, but who would be bold enough to say to someone that he or she just didn't have the intellectual capacity necessary to preach the gospel? Wesley resented the idea that parents felt their "blockhead" child could become a pastor even though they knew their child did not have capacity to become a lawyer or physician.

After taking a long hard look at the natural endowments, Wesley reviewed all the acquired endowments, asking pointed questions about a pastor's knowledge of Scripture, the biblical languages, world history, the sciences, and many other disciplines. The thrust of his argument was that there is no excuse for a minister of God's truth to become a blind guide. Wesley argued that the reason we do not excel in these many areas of knowledge is because we are lazy and we have not taken advantage of the educational opportunities we have been given. Wesley was an activist, a pioneer missionary, an urban evangelist, and tireless preaching pastor. His ministry became the motivation for embracing the truth in all its dimensions. "I am absolutely incapable of teaching my flock what I have never learned myself; no more fit to lead souls to God, than I am to govern the world."[31]

Our tendency today is to skip over Wesley's concern for "intellectual endowments" and jump to the heart issues. How does a person feel about ministry? We seem to think that ministry is all about relationships and if pastors and other believers really have a heart for people and

29. Ibid., 486–87.
30. Ibid., 489.
31. Ibid., 493.

ministry, they need not bother about the intellectual side of life. It seems that faith is more about what you feel than what you know. Wesley disagreed. No one whose passion was for the glory of God and the salvation of the lost would ever sacrifice or belittle the mind to appeal to the heart. Wesley was convinced that a passion for Christ drove out selfish motives and professional egos, not biblical knowledge. He ridiculed the notion that a true "steward of the mysteries" would make a career move to get a higher salary.[32] A real heart for God only meant that everything was done for the glory of God, every thought held captive for Christ, every effort expended for Christ's kingdom.

In contrast to today's emphasis on self-satisfaction and self-fulfillment, Wesley stressed rigorous preparation and personal self-sacrifice. Pastors and congregations tend to labor under the excessive demands imposed on the church from the false expectations of religious consumers, when what we need is a re-commitment to the truth. Wesley ended his address by questioning the reasons for a diminished pastoral vocation. "Is there any necessity laid upon us, of sinking so infinitely below our calling? Who hath required this at our hands? Certainly, not He by whose authority we minister . . . Is not his love, and is not his power, still the same, as they were in ancient days? Know we not, that Jesus Christ 'is the same yesterday, today, and forever?'"[33]

John Wesley's emphasis on a well-trained team of pastors complemented rather than competed with his biblical emphasis on the priesthood of all believers. Methodism was largely a lay movement that thrived on small group Bible studies, person-to-person evangelism, and a host of caring ministries. Wesley saw a changed life and a transformed mind as crucial for the impact of the gospel in all spheres of life.

The Teaching Gifts

All of us share equal responsibility to live a life worthy of the calling we have received. This shared calling—our *one* calling, involves "bearing with *one another* in love." Our shared calling is linked to bearing with one another in love. Likewise, the unity of the body—our *one* body, depends on *each one* receiving spiritual gifts. *"But to each one of us grace has been given as Christ apportioned it."*[34] Everyone who is in the body is gifted to build

32. Ibid., 497.

33. Ibid., 500; Heb 13:8.

34. Eph 4:7.

up the body. We are to bear with one another but everyone is expected to bear his or her own responsibility. We are a household of faith in Christ not a spiritual welfare state. In a family there are various degrees of maturity but all are expected to be maturing. Responsibilities differ but all are responsible. We are interdependent without fostering dependency. We want to strengthen the weak without perpetuating weakness. We want to empower our brothers and sisters in Christ without enabling immaturity. The goal that Paul had in mind is expressed positively and negatively. He wants all of us "to reach unity in the faith and in the knowledge of the Son of God and become mature, attaining to the whole measure of the fullness of Christ. Then we will no longer be infants, tossed back and forth by the waves . . ."[35]

The diversity of gifts distributed to the church derives from a single donor, Jesus Christ. No one can give what he or she has not first received from Christ and no one can out-give God. The stewardship of life means that everything we receive is held in trust. These gifts are not ours free and clear to simply do with as we please. We have been entrusted to use them for building up the body of Christ. In Ephesians, Paul's emphasis is on the identity of the Giver, followed by a short list of five gifts. In this case, the gifts are not skills or abilities or talents, but *people* tasked with the responsibility of declaring the Word of God. They are listed as apostles, prophets, evangelists, pastors, and teachers. Only teaching gifts are mentioned here. These are the gifts that introduce, proclaim, announce, nurture, and instruct people in the Word of God.

John Calvin observed, "We see that God, who might perfect his people in a moment, chooses not to bring them to maturity in any other way than by the education of the Church."[36] Therefore, preaching the Word became instrumental in growing strong Christians, not because it was the only way, but because it was the chosen way. God might have used angels or no means at all, but instead he chose humans and the "ordinary method of teaching" to convey his truth, "that he may thus allure us to himself, instead of driving us away by his thunder."[37] God declared his own love and humility towards us by choosing people like us "to be interpreters of his secret will; in short, to represent his own person."

The method and the means of teaching the Word of God demonstrates both the humility of God and our humility. Calvin calls it "a most

---

35. Eph 4:13–14.
36. Calvin, *Institutes of the Christian Religion*, IV: 1.5, 284.
37. Ibid., IV:1.5, 285.

excellent and useful training in humility." We might think that having described preachers as the mouthpiece of God, "doing God's work by their lips," that Calvin would emphasize the exalted status of the preacher, but he does just the opposite. By divine design, we learn humility by having to listen to God's Word through people like ourselves, "or, it may be, our inferiors in worth." Calvin goes on to say, "When a feeble man, sprung from the dust, speaks in the name of God, we give the best proof of our piety and obedience, by listening with docility to his servant, though not in any respect our superior. Accordingly, he hides the treasure of his heavenly wisdom in frail earthen vessels (2 Cor 4:7), that he may have a more certain proof of the estimation in which it is held by us."[38]

In humility, God chose the ordinary method of teaching to communicate his Word. And in humility, sincere believers must receive the Word of God from people like themselves ("or, it may be, our inferiors in worth"). This humility has implications for the role of women in ministry. We hear in some circles that men are better representatives of the authority of God than women, but if humility is the key concept for preaching and learning, then it may be argued that women are even better suited than men for the task. Or better yet, neither men nor women are inferior or superior when it comes to the preaching ministry. Both genders ought to evidence the humility of God. By divine design, feeble and frail human beings are chosen to proclaim God's glorious Word. And both men and women train us in humility as we listen to them preach the Word.

We need to resist the temptation to digress from Paul's purpose, by dwelling on the differences between apostles, prophets, evangelists, pastors, and teachers. Paul's concern was not to differentiate these five servants as much as to emphasize Christ's singular purpose, namely, "to equip his people for works of service, so that the body of Christ might be built up . . ."[39] This is another example of Paul piling up the evidence to make his case: first, that all spiritual gifts are dependent upon the Word of God for their effective use. There are no spiritual gifts, no works of service, designed to build up the body that can work effectively apart from the wisdom and guidance of the Word of God. The ministry of the Word is essential in the use of all the spiritual gifts. Second, Paul implies that all believers are without excuse. No one can claim to be ill-equipped to serve, because Christ has provided a variety of ministers of the Word to meet the need.

38. Ibid., IV:3.1, 316.
39. Eph 4:12.

Suppose a person says, "I need an effective Bible study teacher before I can effectively serve the Lord." And someone else says, "I can't serve the Lord, because I don't have a nurturing pastor." And a third person says, "When someone shows me how to evangelize then maybe I'll be able to talk to others about Christ." Excuses like these misunderstand Paul's teaching. He is arguing that all the saints are already the beneficiaries of the apostles, prophets, evangelists, pastors, and teachers. Christ has already given these gifts and we have already received their benefits. So instead of lamenting our perceived deficiencies we should acknowledge God's gracious ministry to us.

To equip the saints for works of service involved dynamic *conditioning* rather than indoctrination; it meant meaningful *restoration* in the love of Christ rather than pedantic teaching on procedures and techniques. Paul was not envisioning "how-to" lessons in social justice or creative formulas for church growth or five easy steps for evangelism.

One church member complained to me that the reason he had never served was because he had never been equipped. Although he had listened to forty years of Bible preaching and been involved in countless Bible studies, he lamented that no pastor had ever taken the time to equip him. He had the mistaken notion that equipping the saints meant specialized, how-to-instruction not found in the Bible. He was looking for step-by-step techniques. But the kind of equipping Paul had in mind was designed to cultivate the Christian mind which would in turn lead to Christian action. His word to Timothy parallels this meaning: "All Scripture is God-breathed and is useful for teaching, rebuking, correcting and training in righteousness, so that all God's people may be thoroughly equipped for every good work."[40]

The saints who are equipped "for works of service" are those who allow the Word of God to train and condition them "for every good work." Because they have a hunger and thirst for righteousness they feed on the Word of God. Because they have been called to be "salt" and "light" in the midst of decay and darkness, they have a need for the life and light of the Word of God. The equipping process takes two sincere people: an honest, humble teacher who is submissive to the Bible and capable of communicating its truth effectively and faithfully, and a sincere saint who is ready to do works of service, so that the body of Christ may be built up. After many years of preaching, I believe it is those who are engaged in ministry who get the most out of the Sunday sermon. Those who see themselves as

---

40. 2 Tim 3:16–17.

missionaries in the marketplace or in the classroom or in their families are the ones who get the most out of preaching. *Salt and light* Christians have a hunger for the Word of God and they profit from this equipping ministry.

The diversity of gifts contributes to the unity of the body, not its division. Paul never intended to reduce the bulk of church members to "the rank of mere consumers of spiritual gifts."[41] Nor was his emphasis on teaching gifts meant to produce a division between pastors and people. The responsibility to build up the body of believers belongs to the people as a whole, not to pastors in particular. Paul assumes two important principles, a team-ministry approach for teaching the Word of God and an every-member ministry for building up the church. No single person is responsible for teaching the Word of God. Christ gives his church a variety of people to minister the Word: apostles, prophets, evangelists, pastors, and teachers. The ministry of the Word is indispensable, but never independent from the full-orbed work of the gospel. Strong Bible teaching invariably produces well-equipped servants who demonstrate "the manifold wisdom of God" and the multi-dimensional love of Christ. All truth is God's truth and God's people are equipped by God's Word to be ministers of God's truth in every sphere of life.

41. Markus Barth, *Ephesians: Commentary on Chapters 4–6,* 479

3

Stay in the Story

Christian communication is vital and real when it is deeply rooted in the drama of God's Story of Salvation. The biblical text reveals the tension between our fallen condition and God's redemptive provision. A theology of ministry is shaped and energized by the whole counsel of God and salvation history. The problem of innocuous pulpit speech and religious small talk is overcome by letting the tension in the text lead to the passion of the passage.

The truth-tension is found in the clash between the mystery of God and the mess of the human condition, between humanity's fallen condition and God's redemptive provision. We live in this tension to the degree that we identify with Jesus, his person, and his work. But it is exactly this tension that we have largely lost in contemporary Christian understanding and communication. We have obscured the polarity of Jesus-like lowliness and worldly success. We have blended Jesus-centered truth and cultural correctness. Christianity in our day has taken on a life of its own—divorced from the message and method of Jesus. Instead of teaching people how to follow Jesus, preachers entice them to admire Jesus. There's a difference. When we lose the truth-tension, Christian communication becomes repetitive, boring, and compatible with culture.

David Matlak, a Beeson Divinity student, on leave from his mission work in Africa, poignantly describes his early years in the faith:

> I am the product of the pop-evangelicalism of our current day. For most of my life I have sat in church while being inoculated with low levels of Christianity. With the IV drip-bag labeled 'Self-Help Moralism' connected in one arm and

'Daily-Devotionalism' in the other arm, I spent much of my life drifting on the tenuous edge of a coma . . . Like a waking dream, I was living the 'Christian life.' . . . My world was one where the Bible had no power and where preaching was like a giant pacifier. We were deprived of true sustenance. In looking back, it is no wonder that I was depressed and contemplating suicide by the time I was twenty years old.

God's Linguists

On the road to Emmaus, Jesus reviewed salvation history. "And beginning with Moses and all the Prophets, he explained to them what was said in all the Scriptures concerning himself." I wish we had this conversation verbatim, but even if we did, it wouldn't add anything to what we already know from the Word of God. However, what a wonderful experience it must have been for these two disciples to have Jesus explain "all the Scriptures concerning himself." The seven mile walk gave Jesus time to discuss Abraham at the altar with Isaac, Moses raising the serpent in the wilderness, Job's cry, "I know that my Redeemer lives. . . ," David's prayer, "My God, my God, why . . .?," Isaiah's picture of the suffering servant, and Zechariah's humble king, unappreciated Shepherd, and the mourned martyr. What a conversation that must have been!

The ministry of the Word requires that we comprehend more deeply the drama of God's great salvation history. This is an approach to the Bible that I would have benefitted from at the beginning of my formal theological education. Like so many Bible and theology students I started out by taking language studies and courses in theology and hermeneutics. I enjoyed classes that delved into background information on the text and explored the latest critical studies. I studied works by famous biblical scholars and theologians and did research on higher criticism, form criticism, and the historical-grammatical method of biblical interpretation. I found these courses and my professors fascinating. There was very little in the graduate school curriculum that I did not enjoy or imagine myself teaching someday. I liked it all: biblical and historical theology, church history, evangelism, and missions. But something was missing in my theological education and ministry preparation that I wasn't aware of until years later. I spent several years studying theological German and Latin and exploring every facet of Latin American liberation theology. I read Augustine for the better part of an academic year and sat under brilliant scholars, but I could not have explained to you the importance of the prophet Zechariah or the impact of Isaiah. I knew the trends of modern theology better than I knew God's salvation history.

I grew up in a home that practiced the spiritual disciplines and encouraged a devotional life. For family devotions we read from *The Daily Bread* and a short passage of Scripture that the devotional guide recommended. In my personal devotions I read Oswald Chambers and kept a journal of my daily Bible reading. Thanks to my parents who lived out the kingdom lifestyle long before it was called that in popular evangelicalism, I was nurtured and instructed in a home that embraced the Word of God. But I still didn't have a sense of the big picture of salvation history. Much of the Old Testament was foreign to me, like the old and forgotten stuff that got stored in our attic. I heard a zillion evangelistic messages at our church, but almost nothing from the biblical prophets.

During my junior high years our pastor focused almost exclusively on the apostle Paul, but it was preaching through the narrow lens of our subculture, rather than the great drama of salvation history. I knew a lot about "getting saved" but not a whole lot about the comprehensive meaning of salvation. Looking back, I sense that my family had an intuitive grasp of the message of the prophets and Jesus' kingdom ethic, but I failed to see how it all fit together. I had pieces of the puzzle but not the big picture. Except for a few well-known Psalms, the riches of the Bible's Wisdom literature was lost to me. Biblical books, such as Leviticus or Numbers, were basically ignored or, when thought about at all, regarded as anachronisms for New Testament Christians. Forays into confusing books like Ezekiel or Daniel were usually for the sake of discovering a devotional thought for the day. I used the book of Revelation to fuel my curiosity more than to deepen my courage.

Although good in themselves, my devotional experience of the Word and my graduate theological education conspired to conceal my ignorance of the sweep and drama of salvation history. My experience and my scholarship produced an unintended and hidden deficiency—a trained incapacity to see the big picture and feel the drama of God's story. My well-intentioned devotional subjectivity and specialized expertise had unwittingly obscured the gospel story. I was left with a piecemeal understanding of the Bible and at the time it didn't bother me that large portions of the Bible remained relatively unknown to me. What I was missing was a coherent understanding of the compelling unity of the Word of God.

Comprehending the fullness of the gospel story is imperative for learning how to preach the truth. No matter how much preachers attend to the clarity of their thoughts and the effectiveness of their style, if the driving force of God's truth is not shaping their message they are bound to fail, even if their sermons are well-received. I believe pastors have a "cover-to-cover" responsibility and a "tension-in-the-text" obligation to teach and preach the whole counsel of God. A great deal of preaching tends to rely on incidental anecdotal material. Preachers unintentionally interrupt God's Story with their own human-interest stories and doctrinal expositions. It is time we concentrate on that compelling, convicting, life-saving Story.

Students come to divinity school to learn how to tell the Gospel story from cover to cover, but this is where we often disappoint them. By focusing on prolegomena and technical issues, at the expense of the big picture, seminaries have a way of exhausting students and preventing them from understanding the scope of God's work. Good teachers know this and guard against it. They defy the scribal propensity to overwhelm students with the complexities and intricacies of scholarly opinions. Their primary purpose is positive: to guide students in the powerful story of God's revelation. Their goal is not to debunk students' naïveté. There is a place for careful explanation, where interpretations are weighed, scholarly debates reviewed, and the latest research cited, but spiritual formation works best when the flow of salvation history is understood.

Wisdom dictates that we first hear the story before dissecting the text. By the time many divinity students plow through the scholarly introduction of a biblical book, including authorship, sources, date, setting, redaction criticism, exegetical problems, and all the accumulated debunked theories attached to the text, they have lost the intellectual and spiritual energy to hear the story, much less proclaim it! These academic questions and concerns can be important, but their priority should be reversed. Begin with the story, revel in the truth and when once that storied truth is internalized in the soul, turn to the textual technicalities and complexities. Students find it difficult to proclaim what they have been trained to see as problematic.

To use an analogy, seminary professors are trying to teach advanced auto mechanics to people who haven't even gotten their driver's license. Textual experts need to be careful with the biblical story. Their love of grammar and syntax may cause them to miss the tone and texture, and especially the truth, of this real-life story. Scholars can exegete a biblical passage, and pastors can work up sermons, but never really tell the story and embrace the message.

Literary critic George Steiner explores the ways we distance ourselves from the text. He laments the "parasitic discourse" that feeds off the Living Word.[1] What Steiner says of literature and art in general is especially applicable to biblical studies. "Mandarin commentators" draw our attention away from the primary text of the Bible through their "professionalization of the academic pursuit" and their "humanistic imitation of the scientific."[2]

It is hard to argue with Steiner's thesis that "we crave remission from direct encounter with the 'real presence,'" when you hear a New Testament lecturer analyze Jesus' parables as if they were a math problem.[3] The message of the text is buried under a review of internationally renowned parable scholars. Various categories of parabolic types are listed and multiple theories of interpretation are numbered. The debate as to whether parables have one, two, three, or more "points" is discussed in the abstract for an hour, and at the end of the day the professor and students are tired. There is no time or energy left to explore the parable itself. That is left for the pastor-to-be to work out on his or her own. Above all else Steiner contends for the primary immediacy of the text. The goal is an authentic experience of answerable understanding, an active apprehension of the truth. Instead of acquiring "the immunities of indirection" and distraction, we were meant to ingest the truth, not reduce it to a "digest."[4]

Not only do we want to begin in the biblical story but we want to remain in this story throughout our ministry. On a mission trip to the northern Ghanian village of Carpenter, I was preparing to teach and discuss the pastoral epistles with thirty-five pastors. Going over my material on the flight to Ghana, I was impressed with how much of my slant on the epistles was shaped by my cultural situation. On the day before our sessions began, we paid a ceremonial visit to the chief and I met the tribal linguist. Second only to the chief, the tribal linguist is responsible for telling the story of his people. Like the chief, his position is inherited by birth. He carries the responsibility of being the tribe's spokesperson, the chief's advisor, and, most importantly, the guardian of the tribe's oral history.

Normally a "linguist" refers to a person who is an expert in languages, one who analyzes the syntax and structure of languages. Linguists can

1. Steiner, *Real Presences*, 47.
2. Ibid., 36.
3. Ibid., 39.
4. Ibid., 7–8, 39.

decipher a language. They know how a language works technically. But the term *linguist* in Ghana applies to a person who *uses* language to communicate. The tribal linguist is more of a poet than a technician. Concern over my cultural slant coupled with my encounter with the tribal linguist caused me to change my approach for our teaching sessions together. We began with Genesis and spent five days working through the Bible. I encouraged these bi-vocational pastors to be God's tribal linguists telling the story of God's salvation history. In the process, I realized that I needed a better grasp of the passion and power of God's redemptive story.

Instead of "dumbing down" the gospel story and editing the canon for what we find relevant, we ought to let *salvation history* and the *intensity of the text* shine through in all of its complexity and mystery. The truth of God revealed to us in the Bible and through salvation history deserves our careful attention. It is ironic that as our culture has become more sophisticated in its methods of communication it has insisted on a simplistic message. As the speed of communications has increased so has our apparent impatience with the message itself. But it is here that we have to resist the reduction of the gospel to sound-bites and insist on comprehending the whole counsel of God. I imagine that there are many people in our churches who long for a passionate, in-depth proclamation of God's story from Genesis to Revelation.

In *The Courage to Teach*, Parker Palmer insists that all good teachers discover the DNA of a text. There is a core truth that needs to be understood to make sense of all the data. The "inner logic" of the text "contains the information necessary to reconstruct the whole—if it is illuminated by a laser, a highly organized beam of light. That laser is the act of teaching." Palmer continues,

> No matter what great thing we are studying, there is always an equivalent to the stem section under the microscope. In every great novel, there is a passage that when deeply understood, reveals how the author develops character, establishes tension, creates dramatic movement. With that understanding, the student can read the rest of the novel insightfully.[5]

The challenge for believers is to embrace the scope of the whole counsel of God and accept the strategic significance of the tension in the text as they explore the internal dynamic of the biblical text.

5. Palmer, *The Courage To Teach*, 123.

Jesus Talk

Evading the biblical text is a national crisis. The problem exists in Bible-belt megachurches and in avant-garde emergent churches. The lack of real preaching is systemic to the American church from coast to coast, in all categories, rural, urban, and suburban. Denominational affiliation makes little difference and variety in worship styles does nothing to conceal the problem. There is a famine in the land, "not a famine of food or a thirst for water, but a famine of hearing the words of the Lord."[6]

There is a growing inability of Christians to talk about the faith in any kind of meaningful way, especially outside the bounds of Sunday school, sermons and small group Bible studies. Sermons have largely become a recital of evangelical platitudes, privately prepared, without interaction with the thinking, praying community, and publicly performed without lasting impact, usually in a style that does not flow from or serve the text. And these days it seems that most Christians are listening to sermons designed for someone else—the seeker or the brand new Christian.

Thousands gather every Sunday to hear what they have heard many times before. There is a large and appreciative market of religious consumers who want to be given a recital of familiar truths. The impact of this kind of preaching is bigger auditoriums, filled with strangers who rarely fellowship beyond their familiar cliques. Consequently, it is becoming more difficult to distinguish between that which is done for spiritual growth and that which is done for public relations. George Orwell's line may be truer than we care to admit, "Orthodoxy, of whatever color, seems to demand a lifeless, imitative style."[7]

Christian communication has virtually no context outside of the pulpit. This is tragic. No one wants to hear from the pastor about these things over lunch or in casual conversation, and most pastors only want to talk about administrative matters, church politics, visionary programs and new trends. Any attempt to bring Jesus up in any kind of meaningful way outside the prescribed bounds feels like a violation of social etiquette. Gossip and small talk have largely replaced the gospel in every arena but the pulpit, and even there the danger now exists for the sermon to be co-opted by mere sentiment and self-expression.

We talk freely about sports, fashions, stocks, personalities, and politics, but serious talk about the kingdom of God is almost non-existent.

---

6. Amos 8:11.
7. Orwell, "Politics and the English Language," 5.

We should not be surprised. Vast numbers of believers attend church in anonymity. One can go to church without ever uttering a word or making meaningful eye contact. An awkward greeting time will not free us up to talk about following Jesus. On religious matters many are well schooled, but they show little sign of a meaningful relationship with God. They look bored in Sunday School and find it difficult to interact with a pedantic lesson that they have heard hundreds of times before. We have little capacity for meaningful dialogue on the very truths that we say we are so committed to on Sunday.

Whenever Jesus opened his mouth he seemed to be offending someone, but thousands listen to preaching today that causes no offense. There is no tension in the text, no tension between Christ and culture, except in a predictable, non-controversial, and non-offensive way. Sermons are innocuous. They lack personal impact and engagement. We sit through a sermon thinking that this must be good for a new believer or a seeker, but we get nothing. The preaching leaves us bored and restless. And who are we to assume that these bland sermons help the new believer or seeker?

Tension in the Text

So then, what is this tension in the text, that we seem to be so good at avoiding? Everyone has a story, but only one story redeems our story. Therein lies one tension. As long as the preacher and the hearer stay in the small worlds of their own individual stories, they can avoid the tension, but as soon as they place their story in the context of God's salvation history they are invited into the large world of God's making, redeeming, and reconciling. Too much of our preaching stays within the confines of our little worlds because the sermonic scope is limited to our immediate felt needs. But there are other fault lines. To summarize, the fault lines that lead to this tension fall:

> between God's salvation history and our personal story,
> between biblical genres and our familiar styles of communication,
> between the author's intended meaning, along with the canonical
> meaning of the passage, and our expectation of felt-need
> satisfaction,
> between the truth that stands over and against us and our subjective
> selves seeking affirmation and approval,
> between Jesus—living and Incarnate—and innocuous Jesus talk.

The various biblical genres lead us into this tension. If the Bible came to us as lists and lectures we might have an excuse for neglecting the overarching gospel story, but instead it comes to us as historical narrative, wisdom literature, prophetic poetry, God-centered praise and lament, missional epistles, and historical apocalyptic. The Gospel accounts fuse and fulfill these genres. We are drawn into the tension between the Word of God and the way of the world. We wrestle with sin and salvation, judgment and worship, law and grace. Jesus' sermons are the furthest thing you can imagine from today's info-sermon and Christianized self-help. His parables thrive on twist and turns, exposing the fault lines that run between conventional thinking and the gospel.

If the Bible was fiction and fantasy, Schleiermacher's definition of preaching as "self-display with a stimulating effect" would make sense, but it isn't. If we take the Bible seriously, and not as some kind of moralistic manual or Christian Koran, then we cannot help but be drawn into this Salvation Story—the truest of true stories.[8] Our thinking is upended. Our sinful preoccupation with self is confronted. Our religious self-justification is challenged. We are not listing doctrines, we are engaged in a life of discipleship, living for Christ and his kingdom.

The tension in the text leads to the passion of the passage. We have to be careful not to truncate the text and edit out the tension. Many sermons miss the tension, because they skip over what the text is all about. Preachers select what they want to bring out from the text and ignore the context. They feel free to isolate a verse or lift out a line as a springboard into a sermon. They neglect the original tension in the text and preach a positive sermon on how to be a better Christian. They are preaching from the Bible but they ignore the tension that is there in the text between merit and mercy, judgment and salvation, the putting off and the putting on, sin and grace, idolatry and worship. Conventional sermons tell a clever opening story, plow through a text, make a few points and draw a conclusion, but in the process miss the passion of the passage.

We have fallen into the bad habit of reading small portions of the Bible subjectively. Our focus is not on what the text means, but on a more self-centered question, "What does the text mean to me?" Such preachers are more like postmodern artist Jackson Pollock than they are like Rembrandt. They paint what they feel, not what they see. Our subjective experience trumps the tension in the text. After reading the Bible for a few minutes, whatever comes to mind is our devotional thought for the day.

8. Quoted in Barth, *Church Dogmatics*, vol.1:1, 62.

This practice may not be very different from praying the rosary. Surely, God can use these few minutes of Bible reading in the life of a believer, but it is not the best way to read the Bible for all it's worth.

Instead of the text calling the shots and laying down its own terms, many preachers believe that the text can be preached a thousand different ways. They can subjectively encounter any given biblical text and produce a so-called powerful sermon. It is true, they can sermonize any way they want, but the sermon will not be a biblical sermon even though it allegedly comes out of the Bible. If *our* context controls the text then *we* are the text, not the Bible. Much of our devotional and sermonic material fails to identify the tension in the text and thus fails to grasp the true passion of the passage.

Preaching has been defined as truth through personality. That is to say, the tension in the text runs right through the pastor. If that tension does not resonate with the preacher, so that the preacher is disturbed and delighted, comforted and challenged, then the preacher is not ready to preach. If the preacher hasn't experienced the passion of the passage, doesn't feel the dissonance between the Word of God and the human condition, then chances are the congregation will not either. It is important not to confuse the tension in the text with self-doubt and anxiety. The tension is derived from the text, the message intended by the original author, and not the psychological angst of the preacher. All too often, we miss the most obvious sense of the text and bring our own agendas instead.

Poor preaching can be used mightily by the Spirit of Christ to proclaim the gospel and make disciples. It happens every Sunday morning, but that's no excuse for poor preaching. Thankfully, "God in his ordinary providence makes use of means, yet is free to work without, above and against them, at his pleasure"—and for his glory![9] How much better when the preacher is standing on the fault line between the mystery of God and the mess of the human condition and preaches the Word as it was intended to be preached. Good preaching requires discernment and hard work. It doesn't take a genius. It takes someone who will pay attention prayerfully and thoughtfully to God's overarching salvation history, the original intention of the passage, the context of the text, and the people to whom one is preaching.

9. Williamson, *The Westminster Confession of Faith*, 46.

Tell it Slant

If we are going to let the Word of God dwell in us, the way Jesus, the Living Word, dwelled among us, then we will have to re-examine the way we read the text. The Word must be read in the light of the incarnation. Otherwise, we will miss something important. The paradigm for all Christian communication is the Incarnate One: Truth in Person, absolute truth, independent of all contingencies, spoken into the personal, earthy contingencies of daily life. "The Word was made flesh and dwelt among us and we beheld his glory, the glory of the only begotten full of grace and truth."[10] God in the flesh, bears witness in our mundane world. The most real world interfaces with our all-too-real-world. The Incarnate One moves into our neighborhood. There is nothing abstract and theoretical about this. Belief is not a cognitive assent to ideas, but a living relationship of obedience, a daily following after Jesus, our crucified and risen Lord. We don't become Jesus, but we become like Jesus as the Spirit of Christ indwells us. The Word embodied defines us as we follow the Incarnate Word.

Self-emptying is the key. God transcended his own being by becoming human. He emptied himself of himself, his divine attributes and prerogatives, and became obedient to death—even death on a cross. This lowliness produces the contradiction that the truth of the gospel must suffer in a world that makes success and self-achievement into a god, that fashions immortality symbols out of children and houses and adventures. The Creator became a creature. The followers of Jesus are to become like Jesus, unrecognizable by the world, incognito, bearing the truth essential for the world's salvation, all the while living under the radar. For the sake of Christ and His kingdom all worldly triumphalism must be forsaken. The tension in the text is made possible by the Author of life who intervened in the Story he spoke into existence.

Emily Dickinson's "Tell all the Truth but tell it slant" underscores the need to get at the truth in ways that serve the truth, not stifle it. If the Incarnate One, who is the Way, the Truth, and the Life, and the single most important paradigm for all Christian communication, doesn't show us the way to communicate the truth of God, what does? And the method of the Incarnate One is not limited to sermons, but extends to casual conversation, table talk, and lectures. There is too much religious verbiage,

10. John 1:14.

"impotent phrasemongering," and sanctimonious talk in church, and a psychological censorship of the truth everywhere else.[11]

Kierkegaard contended that the truth of the God-man eliminated all direct communication, making it impossible to turn the wisdom of Christianity into some kind of cognitive formula that people only needed to agree to in order to become believers. Instead of agreeing to a few bullet points, we have to honestly, humbly, radically follow Jesus! We have to listen to Jesus. Kierkegaard grieved over the pervasive influence of Christendom on preaching. He wrote,

> One might well weep at the state that Christianity has been reduced to in Christendom, considering what the pastors in their sermons again and again repeat, with the utmost assurance, as if they were saying something most striking and convincing. What they say is that Christ directly affirmed that he was God, the Only Begotten of the Father; they are horrified at any suggestion of concealment, as a thing unworthy of Christ, as vain trifling with regard to a serious matter, the most serious matter of all, the salvation of man . . . Direct recognizableness is precisely the characteristic of the pagan god.
>
> . . . Take away the possibility of offense, as they have done in Christendom, and the whole of Christianity is direct communication; and then Christianity is done away with, for it has become an easy thing, a superficial something which neither wounds nor heals profoundly enough; it is the false invention of human sympathy which forgets the infinite qualitative difference between God and man.[12]

Commenting on "Jesus' fondness for the enigmatic style of speech," Helmut Thielicke wrote, "Jesus is constantly wrenching us out of our self-made dreamworld." And for that reason "he repeatedly becomes an enigma to us, in order that we may listen to what he himself says and perhaps be offended at him, but in this listening and in this offense penetrate more deeply into his mystery. We should not go on being dreamers but rather become realists who discover the real Jesus."[13]

Karl Barth in his little, yet powerful, *Dogmatics in Outline* laments a form of preaching that dismisses faith as knowledge. Such preaching assumes that religious rhetoric rises above the challenge of truth. Preachers

11. Thielicke, *The Waiting Father*, 144.

12. Kierkegaard, *Training in Christianity*, 134, 139.

13. Thielicke, *The Waiting Father*, 149.

need only embellish their platitudes with human interest anecdotes and clever phrases, without the hard work of giving reasons for the hope Christians have in Christ. Barth writes,

> You have probably also suffered from a certain kind of preaching and edifying talk, from which it becomes only too clear that there is talking going on, emphatic talk with a plenteous display of rhetoric, which does not however stand up to this simple question as to the truth of what is said.[14]

Christianity without Christ seems to echo Jesus' unbelieving brothers in John 7. As the Feast of Tabernacles approached, they chided Jesus, saying, "No one who wants to become a public figure acts in secret. Since you are doing these things, show yourself to the world." As if to say, "If you want people to believe in, you have to work for it. You have to run for office. You have to lay out your agenda and make your case." It was obvious to them that Jesus had chosen a radically different method of communication, one that in their opinion was bound to fail. Dependent upon the Father's timing and teaching, every time Jesus made a move or opened his mouth he raised questions and stirred up confusion. His proclamation of the truth was provocative. He caused people to think. He challenged their assumptions and exposed their prejudices. Some even used his awareness of the situation to accuse him of being paranoid. They mocked him, saying, "You are demon-possessed. Who is trying to kill you?"[15]

The crowd at the Feast was divided over Jesus. Some thought he was a deceiver, others thought he was a prophet, and still others that he was the Messiah. For some he was too well known. They claimed to know everything they needed to know about Jesus. They said, "But we know where this man is from; when the Messiah comes, no one will know where he is from."[16] Their knowledge got in the way of their belief. They were hung up on the fact that Jesus was from Galilee. The Pharisees kept their distance. They could hear the crowd whispering but they refused to listen to Jesus.[17]

Yet with all this confusion and chaos generated by unbelief and resistance, Jesus didn't bullet point his message. He refused to clear up the confusion and reduce his message to a list of explicit propositions. He kept coming at the truth paradoxically. "You know me," he says, "but you don't know the one who sent me . . . You will look for me, but you will not find

14. Barth, *Dogmatics in Outline*, 22.
15. John 7:20.
16. John 7:27.
17. John 7:32, 51.

me." He even spoke of the Spirit filling believers with rivers of living water, but the Spirit had not been given yet.[18] Of all the people listening to Jesus or trying not to listen to Jesus, the guards sum it up best, "No one ever spoke the way this man does."[19] The Jesus way of communicating needs to impress us more, so that when people hear us preaching the gospel they think of Jesus.

18. John 7:39.
19. John 7:46.

4

The Unadorned Altar

True worship leads us deeper into fellowship with God and with one another. Golden calf worship is an excuse for self-indulgence and cultural idolatry. Genuine worship strips down the ego, focuses on the Lord, and opens us up to the other, both to those who are in need and those who can lead us and teach us.

WHEN IT COMES TO worship styles, we seem to have more than enough tension—negative tensions that distract us from Christ and divide us from one another. The crux of the worship crisis is not over hi-tech auditoriums versus gothic sanctuaries or a preference for choirs over praise bands. It is not a battle over instruments: organs versus guitars, drums or no drums. If we frame the worship-tension as a debate between innovation and tradition or contemporary versus classical worship styles, we form two camps, two opposing sides, and make worship into a win-lose competition. And before we know it, the unity of the body of Christ rests on whether or not there's a drummer in worship!

We have to find a way of dealing with the worship-tension that lifts us above a squabble over musical styles and places us before the presence of God. We need something of the attitude of Moses standing on holy ground before the burning bush or of Peter in the fishing boat falling to his knees before the Lord Jesus, saying, "Depart from me for I am an evil man."[1] A positive tension in worship fills us with a deep sense of our utter need for the living triune God. Like Isaiah before the throne of God, we ought to feel "woe to me! I'm ruined!"[2] We ought to know that without

1. Exod 3:5; Luke 5:8.
2. Isa 6:5.

Christ we are hopelessly lost. If worship laid out the apostle John flat on the ground ("I fell at his feet as though dead") at least it should drive us to our knees.[3]

When Bible-based verticality in worship is set in tension with Christ-centered neighbor-loving horizontal intensity, we have a positive tension. We need and want this tension between order and spontaneity, head and heart, ancient hymns and contemporary praise songs, so as to strengthen and challenge our worship of the living God. Our goal is the in-depth worship of the triune God with reverent doxology, expressive praise, submissive obedience, evangelistic passion, and ethical impact. We want the worship of God and the mission of God to be inseparable.

Sadly, we may have been too quick to write off the biblical model of the church as a multi-generational, cross-cultural, racially mixed, and socially diverse congregation of followers of Jesus Christ. We have acted as if the dynamic nature of the church is the New Testament equivalent to the Old Testament Year of Jubilee, great in theory but untried in practice. However, if the body of Christ was designed by the Spirit of Christ to reflect this unity in diversity, then we have to be true to the doctrine of the church just as we have to be true to the doctrine of salvation. Faith and practice come together in the fullness of the body of Christ.

Framing the Tension

In *Who Stole My Church*, well-known pastor Gordon MacDonald frames the worship tension as a clash of cultures—"a dark tension between the generations."[4] He does a good job of showing how little it takes to divide the evangelical church along partisan lines. MacDonald describes the small-minded ways of fifty-something baby boomers, who are change-resistant, out-of-date, devoted to pews, neckties, Wednesday night prayer-meetings, three-point sermons, choir robes, and their favorite hymns. Mess with these things and you are in for a fight. MacDonald draws an easy parallel between the resistance of the Pharisees and the church-killing ways of his New England parishioners. He argues that in order for the church to remain relevant she must be in a constant state of re-invention. The "core beliefs" remain the same but everything else is subject to change. "Almost nothing can stay the same for long if you want to connect with people and

3. Rev 1:17.
4. MacDonald, *Who Stole My Church?*, xx.

introduce them to Jesus Christ."[5] MacDonald turns to the conventional wisdom of business expert Jack Welch to make his point, "When the rate of change inside an organization is slower than the rate of change outside an organization, the end [of that organization] is in sight."[6]

What we are to make of Jack Welch's line is unclear, because the church is not like any other organization in history. The Bride of Christ is much more like a family, a household of faith, than a corporation. We don't have a product line; in Christ, we have a whole new way of life. God-centered worship keeps believers praying the psalms, singing old hymns and contemporary praise songs, offering up prayers of confession, preaching the tension in the text, relating to each other personally, showing compassion to the needy, and reaching out to their neighbors locally and globally.

MacDonald's basic assumption is that the "core beliefs" have little to do with the "total re-invention" he is advocating to reach younger generations. Hi-tech auditoriums, rock-out music, video movie clips, mini-dramas, interviews, and casual conversational sermons are the new tools for church growth. Multi-sited churches linked up technologically to listen to the same sermon video, are all part of a huge paradigm shift that needs to happen to bring the church into the twenty-first century. Anything less is status quo, reactionary thinking. Church growth is a matter of strategic product placement, as in changing the name of the church or using technology to present the gospel. MacDonald warns that church innovators have to be prepared to do battle, because there are plenty of "laggards" who are bound by tradition.[7]

Gordon MacDonald is right to critique the narrow-minded, spiritually shallow traditional church, but he offers no parallel critique of modernity's sins. We are not warned of any dangers inherent in embracing technology or adapting to a narcissistic generation. We are not cautioned against change for change's sake. The book blurb on the back cover promises that the reader will "discover how to meet the needs of all believers without abandoning the dreams and desires of any." By framing the worship tension as a clash of cultures, with innovative cultural change the key strategy for transformation, this people-pleasing discovery seems highly unlikely.

5. Ibid., 41.

6. Ibid.

7. Ibid., 177.

Pastor Mark Labberton in *The Dangerous Act of Worship* frames the worship tension differently. The real battle over worship has much less to do with musical genre, liturgical form, cultural tastes, personal preferences, spiritual aesthetics, and technological acoustics than it does with reflecting "the worthiness of God by how we love and serve whomever and whatever God considers to be of worth."[8] The real crisis is that our worship does not "produce the fruit of justice and righteousness that God seeks. This creates a crisis of faithfulness before God and crisis of purpose before the world."[9] Real worship is best judged by righteousness and justice, not by its relevance. Is our personal and communal worship consistent with Christ being the center of our lives? "Worship is to be the one activity that sums up the scope of our lives."[10]

The positive tension of worship holds together loving God with our whole being and loving our neighbor as ourselves. Unless worship calls us "deeper into God's heart and deeper into the world for which Christ died" it is not very good worship. It may be safe and everybody in the congregation may be happy, but God, who is the primary audience of our worship, is not pleased. It would be impossible to read the biblical prophets on Israel's worship and come away with the notion that innovation was the pressing need for our worship. Religious people are capable of going to great lengths to perform high-powered worship services, but if they neglect the widow and the orphan, take advantage of the poor, and turn a blind eye to the needy, their worship is a sham. Labberton writes, "That is the crux of the crisis. I and other Christians I know have been busy tithing the dill and cumin of worship forms while avoiding what Jesus calls the weightier matters of the Law: justice, mercy and faith."[11]

Whenever we try to entice or entertain the world by mimicking the world our silly efforts come across as embarrassing. Secular people are not asking "Why doesn't the church look more like us?" What they're really asking, Labberton suggests, is, "Why doesn't the church look more like Jesus?"[12] In our effort to be relevant "we are willing to make the gospel more accessible than it really is, to remove the scandal, the offense of the cross, to deceive people into thinking that it is possible to hear without

8. Labberton, *The Dangerous Act of Worship*, 27.

9. Ibid., 22.

10. Ibid., 39.

11. Ibid.

12. Ibid., 51.

conversion."[13] If worship is all about being brought before the living God, then we would be better off refusing "to relax the tension between our ways and God's ways."[14]

Robert Webber prayed that the church would "look *less* like culture, not *more* like it." He anticipated a church that would be more counter-cultural, not less. The biblical values of community, relationship, authenticity, and radical biblical discipleship would mean more to the church in the future, not less. He saw the church embracing more fully ethical absolutes and the fullness of the biblical narrative. "My guess is that worship will become more biblical (Word and Table), simpler (not a show with all the cultural stuff), more authentic (real people doing real things like praying, giving testimony, responding to sermons, being participatory), much smaller (neighborhood churches), and quite eclectic in music and arts."[15]

Worship is dangerous *negatively* when we make it about ourselves, rather than about God; when we lie about God and make our "worship" a platform for showcasing our talents or our patriotism. When worship doesn't change us or the world we serve, it is dangerous in a debilitating way. "Millions of American Christians spend hours in worship and yet lead lifestyles indistinguishable in priorities, values and practices from those in the broader culture."[16]

Worship is dangerous *positively* when we encounter the living triune God; when it isn't safe, comfortable, or convenient; when it opens us up to the word of God and lays us out in surrender to the will of God. Worship changes the way we see God, ourselves and the world—dramatically so! "The primary lens is no longer our family background, our personality, prejudices, worries or subculture; it is now the love of God for every person."[17] Mark Labberton reframes the worship-tension so that we don't mistake our petty differences for the real issue. Labberton's biblical thesis has proven true in my pastoral experience. The Lord used three key ways to keep our congregation on track worship-wise.

The first was suffering. As a church we found it difficult to be small-minded, opinionated, and selfish, in the company of ordinary saints who remained faithful while undergoing great trials. The impact that their quiet testimonies and evident resolve had on the congregation was amazing.

13. Willimon, *The Intrusive Word*, 19.
14. Ibid., 68.
15. Webber, *Exploring the Worship Spectrum*, 248.
16. Labberton, *The Dangerous Act of Worship*, 74.
17. Ibid., 94.

Their presence in worship made the presence of God more real and prayer more urgent. Does any Sunday go by when a pastor is unaware of brothers and sisters in Christ who are standing strong in spite of battling the world, the flesh, and the devil? I didn't have to talk about these people or make a big deal about them. Their testimony without words was powerful.

The second was mission. A profound sense of God's mission for the Body of Christ is far more important for worship than a great choir or praise team. In fact, I doubt that a church can have a truly great choir or praise team without a strong sense of God's mission for the church. They may be good musically, but without a sense of mission, they will not help the congregation worship. Worship and mission form a dynamic tension, each serving as an energizing and motivating catalyst for the other. Both sides of the equation work equally well. We can worship our way into mission and mission our way into worship. But feelings alone are a poor resource for worship. We worship more consistently when we worship our way into feelings for God than when we use feelings to motivate our worship. Mission produces a powerful incentive to worship because both mission and worship are centered in God. Worship reminds us that "mission is not ours; mission is God's." We worship the triune God who is on a mission and when we worship we are reminded, "it is not so much the case that God has a mission for his church in the world but that God has a church for his mission in the world. Mission was not made for the church; the church was made for mission—God's mission."[18]

The third element that kept our worship on track was key people with a passion for praising God. When worship leaders have a passion for Christ and a pastoral concern for people they use their musical gifts in profoundly redemptive ways. The body of Christ is best served by people who are more God-centered than musically oriented. At times the distinction may be difficult to discern, but it is crucial. People who make it mainly about musical performance end up hurting worship and body life. I have had the privilege of working with musicians who are first and foremost disciples of the Lord Jesus who pastor their choirs and praise teams with wisdom and love. They are vitally interested in all aspects of the worship, including the sermon. Musical excellence is important to them, but never as a substitute for humble, Christ-centered worship.

We need to reframe the worship-tension and lift the conversation to a higher plane than our cultural and generational differences over worship styles and liturgy. The issue is not as much about contemporary versus

18. Wright, *The Mission of God*, 62.

traditional musical styles as it is about faithfulness and mission. It is not about religion; it is about justice and righteousness.

God's Worship Instructions

A theology of ministry seeks to understand how God wants to be worshiped and there is no better place to begin than with God's altar building instructions in Exodus 20.

> Then the Lord said to Moses, "Tell the Israelites this: You have seen for yourselves that I have spoken to you from heaven: Do not make any gods to be alongside me; do not make for yourselves gods of silver or gods of gold. Make an altar of earth for me and sacrifice on it your burnt offerings and fellowship offerings, your sheep and goats and your cattle. Wherever I cause my name to be honored, I will come to you and bless you. If you make an altar of stones for me, do not build it with dressed stones, for you will defile it if you use a tool on it. And do not go up to my altar on steps, lest your nakedness be exposed on it.[19]

This is an intriguing and seldom referred to command that broadens the prohibition against idolatry. Does the divine stipulation against dressed stones and a raised platform apply only to the Israelites in the wilderness or is there a principle implied in this command that applies to our worship of God today? If God's altar-building instructions are to be taken seriously, as an enduring guide for understanding how the invisible God makes himself known, how should they impact us today?

We are deep into salvation history before the Lord God gave these basic instructions about obedience and altar building. God-fearing righteous men and women illustrated the meaning of the Ten Commandments and true worship long before these instructions were given. In Exodus, Yahweh makes explicit what was understood from the beginning. In spite of our predisposition to sin, there is an intuitive awareness that God's law is right and good. Since we are made in God's image, our souls resonate with commands against idolatry, adultery, thievery, and envy. The apostle Paul insisted in Romans chapter one that even pagans understand the right way to live. God's will on obedience and altar building is bedrock wisdom on righteousness and spirituality.

Abel was the first to sacrifice an animal but the Bible does not refer explicitly to Abel building an altar. Noah was the first to build an altar,

19. Exod 20:22–26.

several thousand years before the Exodus. He gathered his family around him and celebrated their salvation from the flood with an altar to the Lord. His altar stood for human repentance and divine mercy. We read: "The Lord smelled the pleasing aroma and said in his heart: 'Never again will I curse the ground because of human beings, even though every inclination of the human heart is evil from childhood.'"[20] Roughly a thousand years before the Exodus, Abraham was the next altar builder. He marked the defining moments of his life with an altar. His answer to the promise of God was an altar.[21] He proved his faith in God by his willingness to offer his only son Isaac on an altar on mount Moriah.[22] Isaac continued the practice, but he did not merely copy his father's worship, as if he were maintaining a tradition. Isaac built an altar in response to God's personal revelation and promise. The Lord appeared to Isaac and said, "I am the God of your father Abraham. Do not be afraid, for I am with you . . ."[23] Likewise, when God revealed himself to Jacob, Jacob built an altar.[24]

The human response to a personal saving encounter with the living God was intuitively simple and inherently sacrificial. When the Lord rescued the Israelites from their enemies the Amalekites, Moses built an altar and called it *The Lord is my Banner.* All of these altars were built without explicit instructions. Why then did God decide several thousand years into salvation history to give instructions on how to build altars? The Ten Commandments and God's altar building instructions establish a divine principle that ought to be followed by the people of God in every generation. The Ten Commandments institute life's priority—obedience. The altar building instructions establish worship's simplicity and sacrifice. Left to ourselves, religion evolves into something we create. Human initiative distorts obedience and worship into something complex and confusing, but true spirituality involves an immediate and personal *sacrificial* encounter with the living God who redeems us from sin and death. Our human tendency is to make life complicated even though God has commanded it to be simple and straightforward.

We invariably distract ourselves from the real work and worship that God intended and substitute our own will and work in its place. The Westminster Confession seeks to honor the principle of the unadorned altar

20. Gen 8:21.
21. Gen 12:7; 13:18.
22. Gen 22.
23. Gen 26:24.
24. Gen 35:1, 7.

by stating that "the acceptable way of worshiping the true God is instituted by himself, and so limited by his own revealed will, that he may not be worshiped according to the imaginations and devices of men, or the suggestions of Satan, under any visible representation, or any other way not prescribed in the holy Scripture."[25] True worship is instituted by God and limited to what God has commanded in his Word: prayer, praise, proclamation of the Word of God, celebration of baptism, and the Lord's Table. Worship is both *prescribed* and *limited*. For some this stipulation raises a question: Does this mean that the celebration of Advent and Lent are unacceptable because they are not explicitly prescribed by Scripture? On the contrary, these times of worship are consistent with a biblical prescription and a Christ-centered focus. When they are done well they strengthen the worship and witness of the church. The Westminster Confession raises our sensitivity to false worship and underscores the truth that worship is limited to what God prescribes, not what humans propose. "To worship in the way that we will, without proof that it is God's will, is to worship our own will rather than God."[26]

God's altar building instructions have implications beyond saying "no" to designer stones and a raised platform. The principle established in the wilderness becomes a pattern throughout salvation history. The invisible God insists on a simplicity of spirituality that does not distract from the act of worship. The purpose of the altar was sacrifice, not self-expression, and the sacrifice stood for human repentance and divine mercy.

The Principle

Several observations underscore the principle of the unadorned altar:

1. "You have *seen* for yourselves that I have *spoken* to you from heaven." The people's vision of God was not visual but audio. Instead of a physical representation of God there was a spiritual understanding of God. God defined himself linguistically, not visually. In a visual and visceral sense God remained hidden. Yahweh refused to be reduced to an object that could be worshiped. God reveals himself as the living subject, who is rationally, spiritually, and emotionally comprehensible. The hidden God is present among his people personally, but not materially. Instead of projecting himself in a shrine, Yahweh insisted on a conversation with his people.

25. Williamson, *The Westminster Confession*, 158.
26. Ibid., 160.

The order of God's revelation is also instructive. Altar building instructions follow the Ten Commandments. Spirituality is rooted in objective obedience. Explicit commands describe the visible righteousness of a person who loves and obeys God. The altar-building commands apply to authentic worship and follow up the description of righteousness in the Ten Commandments. Piety always follows obedience. Spirituality and ethics are inseparable. This same pattern is evident in the Sermon on the Mount. Jesus spoke first of visible righteousness. Beatitude-based belief was evident in practical obedience: love instead of hate, purity instead of lust, fidelity instead of infidelity, honesty instead of dishonesty, reconciliation instead of retaliation, and prayer instead of revenge. Then, he spoke of the hidden righteousness of giving, praying, and fasting.

2. "Do not make any gods to be alongside me; do not make for yourselves gods of silver or gods of gold." The revelation of God ruled out any competing visualizations of God. Note that the prohibition explicitly rules out any images *alongside* God. We might have expected the command to say, "Do not make any gods in place of me," or "instead of me," but the command goes further. Idols can neither substitute for God, nor be placed alongside God. Those who use visual representations of God to make worship of Yahweh more accessible are put on notice that this unacceptable. It is the idolatry *alongside* God that is most troublesome. Pagans are expected to worship idols, but when those who follow the one, true and living God place something *alongside* God to make worship more exciting or more visceral, they expose an even greater problem than pagan idolatry. The "alongside" variety of idolatry is a far greater problem for us than we may wish to acknowledge. When we place something alongside God to make the gospel more exciting or more attractive, we say in effect that Jesus and his sacrifice are not enough. We need a value-added gospel. We feel the necessity of offering our visual enhancements to the gospel.

3. "Make an altar of earth for me . . ." The altar was nothing to look at. The altar, the physical setting for sacrificial worship, was not important, any mound of dirt would do. The heart of the worshiper was not revealed in the altar, but in the quality of the animal sacrifice. The perfect sacrifice was always created by God not humans. The sacrificial lamb could never be an object of human pride.

4. "Wherever I cause my name to be honored, I will come to you and bless you." From this line we learn that the initiative always lies with

God. God goes before the worshiper revealing his will and accomplishing his purposes. The worshiper finds himself or herself in the middle between God's sovereign initiative and God's great blessing. It is not a matter of us going out in our own strength and power to accomplish something great for God, as if God were waiting for us to get to work. No, God honors his name where and when and how God chooses. Blessing flows from God's work, not ours. The true worshiper is disciplined in willed passivity, in wise passivity. He or she is attentive to God's will and work and receptive of God's blessing.

5. "If you make an altar of stones for me, do not build it with dressed stones, for you will defile it if you use a tool on it." We are in the habit of linking defilement with flagrant sin and disobedience, but the Lord warned that desecration goes up as well as down. Well-intentioned people may pour their heart and soul in doing something for God and end up desecrating worship. Blasphemy and profanity are blatantly sinful, but equally repulsive to the Lord is obsequious piety that draws attention to itself. When worship is used to display our skills and talents, we are calling people's attention to ourselves instead of to the Lord. Such worship is really not worship at all, but an egocentric performance. The danger is that we become very busy doing for God what God has not asked us to do, and even warned us against doing, while avoiding the very things that God has commanded us to do. Consistent with this concern is the prohibition against putting the altar up on a raised platform. "And do not go up to my altar on steps, lest your nakedness be exposed on it." The issue here is not raised platforms per se, but our vain attempt to bring something special to worship that distracts from the true meaning of worship. The invisible God does not want our visual special effects to obscure the real meaning of sacrificial worship. Well-intentioned but misguided spirituality invariably calls attention to itself and not only distracts, but defiles true worship.

6. The necessity for God's altar building instructions became apparent as Moses descended the mountain. Impatient with Moses' delay, the people demanded that Aaron make a visible image of divine power. Instead of waiting in dependence upon Yahweh, they filled the void they felt with their own willful desires and human effort. As we said earlier, Aaron dedicated the golden-calf idol to the Lord and called the occasion "a festival to the Lord," but labeling it didn't change it. Undoubtedly, Aaron was well-intentioned. His purpose was to give

to the people a visible manifestation of Yahweh in order to build morale as they waited for Moses to come down the mountain. But idolatry is idolatry, regardless of the subjective motive. "The calf represented Yahweh on *their* terms."[27]

The invisible God is iconoclastic. God takes a dim view of the visual aids that we use to enhance worship. The biblical word used to describe these special effects is not "distraction" but "defilement." The warning against dressed stones and raised platforms applies to Western Christianity's propensity to build impressive buildings, celebrate high-profile personalities, glory in large anonymous audiences, deliver entertaining self-help sermons, and focus on one's own denomination or association to the exclusion of other believers. The visual, visceral, impact of all of these things ends up placing an idol *alongside* the living God.

The principle of the unadorned altar applies on a personal level as well. In *Death by Suburb*, David Goetz warns middle class Christians of their tendency to create "immortality symbols" out of their suburban lifestyle. We attach intangible significance and self-worth to tangible objects like cars, homes, children, sports, sex, vacations, etc. The unawakened self is dominated by visual material objects and visceral experiences. Goetz writes, "The unawakened self lives only in the flat, mysteryless, empirical world, pursuant only of what psychologist Ernest Becker called 'immortality symbols.' . . . An immortality symbol is not really about the thing (bank balance, home, car, child, job, etc). It's about the glory that the thing bestows on me."[28] The principle of the unadorned altar is in conflict with the experience of the unawakened self. Life is all about the dressed stones and raised platform, instead of a sacrificial encounter with the living God.

The Pattern

Yahweh's altar-building instructions are consistent with a pattern that emerges throughout salvation history calling for simplicity and sacrifice. In worship, Yahweh allowed nothing to compete with human repentance and divine mercy. Biblical iconoclasm ruled out visual and emotional competition with the true focus of worship. Three important phases of salvation history affirm the principle of the unadorned altar: the tabernacle, the temple, and the table.

27. Durham, *Exodus*, 422 (emphasis his).

28. Goetz, *Death by Suburb*, 42.

The Tabernacle

The sheer volume of detailed instruction on how to make the Ark of the Testimony, the Table for the Bread of the Presence, the Seven-branched Lampstand, and the Tabernacle emphasizes the invisible realities of salvation, forgiveness, and holiness. The Ark of Testimony was the most important symbol of God's presence. Although it was lined and covered with pure gold, and it was not to be touched by human hands but moved by specially made poles, it was but a box. And not a very big box at that. It measured three feet, six and a half inches long and two feet, two and a quarter inches wide and high. Everything else, from the Table of the Bread of Presence to the Altar of the Burnt Offering, was placed in reference to the Ark of the Covenant. Its lid was called the atonement cover and its contents included a copy of the commandments. It signified the Word and Sacrament of God.

The notion that the tabernacle replicated the garden or paradise is speculative and misleading. When Yahweh said to Moses, "Make this tabernacle and all its furnishings exactly like the pattern I will show you," he gave him verbal instructions.[29] God didn't take him on a virtual tour of his heavenly home, because there would have been no "sacred space" to show him. Nor does the author of Hebrews imply that there is a heavenly ideal generating the form or shadow on earth.[30] The stress here is on understanding the Lord's instructions, not copying a heavenly sanctuary.

We are given no hint in the New Testament that the tabernacle serves as a guide for constructing church buildings and sanctuaries. Everything the tabernacle represented and stood for pointed forward to Christ and was fulfilled in Christ. By design, the way the church focuses people's attention on the Lord is not by a building but by how the church honors and obeys the Lord in everyday living. It is the body of Christ, not the church building, that points true worshipers to the living God. If the testimony of the body of Christ depends on our buildings and sanctuaries we are serious trouble. Since Christ, the emphasis has shifted from architecture to relationships, as the author of Hebrews makes plain: "Let us draw near to God with a sincere heart in full assurance of faith . . . Let us hold unswervingly to the hope we profess, for he who promised is faithful. And let us consider how we may spur one another on toward love and good deeds, not giving up meeting together, as some are in the habit of doing, but encouraging

29. Exod 25:9.
30. Heb 8:5.

one another—and all the more as you see the Day approaching."[31] From its name, shape, and contents, the Ark of Testimony symbolized Yahweh's presence and pointed to the divine work of redemption and revelation necessary for the salvation of God's people. It was never thought of as a substitute for the invisible reality of God or as an object of worship and devotion. At the center of Israel's worship life, in the Most Holy Place, the Ark was not a sacred relic, but a symbol of the Presence of God. The Ark of Testimony pointed away from idolatry to the invisible reality of the God who is.

The Temple

Whatever glory was invoked by the massive and majestic buildings of the temple was overshadowed by the tragedy of Israel's disobedience and apostasy. Seven years in the making, the temple required tens of thousands of enslaved workers hewing Lebanese cedar, mining gold, silver, iron and precious stones, and hauling huge blocks of high-grade stone to Jerusalem. From the beginning we sense that this massive project was more for Solomon's ego than for God's glory. Solomon's own palace took thirteen years to build and was bigger than the temple. He continued his building projects by constructing a palace for his Egyptian wife and building shrines for his other foreign wives to the child-sacrificing gods of his neighbors, the Moabites and the Ammonites.[32] Israel had come a long way from the unadorned altar in the wilderness to Solomon's altar. The bronze altar in the outer courtyard of Solomon's temple was the size of a small house. It measured thirty-four feet long and wide and seventeen feet tall.

Roughly four hundred years after Solomon, Jeremiah showed real courage when he stood his ground at the gate of the temple and said, "This is what the Lord Almighty, the God of Israel says: Reform your ways and your actions, and I will let you live in this place. Do not trust in deceptive words and say, 'This is the temple of the Lord, the temple of the Lord, the temple of the Lord!'"[33] In Jeremiah's day, ritual practices were well attended. The temple liturgy was lively. Priests were popular. Religious diversity was in vogue and cultural inclusiveness was trendy. The long tradition of

31. Heb 10:22–25.

32. 1 Kgs 6–7, 11.

33. Jer 7:3–4.

respect for the house of the Lord was pretentiously maintained while despising everything the Name of the Lord stood for.[34]

When Jeremiah stood at the gate of the temple to proclaim the Lord's message against blatant idolatry and false sacrifice, he took his stand in a long tradition that valued obedience over ritual and humble devotion over religious performance. He stood with Abel and his sacrificial lamb, against Cain's offering of choice produce.[35] He stood with faithful Samuel against Saul's religion of convenience.[36] He stood with a repentant King David when he prayed, "You do not delight in sacrifice, or I would bring it; you do not take pleasure in burnt offerings. The sacrifices of God are a broken spirit; a broken and contrite heart, O God, you will not despise."[37] He stood with Amos, who declared the word of the Lord, "I hate, I despise your religious feasts; I cannot stand your assemblies. Even though you bring me burnt offerings and grain offerings, I will not accept them. . . . But let justice roll on like a river, righteousness like a never-failing stream!"[38]

Jeremiah stood in the tradition of Hosea, who spoke for God when he said, "For I desire mercy, not sacrifice, and acknowledgment of God rather than burnt offerings."[39] He stood with Micah, when the prophet contrasted hyper-religiosity with simple obedience, saying, "He has showed you, O man, what is good. And what does the Lord require of you? To act justly and to love mercy and to walk humbly with your God."[40] He stood with the prophet Isaiah when he said hear the word of the Lord, "Stop bringing meaningless offerings! Your incense is detestable to me. . . . I cannot bear your evil assemblies . . . Stop doing wrong, learn to do right! Seek justice, encourage the oppressed. Defend the cause of the fatherless, plead the case of the widow."[41]

Jeremiah kept this long tradition going, but his most important connection was not to the past but to the future, not to the prophets he echoed but to the Savior he preceded. Jesus forcibly drove out "all who were buying and selling" and "overturned the tables of the money changers." He leveled a stinging accusation, quoting the prophets, he said, "It is

34. 2 Sam 7:12–13; Ps 132:13–14.
35. Gen 3.
36. 1 Sam 13.
37. Ps 51:16–17.
38. Amos 5:21–24.
39. Hos 6:6.
40. Mic 6:8.
41. Isa 1:13–17.

written, 'My house will be called a house of prayer,' but you are making it a *den of robbers*."[42] By drawing on Isaiah and Jeremiah, Jesus equated the religious crisis of his day with the false temple religion that the prophets had confronted. His words and actions vindicated the work of the prophets through the centuries as they sought to drive out empty religiosity, meaningless ritual, and self-righteousness.

One incident in particular symbolizes Jesus' attitude toward temple religion. One day as Jesus and the disciples were leaving Herod's temple, Jesus noticed a poor widow putting two very small copper coins into the temple treasury. He commended her to the disciples as an example of sacrificial giving. She gave more than all the others. Meanwhile, one of his disciples excitedly exclaimed, "Look, Teacher! What massive stones! What magnificent buildings!" He was awed by the beauty of the buildings and proud of what they symbolized, the enduring status and significance of Israel's greatest institution. Jesus however did not share his disciple's enthusiasm. "Do you see all these great buildings?" he replied. "Not one stone here will be left on another; every one will be thrown down."[43] For Jesus the buildings symbolized what must come down. The temple did not represent the future of the faith but the end of religion. However, there was an even greater contrast than the one between the present and the future. One that was clearly in the mind of Jesus when he said, "Destroy this temple, and I will raise it again in three days."[44] In his own person he rendered the temple obsolete and its adoration inappropriate. In the light of salvation history a disciple's enthusiasm for an edifice or an institution is at best embarrassing and at worst idolatry.

The Table

Jesus instituted the Lord's Supper in the upper room on the night that he was betrayed. Having washed his disciples' feet, he said to them, "Very truly, I tell you, servants are not greater than their master, nor are messengers greater than the one who sent them."[45] The setting was simple, as were the words of institution: "Take and eat; this is my body" and taking the cup, "This is my blood of the covenant, which is poured out for many." Jesus commanded his followers to remember his atoning sacrifice in a

42. Matt 21:13; see Isa 56:7; Jer 7:11.
43. Mark 13:1–2.
44. John 2:19.
45. John 13:16.

simple and reverent way. He embodied the principle of the unadorned altar: "No dressed stones and no raised platform."

The ecclesiastical special effects that surround today's celebration of Holy Communion are out of sync with our Lord's institution. Protestants, Roman Catholics, and Orthodox alike have elaborated a ceremonial ritual that draws attention away from Christ and emphasizes the presiding pastor or priest and the pageantry of a ceremony. Luther was a strong advocate for the simplicity of the Lord's Supper. His perspective was in keeping with the principle of the unadorned altar, when he wrote,

> In the first place, in order that we might safely and happily attain to a true and free knowledge of this sacrament, we must be particularly careful to put aside whatever has been added to its original simple institution by the zeal and devotion of men: such things as vestments, ornaments, chants, prayers, organs, candles, and the whole pageantry of outward things. We must turn our eyes and hearts simply to the institution of Christ and this alone, and set nothing before us but the very word of Christ by which he instituted the sacrament, made it perfect, and committed it to us.[46]

We act as if we must make something special of Christ's sacrifice. The pastor raises high the gleaming silver pitcher and dramatically pours out the wine into a cup, sanctimoniously repeating the words of institution. In flowing robes, priests parade up to the altar, swaying incense urns and chanting in Latin. What Jesus began as a climax to his table fellowship with his disciples and as a memorial to his atoning sacrifice on the cross, has evolved into a religious show.

The principle of the unadorned altar is evident in the tabernacle, temple and table, and can be found as a pattern throughout salvation history. The trajectory of humility during the second exodus, when the Israelites returned to Jerusalem from their captivity, is consistent with the principle of the unadorned altar. It is also evident in Jesus' promise of an easy yoke and in how the apostle Paul uses the analogy of jars of clay. Throughout the Bible, the message is clear, no dressed stones, no raised platforms. Nothing belongs *alongside* the Lord Jesus. The vain attempt to "dress up" the gospel to make it more attractive or more exciting, only defiles it. When religion is the product of human effort, it invariably moves toward manipulation, bureaucratic control, or whimsical subjectivity, cultural conformity, and false complexity.

46. Luther, *The Babylonian Captivity of the Church*, 153.

The Picture

The unadorned, undecorated pile of rocks in the wilderness stood there in earthy simplicity as a symbol of human need and divine acceptance; humility and mercy, repentance and redemption. The Lord insisted that the altar must not be turned into a shrine to human effort and religious pride. To decorate the altar was to desecrate it. To put it high up on a platform was to exalt man and debase God. "Whatever you do," the Lord said in effect, "don't work on it religiously. Keep it simple. It's just a pile of rocks. Worship me in humility and depend upon my mercy."

How does the principle of the unadorned altar apply to our church buildings? Nothing is said in the Bible about church buildings, but many churches identify themselves with their buildings. Wang Mingdao, respectfully remembered as the dean of the house church movement in Communist China, called for simplicity and integrity. "I have no desire to do something great," Wang Mingdao wrote. "It is not so much a large church that I want to build; it is rather to build up a church according to the mind of God."[47] In 1936, the church he led bought property and built a building, which they named the Christian Tabernacle. Later, Wang recalled their concern to keep the building and the liturgy simple:

> The equipment and furnishings inside the hall were marked by simplicity, cleanliness and dignity. The walls were as white as snow and no words or pictures were hung on them. This was so that nothing should distract the attention of the worshipers so that they could worship God with singleness of heart. Neither outside the building nor inside did we have a cross . . . A white stone on the southeast corner carries an inscription of four sentences which indicate our faith and the truths we emphasize. . . . "He was wounded for our transgressions." He rose again from the dead. He has already been received into heaven. He will come again to receive us.[48]

The contrast between Wang Mingdao and Pope Nicholas V could not have been greater. In 1450 as he lay dying, Nicholas shared his dream with his cardinals of a Vatican that would be greater than any emperor's palace:

> A popular faith, sustained only on doctrines, will never be anything but feeble and vacillating. But if the authority of the Holy See were visibly displayed in majestic buildings, imperishable

47. Harvey, *Acquainted with Grief*, 42.
48. Ibid.

memorials, and witnesses seemingly planted by the Hand of God Himself, belief would grow and strengthen like a tradition from one generation to another, and all the world would accept and revere it. Noble edifices, combining taste and beauty with imposing proportions, would immediately conduce to the exaltation of the Chair of St. Peter . . .[49]

R. A. Scotti traces the history St. Peter's Basilica, "a work in progress for more than two centuries." She gives the fascinating story of intrigue, conflict, sacrifice, and scandal that lies behind what Edward Gibbon called, "the most glorious structure that ever has been applied to the use of religion."[50] "The ideal remained constant," Scotti concludes, "to construct a metaphor in stone for the leap of faith that is at the heart of the gospel of Christ . . . Gothic cathedrals reach up to heaven. St. Peter's—muscular, sublime, irrevocable—brings heaven to earth."[51]

Visual support for New Testament faith stands in stark simplicity to Medieval Christianity with its elaborate rituals, vestments, indulgences, paintings, statutes, cathedrals, feast days, plays, and images of saints. The church promoted these visual aids to faith, including pilgrimages and the veneration of relics, but resisted giving people the Bible in their own language. Priests re-enacted Christ's crucifixion in the Mass, but neglected to preach the Word of Christ. The high point of the Mass in the Medieval church was *seeing* the Host raised up and consecrated by the priest with the words of institution, "This is my body," but one wonders whether they were taught what it meant to take up their cross and follow Jesus.

The invisible God's altar building instructions prepared the way for the revelation of God. God ruled out the clutter, diversion, and defilement that humans insist on bringing into their religion. Nothing was meant to distract from the incarnation of God and the atoning sacrifice of Christ on the cross. The Lord God's insistence on invisibility until the revelation of Christ focuses our attention where it belongs, on the crucified and risen Lord.

Two verses by the apostle John summarize the unique and humble visibility of the revelation of God: "No one has ever seen God, but the one and only Son, who is himself God and is in closest relationship with the Father, has made him known."[52] Salvation history is fulfilled in the one

49. Scotti, *Basilica*, 21.
50. Ibid., 269.
51. Ibid.
52. John 1:18.

who "being in very nature God . . . made himself nothing."[53] The invisible visibility of the hidden God made known in Jesus offers the most profound rationale for the unadorned altar. From the beginning and throughout salvation history everything was carefully orchestrated by God to prepare for the stark simplicity of Jesus in the manger and the cross of Christ. This is the unadorned sacrifice that saves us from our sin and redeems us for the very presence of God. In the coming of Jesus, God remained true to the principle and pattern of the unadorned altar.

The second verse is in 1 John 4:12: "No one has ever seen God; but if we love one another, God lives in us and his love is made complete in us." The invisible God's visibility is revealed today in and through the body of believers marked by the love of Christ. John is careful to define the meaning of this love. "This is love: not that we loved God, but that he loved us and sent his Son as an atoning sacrifice for our sins. Dear friends, since God so loved us, we also ought to love one another." Like the Israelites in the wilderness, the human propensity is to add something alongside God that we can control and glory in, whether it be basilicas or budgets. Instead of loving one another in Christ we build shrines and power-bases. We have our own institutionalized golden-calf religion. We need to be reminded of God's timely message and apply the principle of "no dressed stones and no raised platforms" to the church today. Much of our effort is not just a distraction but a defilement. In the body of Christ, we want to remain true to the principle of the unadorned altar. The only way to do that is for each of us to offer our whole self "as a living sacrifice, holy and pleasing to God—this is true worship."[54]

Paradise or Passion

Beautiful churches are impressive, but not nearly as impressive as Colorado's Rocky Mountains. On the whole we do a pretty poor job of building beautiful churches and when we do succeed we invite idolatry. We encourage people to identify with a building, give to a building, maintain loyalty to a building, and ooh and ah over a building. It is not the building that reflects the priorities and procedures of the worshipers, but the body-life of the believing community.

Architectural design and great craftsmanship is a limited medium for devotion to God. True worship is reflected in discipleship, not sacred

53. Phil 2:6–7.
54. Rom 12:1.

decor. The power of the gospel may be evident in sacred rituals, but only when backed up by relationships made real in Christ. It is not our vaulted ceilings, but our humility that counts for Christ. We were not meant to flee the mundane world or forsake the ordinary world of needy souls. In Christ, we are invited to turn the neighborhood into sacred space. "Believe me," Jesus said to the Samaritan woman at the well, "a time is coming when you will worship the Father neither on this mountain nor in Jerusalem . . . Yet a time is coming and has now come when the true worshipers will worship the Father in the Spirit and in truth, for they are the kind of worshipers the Father seeks. God is spirit, and his worshipers must worship in the Spirit and in truth."[55]

True worship and mission centers on the Passion of Christ. It does not retreat to paradise. A church that preaches the cross must itself be marked by the cross.[56] Stephen, the church's first martyred missionary, gave the first word on New Testament church architecture, "the Most High does not live in houses made by human hands." He then extended his missional principle of holy ground to include the cosmos. Quoting the prophet Isaiah he declared, "'Heaven is my throne, and the earth is my footstool. What kind of house will you build for me?' says the Lord. 'Or where will my resting place be? Has not my hand made all these things?'"[57] If Stephen gave us the first word on church buildings, the apostle John gave us the last word: "I did not see a temple in the city, because the Lord God Almighty and the Lamb are its temple."[58]

55. John 4:21–24.

56. Douglas, "The Lausanne Covenant," 5.

57. Acts 7:48–49.

58. Rev 21:22.

5

The Sacraments

Worship is anchored in the identifying act of baptism and in the praise and fellowship of Holy Communion. Baptism seals our solidarity with Christ and the eucharist signifies the real presence of Christ in us and for us. Through these two sacraments the Body of Christ is set apart and nourished by the saving, sanctifying, and sustaining grace of the triune God, who is Father, Son, and Holy Spirit. That which God ordained for our strength and unity must be embraced and celebrated, not debated and neglected.

Since we tend to worship the Lord in our separate ecclesiastical camps, we may be unaware that the sacraments generated serious theological controversy and led to disunity and hatred among Christians. Negative tensions over the sacraments contributed to splitting the Christian tradition and forming denominations. God's worship instructions and the principle of the unadorned altar, along with the apostolic simplicity of the New Testament were all but forgotten in the debate over the baptism and the Lord's Supper.

For many believers in the twenty-first century it is the sacraments themselves that are marginalized, if not almost forgotten. Sometimes it seems that they are awkward appendages to a user-friendly, seeker-sensitive worship service. At various times, the church has been guilty of over-thinking, under-thinking, and not knowing what to think about the sacraments. Throughout the history of the church, the sacraments have been the catalyst for negative tension, but by God's design and grace they have worked to sustain the identity and viability of the Body of Christ down through the centuries. The purpose of this chapter is to better understand how the church has understood baptism and the Lord's Supper. We want to draw out the meaning of the sacraments and the impact of their witness in order to counter the casual and dismissive attitude toward them that many experience today.

The Mystery

"Beyond all question," the apostle Paul wrote, "the mystery of godliness is great: He appeared in a body, was vindicated by the Spirit, was seen by the angels, was preached among the nations, was believed on in the world, was taken up in glory."[1] Paul called the relationship between Christ and the church a "profound mystery."[2] This deeply personal and essentially corporate relationship is celebrated in the sacraments. Neither baptism nor holy communion can be understood Christianly apart from the Body of Christ. The first person plural is decisive: "In him *we* have redemption through his blood, the forgiveness of sins, in accordance with the riches of God's grace that he lavished on *us* with all wisdom and understanding. And he made known to *us* the mystery of his will according to his good pleasure, which was purposed in Christ . . ."[3]

Since the apostle Paul disassociated the gospel from the mystery religions, we know he did not mean to imply that the gospel was mysterious or secretive. Nor did he use the word *mystery* to condone ignorance or discourage reflection. On the contrary, Paul was exuberant over the wisdom of the gospel. "O the depth of the riches and wisdom and knowledge of God! How unsearchable are his judgments and how inscrutable his ways!"[4] Like Paul, we seek to revel in the knowable, yet unfathomable truth of the gospel. We resist the rationalistic impulse to reduce the reality of God's truth to a neat formula. We want to grasp the meaningfulness of God's revelation. The mystery is no longer hidden, but revealed, made known through the proclamation of the gospel.[5] It is neither mundane nor magical. This is the mystery that is filled with expressible, articulate meaning. We approach the mystery of the gospel of Christ, not as a problem to be solved, but as a truth to be embraced and proclaimed. "Mystery is not the absence of meaning, but the presence of more meaning than we

1. 1 Tim 3:16.
2. Eph 6:32.
3. Eph 1:7–9.
4. Rom 11:33.
5. Rom 16:25; Eph 3:6; Col 1:26; 2:2; 4:3.

can comprehend."[6] This knowable, yet inexhaustible mystery, can be comprehended by believers, whether they are nine or ninety, in the physical, spiritual, intellectual, emotional, and relational experience of the sacraments. Through them, we are identified, defined, inspired, and embraced by the body of Christ.

Sacramentum

The Greek word *mysterion* was translated in Latin *sacramentum* and came to be associated with the rites of Baptism and Lord's Supper, spoken of as *sacramenta*.[7] In classical Latin it referred to a military oath of allegiance and conveyed the idea of a sacred vow. Ironically, the Latin notion of a solemn vow overshadowed the biblical notion of mystery as the church began to elaborate on the meaning of the sacraments. This shifted attention away from the Body of Christ to an individual's spiritual journey. Medieval theologian Peter Lombard, best known for his *Book of Sentences* (1158) called a sacrament "a sign of the grace of God and a form of invisible grace, so that it bears its image and exists as its cause." Under the Old Law, he reasoned, physical sacrifices and ceremonial observances signified but did not sanctify, but under the New Law, the sacraments both signify and sanctify. Lombard identified seven sacraments, "baptism, confirmation, the bread of blessing (that is, the eucharist), penance, extreme unction, ordination, and marriage."[8]

According to Roman Catholic theology, confirmation is administered by a bishop before children receive their first Communion. Confirmation increases sanctifying grace and bestows the seven gifts of the Holy Spirit. It is a sacramental rite completing Baptism.[9] Penance was officially accepted as a sacrament at the Council of Trent (1545–63). By complying with the church's disciplinary procedures believers could be assured of pardon for certain sins.[10] The Reformers distinguished between penance and penitence or repentance. Extreme Unction is the last of the three sacramental unctions, preceded by baptism and confirmation. "Oil, consecrated by the bishop, is the matter; unction with prayer by the priests the sign; the grace given on condition of repentance and faith is forgiveness of sins, renewed

6. Covington, *Salvation on Sand Mountain*, 203–4.

7. Wallace, "Sacrament," 965.

8. McGrath, *The Christian Theology Reader*, 299.

9. See Acts 8:14; 19:6.

10. See John 20:21–23.

health, and strength of soul and also of body if God sees fit."[11] According to Roman Catholic and Orthodox churches, ordination is a sacrament and confers grace upon the recipient.[12] Marriage as a sacrament of the church is sanctified and consecrated to fulfill its distinctively Christian elements.[13] These seven sacraments were employed as a spiritual road-map charting the course of a believer's life.

Zwingli offered a decidedly different perspective. In his 1525 treatise *On Baptism*, he wrote,

> To us Germans, the word 'sacrament' suggests something that has power to take away sin or to make us holy. But this is a serious error. For only Jesus Christ and no external thing can take away the sins of us Christians or make us holy . . . As used in this context the word *sacrament* means a sign of commitment. If a man sews on a white cross, he proclaims that he is a Swiss Confederate . . . Similarly the man who receives the mark of baptism is the one who is resolved to hear what God says to him, to learn the divine precepts and to live his life in accordance with them. And the man who, in the remembrance or supper, gives thanks to God in the congregation, declares that he heartily rejoices in the death of Christ and thanks him for it. So I ask these quibblers that they allow the sacraments to be real sacraments, and that they do not describe them as signs which are identical with the things which they represent.[14]

Zwingli and Lombard held such different perspectives on the meaning of the sacraments and their significance for the church that we are encouraged to retrace our theological steps back to the Bible and see for ourselves the nature and role of the sacraments.

Biblical Foundation

The New Testament does not argue a case for either baptism or the Lord's Supper. The significance of these two sacraments is simply accepted and celebrated. No big deal is made of them. No reasoned defense or elaborate description of how these sacraments are to be practiced is given, but they are treated as essential for the body-life of the church. They exist quietly,

11. Coates, "Extreme Unction," 398; see Jas 5:13–15.
12. See Luke 22:19; 1 Cor 11:26.
13. See Matt 19:4–9; Eph 5:21–32.
14. McGrath, *The Christian Reader*, 311.

powerfully, at the center of our worship, pointing to Christ, affirming the body of Christ.

Both rituals were appointed and modeled by Jesus without much elaboration or explanation. Baptism and the Lord's Supper are defined by the proclamation of the gospel. The words and actions of Jesus are foundational for both sacraments. Through his baptism, Jesus identified with us in our need and with the Father in his redemptive purposes. It was "a baptism into solidarity with sinners and obedience of the Father."[15] The transition from the baptism of repentance, in the tradition of John the Baptist, to baptism in the name of Christ can only be understood in the light of Christ's cross.[16] "Therefore go and make disciples of all nations, baptizing them in the name of the Father and of the Son and of the Holy Spirit, and teaching them to obey everything I have commanded you."[17] Likewise, the transition from the Passover meal to the Lord's Supper was made without elaboration and rests in the words and action of Jesus:

> I tell you the truth, unless you eat the flesh of the Son of Man and drink his blood, you have no life in you. Whoever eats my flesh and drinks my blood has eternal life, and I will raise him up at the last day. For my flesh is real food and my blood is real drink.[18]

Christ and the cross revolutionized and fulfilled the Passover. We move from the Passover to the eucharist. "This is my body given for you; do this in remembrance of me." And again, "This cup is the new covenant in my blood, which is poured out for you."[19] The early church incorporated the celebration of the Lord's Supper into their daily worship. "They devoted themselves to the apostles' teaching and to the fellowship, to the breaking of bread and to prayer."[20] The definite article ("the breaking of the bread") suggests a reference to the Lord's Supper and implies that the early church experienced the eucharist as part of a larger meal in a natural and ordinary way. It would appear that the observance was not accompanied by any ceremony.

Baptism and the Lord's Supper are explicitly linked together by Jesus in a passage that underscores the cost of discipleship. In the context

15. Beasley-Murray, *Baptism In the New Testament*, 64.

16. See Acts 2:38; 10:48.

17. Matt 28:19.

18. John 6:53–55.

19. Luke 22:19–20.

20. Acts 2:42.

of admonishing James and John, the sons of thunder, Jesus pronounced, "You will drink the cup and be baptized with the baptism I am baptized with . . ."[21] Later, the apostle Paul expounded on the significance of our identification with Christ on the Cross through baptism:

> Don't you know that all of us who were baptized into Christ Jesus were baptized into his death? We were therefore buried with him through baptism into death in order that just as Christ was raised from the dead through the glory of the Father, we too may live a new life. If we have been united with him in his death, we will certainly also be united with him in his resurrection. For we know that our old self was crucified with him so that the body of sin might be rendered powerless, that we should no longer be slaves to sin—because anyone who has died has been freed from sin.[22]

In a similar way, the apostle Paul linked the Lord's Supper to our participation in the death of Christ. He wrote, "For whenever you eat this bread and drink this cup, you proclaim the Lord's death until he comes. So then, whoever eats the bread or drinks the cup of the Lord in an unworthy manner will be guilty of sinning against the body and blood of the Lord."[23]

Through the sacraments of baptism and the Lord's Supper we participate through faith in the bodily death and resurrected life of Christ. As Dietrich Bonhoeffer wrote,

> The earthly body of Jesus underwent crucifixion and death. In that death the new humanity undergoes crucifixion and death . . . It is all our infirmities and all our sin that he bears to the cross. It is we who are crucified with him, and we who die with him . . . How then do we come to participate in the Body of Christ, who did all this for us? It is certain that there can be no fellowship or communion with him except through his Body. For only through that Body can we find acceptance and salvation. The answer is, through the two sacraments of his Body, baptism and the Lord's Supper.[24]

The apostle Paul's earnest desire "to know Christ and the power of his resurrection and the fellowship of sharing in his sufferings, becoming like him in his death, and so, somehow, to attain to the resurrection from

21. Mark 10:39.
22. Rom 6:3–7.
23. 1 Cor 11:26–27.
24. Bonhoeffer, *The Cost of Discipleship*, 266–67.

the dead" serves to articulate the purpose and passion of both baptism and the Lord's Supper.[25] New Testament scholar Gerald Hawthorne explains, "Thus, just as knowing Christ in the power of his resurrection is an inward experience that can be expressed in terms of being resurrected with Christ, so knowing Christ in the fellowship of his sufferings is equally an inward experience that can be described in terms of having died with Christ."[26] Through these two sacraments we experience the reality of the cross and the grace of Christ by the power of the Holy Spirit. The cross defines their meaning and their holy practice complements one another. Baptism is a singular event in the life of the believer affirming, testifying and illustrating in a visible act the believer's forgiveness of sins and reception into the Body of Christ. The Lord's Supper is a continual experience in the life of the believer celebrating our participation in the Body of Christ, proclaiming "the Lord's death until he comes."[27]

There are places in Indonesia and in India where believers risk persecution for being baptized in the name of Jesus. They are fired from their jobs, ostracized from their communities and excommunicated from their families. Believers in these places have suffered this way for centuries. Contrast their costly identification with Christ, with our caviler approach to baptism. I recently heard a pastor introduce baptism by saying, "We want to make this as convenient and as non-threatening as possible." This came after thirty minutes of decibel-defying rock and roll "praise" music and a thirty-minute anecdotal talk on friendship sprinkled with a few Scripture references. Up to that point in the worship service, no mention had been made of the cross or baptism and there was no discussion on what it meant to be committed to Christ. Baptism amounted to little more than audience participation.

Visible Sign and Spiritual Value

The Old Testament prepared us for these sacraments by providing visible signs of the will of God, such as the altar of sacrifice, circumcision, the Ark of the Covenant, and the Passover meal. These object lessons of redemption pointed to the grace of God. They shared an idol-resistant quality and an instrumental value. As earthy symbols they served to reveal the will of God for the people of God. They were never intended to become objects

25. Phil 3:10.

26. Hawthorne, *Philippians*, 144; see Rom 6:8; Gal 2:19–20.

27. 1 Cor 11:26.

of worship.[28] Nevertheless, in spite of the iconoclastic character of a pile of rocks and a small box, the Israelites fell into the temptation of turning altars into shrines and using the Ark of the Covenant as if it had magical qualities.[29] A similar temptation was faced by the early church especially as the gospel moved into the Gentile mission field. There were early manifestations of a distorted and spiritualized view of the sacraments. As Michael Green observes,

> Ignatius was a man who came to Christianity from paganism. The sacraments are seen in terms which derive from the Mysteries and verge on magic. The Eucharist is the 'medicine of immortality, the antidote for death' rather than a corporate encounter with the living Christ. It has become static rather than dynamic, physical rather than sacramental. Similarly the water of baptism becomes important in itself rather than in what it signifies . . . When, therefore, Ignatius claims that the coming of Jesus has put an end to magic, one must sorrowfully confess that in some areas of the Church it introduced a new sort of magic . . .[30]

Augustine defined the sacrament as an "outward and visible sign of an inward and spiritual grace." In his struggle with the Donatists, who claimed that the sanctity of baptism and the Lord's Supper depended on the faithfulness of the priest, Augustine argued that the power and validity of the sacrament depended on Christ's holiness rather than upon the priest who administered the sacrament. He reasoned that baptism and the Lord's Supper convey grace "by virtue of the act itself."[31] But this raised an important matter. Does the sacrament serve God's purposes independent of the person's faith and trust in Christ? Does the sacrament dispense the grace of God or does it affirm the grace of God in the life of the believer? It is hard to avoid the criticism of sacramentalism when one argues, as Augustine did, that all unbaptized children are damned. His view of baptismal regeneration made the outward act essential for salvation.

The church has struggled with the relationship between the outward sign and the inward spiritual reality. Is this not what concerned the apostle Paul when he confronted the believers at Corinth? "When you come

28. See Exod 20:24–26; 37:1–5.

29. 1 Sam 4:1–11.

30. Green, *Evangelism in the Early Church*, 138. (This reference is to Ignatius, second century Bishop of Antioch, not to be confused with Ignatius of Loyola, founder of the Jesuits, 1491–1556).

31. Olson, *The Story of Christian Theology*, 266.

together it is not the Lord's Supper you eat, for as you eat, each of you goes ahead without waiting for anybody else."[32] Although they thought they were celebrating the Lord's Supper, Paul contended that they were not receiving the grace of Christ but his judgment. "For anyone who eats and drinks without recognizing the body of the Lord eats and drinks judgment on himself. That is why many among you are weak and sick, and a number of you have fallen asleep."[33]

Calvin argued that the spiritual value of the sacraments was not found in their outward ceremonial performance but "in the promises and spiritual mysteries that our Lord wishes to represent by such ceremonies . . . There is no question of any insistence upon the water and what is done outwardly; what is needed is to lift up our thoughts to the promises of God which are given us in these things."[34] Calvin wrote, "For baptism bears witness that we are purged and washed, and the Supper of the Eucharist that we are redeemed. By the water ablution is symbolized to us, and by the blood, retribution. Both of these things are found in Jesus Christ, who, as St. John says, came by water and by blood (1 John 5:6)—that is, to purge and to redeem."[35] John Calvin elaborated on Augustine's definition "that a sacrament is a visible sign of a sacred thing, or a visible form of the invisible grace." Calvin wrote,

> The sacrament is an outward sign by which God seals upon our consciences the promises of his good will towards us, to confirm our feeble faith, and we give mutual testimony before him and the angels no less than before [people], that we hold to be of God." In other words it is a testimony of the grace of God towards us, confirmed by an external sign, with mutual attestation of the honor we bear him.[36]

Calvin emphasized the close relationship between the Word and sacrament. "The sacrament consists of the Word and external sign." The Word has to be taught in order to explain what the visible sign means. Calvin took issue with those who claimed the sacraments "give no evidence of the grace of God" (Zwinglians) and with those who "attribute to the sacraments I know not what secret virtues" (Roman Catholics). On the one hand, he argued that God instituted the sacraments to strengthen

32. 1 Cor 11:20.

33. 1 Cor 11:29-30

34. Calvin, *Institutes of the Christian Religion*, IV:16.2, 529.

35. Ibid., IV:14.22, 507.

36. Calvin, *Institutes*, IV:14.1, 491; Wendel, *Calvin*, 312.

our weak faith. Through the sacraments the Holy Spirit feeds the believer spiritually and vividly presents the promises of God for our growth. On the other hand, he denies that "the power to justify us and the graces of the Holy Spirit [are] shut up in the sacraments as though they were vessels."[37] For Calvin the meaning of the sacraments was neither mundane nor magical. The true mystery of the gospel was lost in reducing the sacrament to a mere sign or in philosophical speculation about the transformation of the elements. Calvin resisted an objectivity that was either secular or superstitious by underscoring the sacred meaning of the sacrament to be found in its unique presentation and confirmation of the gospel. In a wonderful way he explained the meaning without reducing the mystery.

Real Presence

The debate over what the real presence of Christ means in the Lord's Supper comes late in the history of the church. Italian theologian and Doctor of the Church Thomas Aquinas (1225–1274) saw a parallel between the mystery of the Incarnation and the transformation of the elements.[38] Using Aristotelian logic, Aquinas argued that the "accidents" remain bread and wine but the consecration of the elements transforms their "substance" into the real body and blood of the Lord. ". . . Christ's flesh and blood are set before us to be taken under the appearances of those things which are of frequent use, namely bread and wine. Secondly, if we ate our Lord under his proper appearance, this sacrament would be ridiculed by unbelievers. Thirdly, in order that, while we take the Lord's body and blood invisibly, this fact may avail towards the merit of faith."[39]

Luther reacted strongly to Aquinas' metaphysical speculation in *The Babylonian Captivity of the Church* (1520).

> Therefore it is an absurd and unheard of juggling with words to understand "bread" to mean "the form or accidents" of

37. Calvin, *Institutes*, IV:14.17, 503.

38. Thomas Aquinas wrestled with the kind of literal logic articulated here by Roman Catholic scholar Peter Kreeft: "That thing that looks like a little piece of bread— that's Him. I certainly sympathize with most Protestants, who do not believe that. It is nearly unbelievable. The priest puts God into your left hand, and you pick up God Almighty with your right thumb and forefinger and you swallow God Almighty, and He falls into your stomach. That is crazy—as crazy as the Incarnation. This is 9.9999999999 percent unbelievable. Like the Incarnation." Peter Kreeft, *Jesus-Shock*, 49.

39. McGrath, *The Christian Theology Reader*, 301.

> bread, and "wine" to mean "the form or accidents of wine." . . .
> Moreover, the church kept the true faith for more than twelve
> hundred years, during which time the holy fathers never, at any
> time or place, mentioned this "transubstantiation" (a monstrous
> word and a monstrous idea) until the pseudo-philosophy of
> Aristotle began to make its inroads into the church in these last
> three hundred years.
>
> And why could not Christ include his body in the substance
> of the bread just as well as in the accidents? In red-hot iron,
> for instance, the two substances, fire and iron, are so mingled
> that every part is both iron and fire . . . I rejoice greatly that the
> simple faith of this sacrament is still to be found, at least among
> the common people. For as they do not understand, neither do
> they dispute whether accidents are present without substance,
> but believe with a simple faith that Christ's body and blood are
> truly contained there, and leave to those who have nothing else
> to do the argument about what contains them . . .
>
> Even though philosophy cannot grasp this, faith grasps this
> nonetheless. And the authority of God's Word is greater than
> the capacity of our intellect to grasp it. In like manner, it is not
> necessary in the sacrament that bread and wine be transubstan-
> tiated and that Christ be contained under their accidents in
> order that the real body and real blood may be present.[40]

Undoubtedly Luther would have been unhappy with the label later
church historians gave his understanding of the eucharist. Consubstantiation described the real presence of Christ "in, with and under" the elements of bread and wine. "Just as the incomprehensible and omnipresent
God draws near to a man in the humanity of Jesus Christ, so the incomprehensible and omnipresent humanity of Christ draws near to and can be
grasped by men in the Lord's Supper."[41] Luther and Zwingli met in Marburg
in October 1529 to hammer out their differences on the sacrament of the
Lord's Supper. Zwingli taught that the Lord's Supper is a commemoration
of Christ's death and that there is no "real presence." Zwingli contended,

> We are not given any reason to believe that when the Pope or
> some other human person says: "This is my body," the body of
> Christ is necessarily present . . . Before we use the Word of God
> to justify anything, we must first understand it correctly. For
> example, when Christ says: "I am the vine" (Jn 15:5), we have to

40. Luther, "The Babylonian Captivity of the Church," 147–151.

41. Althaus, *The Theology of Martin Luther*, 399.

consider that he is using figurative speech in the first place. In other words, he is *like* a vine, just as the branches are nourished by the vine and cannot bear fruit without it, so believers are in him, and without him they can do nothing . . . If in Christ's saying: "This is my body," we take the little word "is" in a substantive manner, that is literally, then it necessarily follows that the substance of the body or the flesh of Christ is literally and essentially present . . . If he is literally and essentially present in the flesh, then he is actually torn apart by the teeth and tangibly masticated in human mouths . . .

Notice how utterly unreasonable this position is. On no account will it allow that Christ's words: "This is my body," are figurative or symbolical. It insists that the word "is" must be taken literally. But it then proceeds to ignore the word and to say: "This body of Christ is eaten *in* the bread." . . . How dreadful a thing it is to get out of one's depth!

If the simple meaning of Scripture is that which we maintain through a misunderstanding of the letter, then Christ is a piece of vine wood, or a silly sheep, or a door, and Peter is the foundation-stone of the Church. The simple or natural sense of these words is that which obtains in all similar instances, that which the minds of all believers find the most natural and the most easily understood.[42]

According to Zwingli the value of the sacraments was in their visible witness to the work of Christ. They are object lessons of redemption serving to strengthen the believer's faith. In *An Account of the Faith of Zwingli*, which he wrote in preparation for the Parliament of Augsburg in 1530, he clarified his understanding of the sacraments:

The sacraments are given as a public testimony of that grace which is previously present to every individual. Thus baptism is administered in the presence of the Church to one who before receiving it either confessed the religion of Christ or has the word of promise, whereby he is known to belong to the Church. Hence it is that when we baptize an adult we ask him whether he believes. And only when he answers "yes," then he receives baptism. Faith, therefore, has been present before he receives baptism, and is not given by baptism. But when an infant is offered, the question is asked whether its parents offer it for baptism. When they have answered through witnesses that they wish it

42. McGrath, *The Christian Theology Reader*, 309–10.

baptized, then the infant is baptized. Here the promise of God precedes, that He regards our infants, no less than those of the Hebrews, as belonging to the Church. For when members of the Church offer it, the infant is baptized under the law that, since it has been born of Christians, it is regarded by the divine promise among the members of the Church. By baptism, therefore, the Church publicly receives one who has previously been received through grace. Hence baptism does not convey grace but the Church certifies that grace has been given to him to whom it is administered.[43]

At the Marburg Colloquy, Zwingli argued that "flesh and blood avail for nothing" and Luther countered by accusing Zwingli of attempting to rationalize a mystery.[44] As a result of the meeting both men were more polarized than ever, and as Roger Olson observes, the fundamental theological difference between them was Christological. Zwingli held that because of the incarnation, Jesus Christ remained in heaven and was not everywhere present. Luther, held otherwise, believing in the communication of attributes (*communicatio idiomatum*: whatever can be attributed to either the divine or the human nature in Christ is to be attributed to the entire person) and therefore maintained that "Christ is around us and in us and in all places" at once.[45]

John Calvin took a mediating position between Luther and Zwingli. He rejected transubstantiation and consubstantiation, but was unsatisfied with Zwingli's symbolization. By avoiding speculation and simplification Calvin sought to emphasize the mystery of the gospel. In Calvin's *Treatise on the Lord's Supper* (1541) he wrote, ". . . the bread and the wine are visible signs which represent to us the body and the blood; but that the name and title of body and blood have been given them because they are as instruments by means of which the Lord Jesus distributes these to us. There is good reason for this form and manner of speech. For seeing that it is a thing incomprehensible not only to the eye but to our natural judgment, that we should have communion with the body of Jesus Christ, it is here shown to us visibly."[46]

Calvin used the descent of the dove at the baptism of Jesus symbolizing the Holy Spirit to illustrate the relationship between the visible and invisible. The spiritual reality does not identify with the material elements.

43. Olson, *The Story of Christian Theology*, 405–6.

44. John 6:63.

45. Olson, *The Story of Christian Theology*, 395.

46. Wendel, *Calvin*, 339.

Calvin's understanding is neither Roman transubstantiation nor Lutheran consubstantiation nor Zwinglian symbolization. Calvin held that "Christ comes down towards us not only in the outward symbols but also in the hidden working of his Spirit, so that we can ascend to him by faith."[47]

For Calvin baptism is the sign of our remission of sins. It is not an initiation, but a testimony to the cleansing power of Christ. In itself, the water does not cleanse our souls, but testifies to the power of the blood of Christ to cleanse us from all unrighteousness. Baptism also "shows us our mortification in Jesus Christ."[48] Drawing on Romans 6:1–14, Calvin saw baptism as a sign of our new life in Christ. Baptism is itself a call to discipleship and full commitment to Christ. There is no "next step," such as ordination to "full-time ministry," that proves a greater commitment or a deeper passion for Christ. Baptism says it all. We have died to ourselves and we have been raised to new life in Christ.

Against Roman Catholicism, Calvin argued that baptism does not restore to us Adam's original innocence, that would be to say too much. But baptism does signify the imputed righteousness of Christ. Baptism is linked with our justification by faith. The Reformers sought to correct the notion that put off baptism until the end of life in order to obtain forgiveness of sins for the whole of life. Calvin wrote, "But it must be known that whenever we may be baptized we are washed and purged once for all the time of our life. However, whenever we may fall again into sin, we must return again in the memory of baptism and thereby confirm ourselves in this same faith, that we are always certain and assured of the remission of our sins."[49]

Since Calvin could not produce a single New Testament passage containing a clear reference to infant baptism, he had to be content with indirect inferences and analogies drawn from circumcision and Christ's blessing of the children.[50]

> If it was a reasonable thing to bring the children to Jesus Christ, why should it not be allowable to receive them in baptisms which is the outward sign by which Jesus Christ makes known the communion and society that we have with him? If the Kingdom of Heaven belongs to them, why should they be denied the

47. Ibid., 352.
48. Calvin, *Institutes*, IV:15.3, 514.
49. Ibid., IV:15.4, 514.
50. See Matt 19:14.

sign by which we are introduced to be heirs to the Kingdom of God?[51]

Calvin advanced the idea that God is able to act within children in ways that we do not know about. "'How could this be' say the Anabaptists, 'seeing that faith comes by hearing, as St. Paul says, and infants have no discernment of good and evil?' But they do not see that St Paul is speaking only of the ordinary way in which the Savior works to give faith to his own; not many whom, without ever making them hear a word, he has touched interiorly in order to draw them to the knowledge of his name. . . . It is a thing most uncertain and far from sure, to assert that the Lord cannot manifest himself in them some way."[52]

Calvin rejected Augustine's opinion that children who died without being baptized were destined for hell or limbo.[53] Wendel argues that he could have gone further and argued on the basis of infant baptism's usefulness to the church and for the piety of the faithful, "while frankly acknowledging that one cannot find an acceptable basis for it in the Scriptures."[54] Calvin, however, found the answer in grace, not pragmatism. He felt there was biblical warrant for God bestowing grace on infants who did not have the capacity to intellectually grasp the faith. His thoughts on dying infants are worth quoting:

> For if the fullness of life consists in the perfect knowledge of God, since some of those whom death hurries away in the first moments of infancy pass into life eternal, they are certainly admitted to behold the immediate presence of God. Those, therefore, whom the Lord is to illumine with the full brightness of light, why may he not if he so pleases, irradiate at present with some small beam, especially if he does not remove their ignorance, before he delivers them the prison of the flesh? I would not rashly affirm that they are endued with the same faith which we experience in ourselves, or have any knowledge at all resembling faith (this I would rather leave undecided); but I would somewhat curb the stolid arrogance of those who, as with inflated cheeks, affirm or deny whatever suits them.[55]

51. Calvin, *Institutes*, IV:16.7, 533.
52. Ibid., IV:16.18-19, 541-542.
53. Wendel, *Calvin*, 328.
54. Ibid., 328–29.
55. Calvin, *Institutes*, IV:16.19, 542.

On the subject of the Lord's Supper Calvin emphasized three dimensions: "There are three points to be considered in the sacrament besides the outward sign, which is not at present in question: namely, the signification; then the matter or substance; and thirdly the virtue or the effect which proceeds from the one to the other."[56] "The meaning is in the promises, which are imprinted upon the sign. I call Jesus Christ, with his death and resurrection, the matter of substance. By the effect I mean redemption, righteousness, sanctification, the life everlasting and all the benefits brought to us by Jesus Christ." For Calvin reducing the sacrament to a mere sign was like reducing music to mere notes. No one would ever settle for a scripted score when they could hear the melody. Or to use a closer analogy, it would be like sitting down to a full course recipe instead of a full course meal.

Calvin stressed the importance of the preached Word to shape and define the meaning of the sacrament: "Of what use would it be to us to eat a little piece of bread and drink three drops of wine, if that voice were not sounding from on high, saying that the flesh of Jesus Christ is the true food of our souls and his blood their true spiritual drink? Thus we have every right to conclude that we are not made partakers in Jesus Christ and in his spiritual gifts by the bread, wine and water, but that we are brought to him by the promise, so that he gives himself to us, and, dwelling in us by faith, he fulfills what is promised and offered to us by the signs."[57] To receive the promise is to experience the substance. As in God's pronouncement, "Let there be . . ." and as in the case of the wedding vow, so also in the words of institution. God really communicates what he has promised.

In his *Treatise on the Lord's Supper*, Calvin emphasized that Christ was not only exposed as a sacrifice for us, but now dwells in us. "We are incorporated with him in, so to speak, one and the same life and substance." The purpose of the sacrament is to help us grow in Christ and to confirm his presence in us. "By the hidden and wonderful virtue of the Holy Spirit, Jesus Christ dwells in us, communicates his life to us and makes us share in his virtue. That is how the Supper serves as a memorial, yet this is no mere memorial, not at all like a picture that we contemplate with the eyes, but it is true and sure testimony that Jesus Christ is accomplishing in us what he symbolizes to us; that we do not come to the Supper imagining a vain thing, but to receive in truth all that is pledged to us. Meanwhile we must be ever reaching upward, and let us remember . . . that the sacraments are

56. Ibid., IV:17.11, 564.
57. Wendel, *Calvin*, 337.

not instituted to detain us here below, but rather to draw us towards our Lord Jesus Christ."[58] Calvin declared,

> I say that Christ is the matter of, or, if you rather choose it, the substance of all the sacraments, since in him they have their whole solidity, and out of him promise nothing. . . . In so far, therefore, as we are assisted by their instrumentality in cherishing, confirming, and increasing the true knowledge of Christ, so as both to possess him more fully, and enjoy him in all his richness, so far are they effectual in regard to us. This is the case when that which is there offered is received by us in true faith.[59]

The sacraments do not bestow grace on the believer, but serve as a means of recognizing and affirming the grace of Christ in the life of the believer. The sacraments help to define this grace rather than dispense it.

Experiencing the Sacraments Today

The seriousness with which the church has approached baptism and the Lord's Supper throughout its history challenges the casual and almost cavalier attitude evidenced by many believers today. Like the disciples in the upper room or the early Christians at Corinth we are distracted by peripheral things that do not count for the kingdom and do not deepen our worship of Christ. But this attitude is changing and many churches are taking the sacraments more seriously. Weekly eucharistic celebrations are becoming more common as congregations experience the power of the Table of the Lord to focus our worship on Christ and to form the bond we have in Christ. For all the debate and wrangling about the transformation of the elements, the real issue has always been the transformation of the person in Christ and the building up the Body of Christ. The miracle Christ institutes is not changing wine into blood, but changing sinners into saints.

Our experience of the sacraments, baptism and the Lord's Supper, serves to concentrate our relationship with Christ. Speculation regarding the elements has drawn attention away from the Incarnate One and the grace of justification and sanctification. Certain philosophical notions and doctrinal defenses have confused the mystery of the Gospel with the mysterious, the mythical, and the magical. Although we may not be

58. Ibid., 353–54.
59. Calvin, *Institutes,* IV:14.16, 502.

tempted to impose Aristotelian categories on the meaning of the Lord's Supper, we may be inclined to judge the efficacy of the sacrament on our subjective feelings. I remember as a teenager feeling the burden of working up my emotions whenever we celebrated the Lord's Supper. I felt the need to bring a certain passion to holy communion, but I was relieved of that burden when I realized that the passion to be focused upon was not mine, but Christ's. His actions, rather than my feelings, made the sacrament meaningful.

Christians from all traditions can become *sacrilegious*. Sacrilege goes both ways, up and down. We can desecrate the sacraments by either spiritualizing or secularizing them. Desecration goes upward in the form of embellishment, theological over-thinking, spiritual fantasizing, and obsequious piety. Desecration goes downward in the form of a dismissive and cavalier attitude, theological neglect, and spiritual indifference. True spirituality seeks to neither Christianize the world nor secularize the church. The sacraments are neither the ritualized means of grace, nor the emotional high point of a self-help sermon.

The significance of baptism and the Lord's Supper may be significantly altered by the philosophy of the seeker-sensitive church and its strategy of accessibility. What are the theological and spiritual implications of the diminished role of the sacraments in a church that concentrates on making everything immediately accessible for non-Christians? Are we timid when it comes to the possibility of audience disapproval? Do we yield to the temptation to dilute the message of the gospel and transform it into entertainment so we don't hear from the dissatisfied customer, "I don't get it," or "I'm bored"?

In *The Intrusive Word*, William Willimon notes that, "G. K. Chesterton once said, if you are trying to communicate something to another person and the person says, 'I don't understand,' you will reach for some metaphor. You will say, 'Well, it's like . . .' Then, if the person still responds, 'I don't understand,' you will try another metaphor. If the person still does not understand, then you must say, 'You don't understand.'" William Willimon continues, "We have so little trust in the power of the gospel, through the enablement of the Holy Spirit, to evoke the listeners that the gospel deserves, that we either simplify, simplify, reducing the gospel to a slogan for a bumper sticker, or else we poetically describe, describe, obfuscating the gospel with some allegedly 'common human experience' that is not the gospel."[60]

60. Willimon, *The Intrusive Word*, 24.

The mystery of our union in Christ is sadly overshadowed by a long history of contentious debate and disagreement over the very symbols of Christian unity and the sacraments of Christian faith. As it was in the upper room and in the church of Corinth so has it been throughout the history of the church. Can we not agree to contemplate the mystery of new life in Christ without dividing from and disagreeing with fellow believers who hold to the truth of Christ? The words of the apostle Paul instruct us: "Be completely humble and gentle; be patient, bearing with one another in love. Make every effort to keep the unity of the Spirit through the bond of peace. There is one body and one Spirit—just as you were called to one hope when you were called—one Lord, one faith, one baptism; one God and Father of all, who is over all and through all and in all."[61] The powerful message of unity in Christ needs to be restored to our celebration of the sacraments. Augustine's description deserves to be remembered:

> "The body of Christ," you are told, and you answer "Amen." Be members then of the body of Christ that your Amen may be true. Why is this mystery accomplished with bread? We shall say nothing of our own about it, rather let us hear the Apostle, who speaking of the sacrament says: "We who being many are one body, one bread." Understand and rejoice. Unity, devotion, charity. One bread: and what is this one bread? One body, made up of many . . . Now for the Chalice, my brethren, remember how wine is made. Many grapes hang on the bunch, but the liquid which runs out of them mingles together in unity. So had the Lord willed that we should belong to him and he has consecrated on his altar the mystery of our peace and unity.[62]

Along with this emphasis upon Christian unity, "one Lord, one faith, one baptism," let it be said that the aura of solemn sentimentality surrounding the pseudo-celebration of the eucharist is no substitute for real worship. I have attended ecumenical worship gatherings in which some confessed to be deeply moved by the "experience" of the Lord's Supper, but openly denied the deity of Christ and the efficacy of his atoning sacrifice. The unity we seek is based on our union with Christ and not on present moment feelings or the ambiance of "sacred space." At the 1993 Re-Imagining conference, funded by mainline Protestant denominations, participants celebrated a parody of the Lord's Supper entitled "Blessing

61. Eph 4:1–6.
62. Lubac, *Catholicism*, 92.

over Milk and Honey." The worship leader invoked "Our maker Sophia," and led the audience in a liturgy that could only be described as pagan.[63]

Surely the best way to "guard the table" is not by policing the congregation but by proclaiming the passion of Christ. We agree with the Reformers on the necessity of the preached Word to define and empower the meaning of the sacraments. It is sobering to realize that when Jesus instituted the eucharist he gave the bread and the cup to Judas, knowing that Judas was about to betray him.[64] The integrity of the sacrament depends upon Christ and his Word and is not diminished by even his most deceptive disciple.

Our earnest prayer is that our union in Christ, the hope of glory, may be affirmed and experienced anew through the celebration of the sacraments. May the Holy Spirit use these Christ-inspired sacraments to strengthen our faith and challenge us to let the peace of Christ rule in our hearts and to let the Word of Christ dwell in us richly. Eschewing the mundane and the magical, we embrace "the mystery of God, namely Christ, in whom are hidden all the treasures of wisdom and knowledge."[65] We cannot imagine any of the ancient pastoral theologians who labored to understand the sacraments ever being content to just survey and study various points of view about the sacraments. They were theologians of conviction who earnestly sought to understand the mystery of the gospel and live for Christ and his Kingdom.

From Text to Table

The Table is the altar call for the preached text. The Word proclaimed is the Word remembered, internalized, and eaten as food for the soul. The words of institution, "This is my body broken for you," and "This cup is the new covenant that I pour out with my blood," signify the whole body of revealed truth. They include the whole counsel of God from Genesis to Revelation. The sermon ends with four simple action verbs: take, thank, break, and give. As we partake of the bread and the cup we participate in Christ receiving, thanking, sacrificing, and giving. The mission of God begins and ends at this table in fellowship with the crucified and risen Lord Jesus Christ. A good question for the preacher to ask is did Jesus have to die to preach this sermon? If the preacher moves from the sermon

63. See Edwards, "Earthquake in the Mainline," 38–43.

64. Luke 22:20–21.

65. Col 2:2–3.

to the sacrifice awkwardly or concludes the sermon as if holy communion is an entirely different matter, then chances are Jesus did not have to die to preach that sermon. It may have been a moralistic sermon or an entertaining sermon or an uplifting sermon, but it wasn't an evangelistic sermon—even though it may have called people forward to accept Jesus. All evangelistic sermons are eucharistic sermons. Good sermons bring us to the table of the Lord.

Table fellowship fits into the New Testament narrative so unobtrusively that we can almost miss it. Sharing a simple meal provided the context for much of Jesus' interaction with his disciples. I doubt that it was coincidental that Jesus designed spiritual growth around meal time. In his ministry, physical and spiritual nourishment ran together in the ordinary course of daily life. Jesus' *modus operandi* involved the whole person. He fed the body and the soul. Jesus broke bread with the disciples before instituting the Lord's Supper and before praying for them. He fixed breakfast for Peter before leading Peter to reconciliation. After the resurrection, but before the Ascension, Luke describes the setting this way: "On one occasion, while he was *eating* with them, he gave this command . . ."[66] Jesus promised the Holy Spirit over dinner with the disciples. The ambience must not have been super-spiritual, no incense or prepared liturgy, just a simple meal. Jesus' way of relating to people rules out any method or manner that is either artificially contrived or self-consciously "spiritual." Jesus is real and he models the way he expects us to relate to one another. We need to pay attention. The Table of the Lord is the ultimate family meal and it is hosted by the Lord himself. The preacher moves from the text to the table, bringing the Word home, so we can metabolize it into every fiber of our being.

66. Acts 1:4.

6

The Household of Faith

The household of faith and the solidarity of the saints rests on no other foundation than Jesus Christ and him crucified. Apostolic simplicity encourages relational and spiritual integrity and creates meaningful congregational life.

WE ARE "MEMBERS OF God's household, built on the foundation of the apostles and prophets, with Christ Jesus himself as the chief cornerstone. In him the whole building is joined together and rises to become a holy temple in the Lord. And in him you too are being built together to become a dwelling in which God lives by his Spirit."[1] The imagery used to describe our dwelling with God implies strength, security and intimacy. Our first step toward being a household of faith is a deep-seated, inextinguishable longing, a yearning of the soul, to follow Jesus and belong to the Body of Christ. This is not to be confused with a wishful longing to be "one big happy family," but it is a profound conviction that God makes his presence felt in and through the church.

This chapter focuses on the biblical texts that shape our understanding of the church. The place to begin is with good solid teaching on the household of faith. In an age of recreational spirituality, the prosperity gospel, the commodification of friendship, and competition from "Sportianity," we need to take a breath. We need to pause and reexamine what forms us into a Christ-centered household of faith. State-of-the-art social networking is not a substitute for the body life of the church. Fake

---

1. Eph 2:19–22.

fellowship and shallow enthusiasm can be built on hype, but authentic worship, true preaching, real friendship, and genuine mission cannot.

The church is not an attraction or an event; it is a house of prayer and a place of worship. In the New Testament there is not a single word about facilities, but the apostles enjoyed elaborating on the images and metaphors that describe the community of God's people. Their solidarity was not reflected in structures but in their union with Christ Jesus, their chief cornerstone, and in the presence and power of the Holy Spirit. Down through the ages the people of God used imagery of strength and intimacy to describe the presence of God. Psalm 27 says it well: "The Lord is the stronghold of my life—of whom shall I be afraid? . . . One thing I ask of the Lord and this is what I seek that I might dwell in the house of the Lord all the days of my life, to gaze upon his beauty and to seek him in his temple."[2] And one of my favorite descriptions of dwelling in the presence of God is in Psalm 84:

> How lovely is your dwelling place, O Lord Almighty!
> My soul yearns, even faints for the courts of the Lord;
> my heart and my flesh cry out for the living God.
> Even the sparrow has found a home,
> and the swallow a nest for herself,
> where she may have her young—a place near your altar,
> O Lord Almighty, my King and my God.
> Blessed are those who dwell in your house;
> they are ever praising you.[3]

The description of Christ's followers is entirely communal. Jesus used metaphors and analogies, such as the "little flock" and the vine and the branches to picture the emerging church.[4] The apostles spoke of God's chosen people and members of God's household.[5] Peter emphasized, "But you are a chosen people, a royal priesthood, a holy nation, a people belonging to God, that you may declare the praises of him who called you out of darkness into his wonderful light. Once you were not a people, but now you are the people of God; once you had not received mercy, but now you have received mercy."[6] The apostle Peter certainly spoke the truth when he said we were called out of darkness. He did not exaggerate

2. Ps 27:1, 4.
3. Ps 84:1–4.
4. Luke 12:32; John 15.
5. Col 3:12; Eph 2:19.
6. 1 Pet 2:9–10.

when he said that we were once not a people. We did not always live in the household of faith.

A Church Without Walls

The solidarity of the saints is a consistent theme throughout the book of Ephesians. The apostle Paul refers to Christ creating in himself "one new humanity"; in the Greek, it is literally, "one new person." So real was the oneness of this new humanity that Paul spoke of the church as being one new person. Paul was not interested in individual players as much as in the whole team. Everything he says concerns the family, the holy ones, the community of God's people. The imagery of citizenship, household, and temple imply strength and security, but above all solidarity. In rapid succession, Paul stacks the metaphors: God's kingdom, God's family, God's temple. His purpose is not to preach a three-point sermon, but to deliver a single message: our identity in Christ is not individualistic but corporate. We are this third race—holy ones, members of God's household, and joined together to become a holy temple. We used to be foreigners and strangers but now we have immigrated to a new country, we have been adopted into a new family, and we belong to a holy temple in the Lord.

Early Christians had a sense of place, a feeling of being at home, not in a facility but in a family of shared faithfulness to the Word of God. There was no outward temple or tall steeple to symbolize their place, but as they met together there was a powerful presence of the risen Lord Jesus. The early Christians knew that "the Most High does not live in houses made by men."[7]

All the metaphors in Ephesians chapter two are relational, even the building metaphors. The foundation is made up of people—the apostles and the prophets. Most likely this is a reference to the limited group of disciples who witnessed the risen Lord Jesus together with the expanding circle of preachers and prophets who declared the gospel. The chief cornerstone is Christ Jesus. The "chief cornerstone" is not a ceremonial cornerstone, inscribed with the date of the building, nor is it likely that Paul intended it to refer to the keystone or capstone crowning the top of the building. "Cornerstones in ancient buildings were the primary load-bearing stones that determined the lines of the building. Such stones have been found in Palestine, one weighing as much as 570 tons."[8] The

7. Acts 7:48.
8. Snodgrass, *Ephesians*, 137.

third relational metaphor is "the holy temple in the Lord" described as a dwelling in which God lives by his Spirit. Paul had in mind the people of God, not the Jerusalem temple built by Herod. He used the same imagery with the believers at Corinth, when he said, "Do you not know that your bodies are temples of the Holy Spirit, who is in you, whom you have received from God?"[9] In each case the meaning of the metaphor is personal and relational.

With the literary care of a poet, Paul orchestrated a word play on the Greek word for "house" (οικος). In Christ we are no longer *aliens* (πάροικοι), but members of God's *household* (οἰκεῖοι), *built on* (ἐποικοδομηθέντες) a sure foundation, and the *building* (οἰκοδομὴ) is *built together* (συνοικοδομεῖσθε) into a *dwelling place* (κατοικητήριον) of God.[10] Paul's intentional selection of the household of faith language underscores the relational nature of the church.

The relational and spiritual character of this "house" built by God *of people* is no less material, temporal, spatial, and concrete than if it had been built with stone and steel. "The accent of Ephesians 2 lies not upon intangibleness but upon the fact that the church of God is made of people, rather than of bricks."[11] The good news is proclaimed and lived through the local church, through the community, rather than through the individual. In a world of hostility the church is an alternative society, a visible sign of the kingdom of God in a fallen world.

Since the walls of ritual, tradition, laws, and regulations have been broken down in Christ, we must be careful not to re-erect those old walls. For much of his life the apostle Paul prided himself on his religious heritage, ethnicity, family background, spiritual discipline, and righteous zeal. But "the blinding light of the Christ-encounter (Acts 9:3–5) paradoxically opened Paul's eyes to see everything clearly and in proper perspective."[12] He experienced "a radical transvaluation of values."[13] From then on, Paul "considered everything a loss" compared to the "surpassing worth of knowing Christ."[14] Paul no longer lived at the old address of self-reliant self-righteousness. He had moved to an entirely new address. Mark Labberton describes it this way:

9. 1 Cor 6:19.
10. Snodgrass, *Ephesians*, 137.
11. Barth, *Ephesians*, 320.
12. Hawthorne, *Philippians*, 147.
13. Ibid.
14. Phil 3:8.

When we live in God in the world, we see everything, whether on the other side of the world or down the street, in a new way. The primary lens is no longer our family background, our personality, prejudices, worries or subculture; it is now the love of God for every person. Only when I practice living in God do I realize that I am secure enough to not be self-absorbed, I am free enough to not exploit it. I am gifted and called to express the passions of God's heart for the poor and needy, the oppressed and the suffering.[15]

From the vantage point of being in Christ, people in need become more fascinating to us than those who can advance our career or enhance our pleasure. Showing compassion means more to us than achieving success. It is indeed a strange new world. Our relationship to the world is essentially positive. The gospel is not about what we are against, but what we are for. We must never lose sight of the glory of God and this wonderful news that the walls of hostility have been broken down in Christ. Paul pictures open borders in the kingdom of God, a more-the-merrier household of God, and an organically growing temple in the Lord. People who are saved by grace through faith don't major on denominational distinctives or religious rituals. I have pastored four different churches in four different denominations. I am grateful that my ministry has not been limited by man-made distinctions or boxed in by religious traditions. What is important is that we know Christ and seek to follow him and obey his word. Those who have become one new humanity—this third race in Christ—don't make it hard for others to follow Christ. They don't erect "dividing walls of hostility."

A church member wrote to me about her personal experience. She started her letter with a verse from Psalm 27: "Though my father and mother forsake me, the Lord will receive me." She explained how she had grown up in a mean-spirited, negative home environment. She identified with those who have felt forsaken by father or mother. "Even as adults," she said, "the pain may linger." But God can take that place in our lives, fill that void, and heal that hurt. He can direct us to adults who may take the role of father and mother for us. His love is sufficient for all our needs. Her parents made life more difficult by wrapping up their twisted and negative attitudes "in their brand of Christianity." Over time she absorbed their negative and condemning attitude, which made it extremely difficult for her to relate and find her place in the Body of Christ. But because of God's

15. Labberton, *The Dangerous Act of Worship*, 94.

help, she has slowly overcome this deeply rooted judgmental attitude. She concluded her letter with these words, "So many people in this church have been so loving, caring and kind to me. Their behavior is truly Christ-like. Because of my fellow church members, I am slowly letting down the walls I've built around myself over the years. Please continue to pray for me."

God's purpose is that we not divide along ethnic, cultural, racial, social, gender, and generational lines. We were meant to be fellow citizens with God's people and members of God's household, built on the foundation provided by the apostles and prophets, with Christ Jesus himself as the chief cornerstone. "The church gathers around the character of Christ, not the characteristics of people."[16] It is important to maintain the distinction between being in Christ and being of the world. It is the difference between being guided by God's indwelling Spirit for the good of the world and being shaped by the spirit of the times. Paul became all things to all people "so that by all possible means [he] might save some."[17]

This is different from becoming all things to all people in order to win their favor. Paul insisted on doing everything for the sake of the gospel. His refusal to be judgmental did not discredit discernment. His rejection of prejudice did not sanction disobedience. This is why he said to the Ephesians, "So I tell you this, and insist on it in the Lord, that you must no longer lives as the Gentiles do, in the futility of their thinking. They are darkened in their understanding and separated from the life of God because of the ignorance that is in them due to the hardening of their hearts. Having lost all sensitivity, they have given themselves over to sensuality so as to indulge in every kind of impurity, and they are full of greed."[18]

The borders of the kingdom of God are wide open. The gospel message is all encompassing, "whosoever will may come." No matter how deep the depravity or painful the social alienation, there is room at the table of the Lord in the household of faith. There are no walls of hostility keeping anyone out of the temple of the Lord. Markus Barth calls the message of Ephesians chapter two "the key and high point of the whole epistle."[19] In a world of evil and hostility, the gospel of Jesus Christ is an inclusive invitation to an exclusive Savior and Lord. We come as we are but we do not

16. Snodgrass, *Ephesians*, 155.

17. 1 Cor 9:22.

18. Eph 4:17–19.

19. Barth, *Ephesians*, 275.

remain as we were. We are new creations created in Christ Jesus. We have a new citizenship, a new family, and an entirely new indwelling Spirit.

Unless the Lord Builds the House

Solomon's simple one-liner serves as both admonition and promise, warning and blessing, and should echo through the minds and hearts of everyone in the household of faith. "Unless the Lord builds the house, its builders labor in vain." Explicit in the opening line of Psalm 127 is the emptiness of human achievement independent from the Lord. It was one of the Psalms the Hebrew pilgrims prayed as they ascended to Jerusalem to celebrate the special days of worship, such as Passover and Pentecost. They reminded themselves in song of God's sovereign care over every sphere of life. They were dependent upon the Living God who was their source of security and significance. They traveled to Jerusalem to worship their God, unencumbered by the myth of human self-sufficiency. These Jerusalem-bound sojourners dedicated their efforts and their relationships to God.

> If Yahweh doesn't build the house,
> the builders only build shacks.
> If Yahweh doesn't guard the city,
> the night watchman might as well nap.
> It's useless to rise early and go to bed late,
> and work your worried fingers to the bone.
> Don't you know he enjoys
> giving rest to those he loves?
> Don't you see that children are Yahweh's best gift?
> The fruit of the womb his generous legacy?
> Like a warrior's fistful of arrows
> are the children of a vigorous youth.
> Oh, how blessed are you parents,
> with your quivers full of children!
> Your enemies don't stand a chance against you;
> you'll sweep them right off your doorstep.[20]

When we pray this Psalm today, we acknowledge from beginning to end that the work of the church is God's work. We can only claim it as our own to the extent that we follow God's lead. This means that in our work and effort we draw our wisdom and energy from God. What holds true for

20. Ps 127, *The Message*.

our salvation is also true for our lives as a church. Apart from God we can do nothing and the model for this dependency is Jesus, who said,

> My Father is always at his work to this very day, and I, too, am working. . . . I tell you the truth, the Son can do nothing by himself; he can do only what he sees his Father doing, because whatever the Father does the Son also does. For the Father loves the Son and shows him all he does.[21]

In Psalm 127, the psalmist proposes a new scale for measuring the meaning of ministry. His prayer helps us to picture the spiritual health, physical well-being, and relational strength that comes from God-centered communion. This is the divine defense against the vanity of soul-draining self-effort, competitive insecurity, and restless hyperactivity. The psalmist centers home and city, work and family in God and celebrates the blessing of God's presence and provision. This poetic picture of blessing finds its culmination and fulfillment in relationships. The metaphors paint a beautiful picture of balance, wholeness, health, and happiness. We lay aside our pride and no longer boast of what we have built or done for God. Instead, we humbly declare what God has done for us, in us, and through us. It is a work of grace, thanksgiving and praise. "For he grants sleep to those he loves."

Working from God's blueprint, church and family do not compete, but *unite* and prosper in the household of faith. Church work can erode people's spirituality and love for God, but under the Lord's direction the work of the church builds people up spiritually and physically. Health and holiness are meant to come together in the household of faith. At the end of this beautiful picture of blessing and holy ambition, the psalmist offers a quick sketch of familial protection and support in the public arena. In place of human self-sufficiency the psalmist bears elegant testimony of God's blessing in the family and among friends. In keeping with the poetic metaphor of the psalmist, children are the best protection against enemies and a sure defense against shame. God provides a new generation as a sign of his blessing, who are called to defend and protect the previous generation and carry on the faith. This interdependence is both divine and human, *communion* with God and *community* with one another. The practical implications of this short Psalm are enormous. They encourage us to reexamine the clear goals of the church and turn to the biblical basics. We may find that more becomes less and less becomes more.

21. John 5:19–20.

When I was in middle school we lived in a predominantly Roman Catholic neighborhood and not far from our home there was a large Catholic church. On Saturday night and Sunday morning people attended mass in waves. One of my father's favorite coffee shops was across the street from the church and I remember watching hundreds of people stream in and out for what seemed to me a very short service. My friends told me the service was in Latin, which made it seem all the more strange (this was before Vatican II). I had trouble understanding how such a quick ritual constituted belonging to a church, because our church experience was so much more involved. We spent the morning at church. There was Sunday school, the morning service and a whole lot of interacting with people before, during, and after. At night we returned for another service which was more laid back and informal. And on Wednesday night we attended a prayer meeting. In a church setting like this there were several things that took place without a great deal of effort. We learned a lot of Bible and we learned how to pray. We knew one another and to a certain extent we cared for one another.

It was not an ideal church by any means, but my family and I truly belonged to this group of saved sinners. We knew the pastor and the pastor knew us. New people were easily identified and related to. Members made eye contact with strangers and struck up a conversation. Church was not a place to go for services so much as a place to belong to as a community of believers. It sounds idealistic or pious to say we sought to grow in the grace and knowledge of the Lord Jesus Christ, but given our many weaknesses, sins, and the mess of the human condition this was true. At times it was a frustrating community, conflicts arose and people got upset with one another, but in spite of the problems, worship and witness prevailed, preaching and prayer continued, and believers experienced real fellowship. It was hard to get lost in the crowd and it wasn't easy to remain aloof from the realities of being a church. There is considerable concern today to re-invent the church, but I am convinced that there is no better pattern for building the household of faith than the blueprint followed by the New Testament church. We don't have to design new structures to meet ever-changing demands. We need to build the household of faith from the Lord's blueprint.

God's Blueprint

> They devoted themselves to the apostles' teaching and to the fellowship, to the breaking of the bread and to prayer.[22]

A wise architect knows that the basic functions of a home are universal. We all need places to sleep, eat, congregate, and bathe. A custom home that does not provide for these basic functions may be a spectacular house to look at, but not a very good one to live in. Churches that are preoccupied with target audiences and niche marketing are more like the beautiful homes displayed in *Better Homes and Gardens* and *Architectural Digest*. They are outwardly impressive for their innovative extras, fresh designs, and creative features, but do they enhance family life? The missing element in these pictures of beautiful homes is the lived-in look. They're great for spectators, but how do they work for a family working, sleeping, playing, living, and eating together? Are they designed to make a house a home?

The real test for an authentic, viable church remains outlined for us in the second chapter of Acts. Herein lies the key to turning a crowd into disciples, an audience into a congregation, and isolated individuals into the family of God. In Acts 2 we find the nexus between God's work and our work, rendering everything else superfluous and extraneous. If we don't pay serious attention to these basic functions that are universally necessary for all churches everywhere, we will never find our place in the household of faith.

Almost every church's denominational distinctives appear represented in the experience of Pentecost and the description of the early church. Roman Catholics see the history of apostolic succession commencing with Peter. Baptists point to the baptism of new converts and Pentecostals to the outpouring of the Holy Spirit. The Reformed tradition resonates with Peter's proclamation of the Word and the believers' devotion to the apostles' teaching. Anglicans and Episcopalians may choose to focus on the breaking of the bread and Methodists on small group fellowships. Mennonites see themselves in the early church's social concern and simple lifestyle. Certain Brethren denominations may emphasize prayer and the Nazarenes may see themselves in the quest for personal holiness. Megachurches identify with the early church's explosive growth. However, what the Book of Acts emphasizes is not what sets believers apart in

---

22. Acts 2:42.

denominations, but what holds the followers of Jesus together as the body of Christ. The issue is not our separate denominational distinctives, but our shared commitment to all that the Lord seeks to build in his body, the church.

Luke describes what happened in the First Church of Acts. The early believers "devoted themselves to the apostles' teaching and to the fellowship, to the breaking of bread and to prayer." These four practices constitute the basic needs that are universal to the church at all times, in every age, everywhere. The early church was *devoted* to these four spiritual disciplines. The word *devoted* deserves some explanation, lest we pass over it too quickly and miss its significance. I imagine most churches include these four disciplines somewhere in the life of the church, but are they as much a priority as they were to the early church? By devoting themselves "to the apostle's teaching and to the fellowship, to the breaking of bread and to prayer," the early church gave themselves with great constancy and purpose to these practices. They persisted in and held fast to this basic blueprint for spiritual and evangelistic growth.

They devoted themselves to the apostles' teaching. All the believers became students of the Word of God, not for the sake of acquiring a head knowledge or satisfying intellectual curiosity, but for the purpose of being transformed by the truth of God's Word. The teaching ministry of the apostles was confirmed by "many wonders and miraculous signs done by the apostles."[23] But the great outpouring of the Holy Spirit did not in any way lessen the importance of listening intently and learning personally the truth of God's Word.

The early church affirmed what the apostle Paul later emphasized to Timothy. "All Scripture is God-breathed and is useful for teaching, rebuking, correcting and training in righteousness, so that the person of God may be thoroughly equipped for every good work."[24] We believe in the divine inspiration of Holy Scripture and its entire trustworthiness and supreme authority in all matters of faith and conduct. We do so, not in theory, but in practice. We seek to submit our personal lives, as well as the life and ministry of our church, to the authority of God's Word. We believe that we have no other message than the message revealed in God's Word, the Bible. It is our goal to preach Jesus Christ and him crucified.[25]

23. Acts 2:43.
24. 2 Tim 3:16–17.
25. 1 Cor 2:2.

To that end, "We proclaim him, admonishing and teaching everyone with all wisdom, so that we may present everyone mature in Christ."[26]

This is why God's Word is proclaimed from the pulpit and made the subject of study in Sunday school and in small groups. This is why the music ministry reflects the truth of God's Word and the children's ministry encourages Bible memorization and seeks to teach and apply the Word of God. This is why the Word of God is preached in our ministry to the poor and needy and why ministries that translate the Bible into indigenous languages are supported. This is why missionaries faithfully proclaim the Word of God throughout the world. The body of Christ accepts the admonition to "Let the word of Christ dwell in [us] richly as [we] teach and admonish one another with all wisdom, and as [we] sing psalms, hymns and spiritual songs with gratitude in [our] hearts to God."[27]

My prayer is that the children of the church will understand how valuable the Word of God is to us. I remember my fourth and fifth grade Sunday school teacher Mr. Knuen. Monday through Friday he was a milkman, but on Sunday, he patiently and methodically delivered the "pure milk of the Word" without fail. Maybe he is one reason why I believe so strongly in the priesthood of all believers. I don't remember him as a fun, exciting teacher, but I do remember that he was very sincere about the Word of God. He taught us to memorize verses, and we all knew that he really wanted us to understand the Bible and apply it to our lives. I can't remember a single sermon I heard during my adolescence, but the Word of God shaped my existence and had a profound influence on me. The preached Word, the parented Word, the devotional Word, slowly transformed me.

No preacher in those early years had as profound an effect on me as did Grace Baird. She was one of my grandmother's friends, a large woman in her seventies who commanded respect and taught the Word with authority. She came to church on a mission and that was to teach children how to worship God for real. The hymns I sing on key I learned in Grace Baird's primary church, and I'm glad Grace Baird came to our church and served as my pastor in our primary church. The early church devoted themselves to the whole counsel of God and sought to apply the Word of God in every area of life from their understanding of the fullness of God to their love and support for one another.

26. Col 1:28.
27. Col 3:16.

They devoted themselves to fellowship (koinonia). The basic blueprint of the Lord's church calls for fellowship in two senses. The word *koinonia* means "sharing in" or "causing to share in" something or someone. First, we share together a common fellowship with the triune God, Father, Son, and Holy Spirit. As Paul said, "God, who has called you into fellowship with his Son Jesus Christ our Lord, is faithful."[28] The blessing of our life together depends exclusively on this fellowship. "May the grace of the Lord Jesus Christ, and love of God, and the fellowship of the Holy Spirit be with you all."[29] The fellowship we share is "our fellowship . . . with the Father and with his Son, Jesus Christ."[30] Secondly, the New Testament church used the word fellowship (*koinonia*) to refer to sharing together their material resources. In the NIV the word is translated as "sharing," but it is the same word that is used for fellowship with God.[31] It is this second meaning of fellowship that Luke emphasizes here. The reality of Christian conversion was especially evident in the generous sharing that went on among Christians. Luke writes, "All the believers were together and had everything in common. Selling their possessions and goods, they gave to anyone as he had need." The range of meaning encompassed in the fellowship of the early church ought to be a powerful incentive to build the household of faith on solid theology and practical sharing.

Fake fellowship is a big turnoff. We cannot program fellowship the way we upload our computers with new software and even the most sophisticated social networking does not substitute for authentic body life. Fellowship, like friendship, is born of mutual respect, shared concern, and common cause. The give and take of true fellowship is innocent and uncalculated, uncoerced and spontaneous. That is not to say that genuine fellowship lacks commitment and structure, but like love itself it is not engineered or programmed. Fellowship involves a meeting of the minds, shared ministry, an enjoyment of one another's company, and the freedom to feel at home with one another. What C. S. Lewis says about friendship applies to fellowship. He pictures friends standing side by side with their eyes looking ahead, unlike lovers who look at one another face to face. Fellowship "must be about something," Lewis observes. "That is why those pathetic people who simply 'want friends' can never make any. The very condition of having friends is that we should want something else besides

28. 1 Cor 1:9.
29. 2 Cor 13:14; see Phil 2:1.
30. 1 John 1:3.
31. 2 Cor 8:4; 9:13.

friends . . . Those who have nothing can share nothing; those who are going nowhere can have no fellow-travelers."[32] For the household of faith the matrix of fellowship is the Word and worship, prayer and mission.

They devoted themselves to the breaking of bread. The third characteristic of the early church was worship. Biblical scholars agree that Luke's reference to "the breaking of the bread" implies the celebration of the Lord's Supper. This is an especially relational and intimate way of characterizing worship. The early church moved easily from enjoying each other's fellowship around the table to celebrating holy communion. The apostle Paul gives us a glimpse of some of the practical problems that arose over combining the fellowship meal and celebrating the eucharist, but Luke describes the experience positively.[33] "They broke bread in their homes and ate together with glad and sincere hearts." The believers enjoyed a oneness of fellowship that easily blended and integrated family and home life with the household of faith. It was not unusual for them to enjoy table fellowship and naturally move into worship. They regularly concluded their *agape* meal with the words of institution: "This is my body, which is for you; do this in remembrance of me." And, "This cup is the new covenant in my blood; do this, whenever you drink it, in remembrance of me."[34] If our personal lives and our worship life were so united and conjoined as to be one, we would undoubtedly experience the strength and encouragement of belonging to the church. The worship experience of the early church was far different from just going through the motions. Surely those who experienced the Lord's Supper in the early church did not remain as strangers to one another.

They were devoted to prayer or the prayers. Luke's description includes the definite article before prayer as it does with the breaking of the bread. This reference to *the prayers* indicates that the early church met together for prayer services. Personal prayer was followed up by specific times of prayer. These may have corresponded with the regular Jewish times of prayer. This is suggested by the fact that "everyday they continued to meet together in the temple courts."[35] It is also suggested by the reference to Peter and John "going up to the temple at the time of prayer."[36] Once again Luke's description implies a range of meaning, from personal prayer to corporate prayer,

32. Lewis, *The Four Loves*, 66–67.

33. See 1 Cor 11:17–34.

34. 1 Cor 11:24–25.

35. Acts 2:46.

36. Acts 3:1.

from prayer in the temple courts to prayer in their homes. Psalm 127 is a great example of a prayer that reminds us of our dependency upon the Lord and our partnership with Christ in being his church.

Working from this blueprint means that the church is shaped by the Word of God, united in fellowship with God and with one another, focused in Christ-centered worship, and abiding in prayerful communion with the Lord. Luke's description is not a formula for success but it is a pattern to be followed in experiencing life together in Christ. Formulas may be imposed on people, but a pattern emerges from believers influenced by the Holy Spirit. It is a portrait that helps us see the practical and human side of being spiritual. The nexus between God's work and ours is formed in the Word, in fellowship, in worship, and in prayer. Building the household of faith according to this blueprint makes for a dynamic and exciting fellowship of believers. Such a church becomes a learning, loving, caring, praying, rejoicing, and evangelizing community of disciples.

These four vital elements are held in dynamic tension with one another. Instead of seeing the Word, fellowship, worship and prayer as four categories under which every conceivable ministry program can be conveniently located, we are better off seeing our devotion to God expressed in a four-fold healthy and holistic pattern of life. Church is not made up of four departments with each vying for the attention of the congregation. There is an attractive simplicity to this Spirit-synchronized, four-part harmony. In some sense these four must be seen as the unifying devotion of the Body of Christ. The one thing that we all do all the time all together (Psalm 27:4).

Luke's description is bracketed by two references to church growth. The impact of Peter's message resulted in three thousand baptized individuals "added to their number that day." And the impact of the positive testimony of the church led to a pattern of personal transformation (repentance, baptism, and inclusion). "And the Lord added to their number daily those who were being saved." John Stott observes, "Those first Jerusalem Christians were *not* so preoccupied with learning, sharing and worshiping, that they forgot about witnessing . . ." It is also important to note that the "the Lord added to their number daily those who were being saved." Stott writes, "Doubtless he did it through the preaching of the apostles, the witness of church members, the impressive love of their common life, and their example as they were praising God and enjoying the favor of all the people. *Yet he did it!*"[37] "Unless the Lord builds the house the builders labor in vain" remains as true today as it ever was. If we build

---

37. Stott, *The Spirit, The Church, and The World*, 86.

the household of faith according to the blueprint followed by the emerging church we will discover the wisdom of the Architect and the Lord will receive all the credit.

Building on the Foundation

> For no one can lay any foundation other than the one already laid, which is Jesus Christ.[38]

As any builder will tell you the foundation is extremely important. I grew up in western New York where no builder would ever construct a house on a four-inch slab of concrete as builders do in southern California. When my father built an addition onto our home, the foundation of gravel and concrete went down four feet below the frost-line. Most houses in cold climates are built on cinder block basements. Since builders have to excavate four feet of earth anyway, they might as well go down another four feet and use the space. In southern California builders don't worry about the ground freezing, but they do think a lot about earthquakes. Foundations for taller buildings are sunk all the way down to bedrock, in order to anchor buildings into the outer crust of the earth. Contemporary high-rise buildings are constructed on a suppression system, which are designed to function like a giant shock absorber, isolating the up and down and side to side shock waves of an earthquake. Engineers at the Powell Structural Lab, the University of California at San Diego's seismic testing facility, explore ways to construct foundations and buildings to withstand the destructive forces of an earthquake. They know the importance of a good foundation.

When the apostle Paul wrote to the church at Corinth he detected shock waves that threatened to divide the church. Instead of a community devoted to the apostles' teaching, to fellowship, to the breaking of bread and to prayer, he found a church that was acting like any other human institution. He realized that the church was divided, competitive, and compromising. It was a bad, human organization and yet it was still known as the body of Christ. The spirit of the age was crowding out the Holy Spirit. This was evident in the way they looked at leadership. They began by choosing sides. As Paul explained, "One of you says, 'I follow Paul'; another, 'I follow Apollos'; another, 'I follow Cephas'; still another, 'I follow Christ.'"[39]

38. 1 Cor 3:11.
39. 1 Cor 1:12.

Their apparent embarrassment over the message of the cross was evident in their striving for recognition in the court of public opinion. They were trying to become more popular and improve their social standing. They had grown tolerant of sexual immorality in the church and resorted to the secular law courts to settle disputes among themselves. Claiming their freedom to eat food offered to idols, they were insensitive to those who were new in the faith. Paul linked their lack of stewardship and their indifference to the mission of the church to the cold, hard-hearted Israelites in the wilderness. Instead of becoming one, they were accentuating their social and economic differences. This was especially evident in how they celebrated the Lord's Supper. "When you come together; it is not the Lord's Supper you eat, for as you eat, each of you goes ahead without waiting for anyone else. One remains hungry, another gets drunk."[40] Their worship services appeared confusing and contentious, and speaking in tongues led to pride rather than praise. Private spiritual ecstasy replaced thoughtful evangelism, and some were claiming that there was no resurrection of the dead.

This explains why Paul could not address them as "spiritual but as worldly—mere infants in Christ." This is why he insisted on reminding them that "no one can lay any foundation other than the one already laid, which is Jesus Christ." Sadly, they were living as if the foundation did not exist and they were intent on building according to their own plan.

If the church is a worldly organization, it makes sense to build on human charisma, for the world is comfortable with personality cults. Accommodation to the world promotes personal moral autonomy and tolerates sexual immorality. Good public relations seeks social and cultural prestige. Spiritual ecstasy adds a sense of excitement and private satisfaction, and doctrinal disputes and heretical conclusions prove how free-thinking and tolerant the church is. If the foundation is other than Christ then all these Corinthian features make church growth sense. But if the foundation is Jesus Christ, they have no place in the Body of Christ.

In every age and in every place the church must remember that "no one can lay any foundation other than the one already laid, which is Jesus Christ."[41] We also face the temptation of substituting Herodian methods for Christ's message. The danger lies in wanting to impress people with things other than the gospel, things that we have accomplished. Some also want to prove that the church merits respect in the world for its spirituality, its religious services, its tolerance, and its social relevance. But Paul

40. 1 Cor 11:20–21.
41. 1 Cor 3:11.

argues that the world can never understand the meaning and value of the church outside of Christ. The message of the cross is foolishness to the world. That is why Paul said, "We preach Christ crucified: a stumbling block to Jews and foolishness to Gentiles, but to those whom God has called, both Jews and Greeks, Christ the power of God and the wisdom of God."[42] The apostle Paul spelled out what this means.

First, it means that the wisdom of God is not subject to the spirit of the age. "Where is the wise man? Where is the scholar? Where is the philosopher of the age? Has not God made foolish the wisdom of the world?"[43] The wisdom of God receives no confirmation or commendation from the world.

Second, it means that no one is too inferior, too weak, too foolish, to be chosen by God. "God chose the foolish things of the world to shame the wise; God chose the weak things of the world to shame the strong. He chose the lowly things of this world and the despised things—and the things that are not—to nullify the things that are, so that no one may boast before him."[44] According to what Paul said, the church is by definition a strange mix of people, often drawn from society's outcasts. The church in the eyes of the world is considered both unwise and uncool.

Third, it means that we are no longer defined by what we were, but by who we are *in Christ*. The unity-in-diversity that the world celebrates contradicts the unity-out-of-diversity that the church celebrates. The world says accept everyone as they are and let them be what they want to be. The gospel says come as you are, but don't remain as you were. In Christ you'll never be the same again. What we were, is not who we are in Christ. "[We] were washed, [we] were sanctified, [we] were justified in the name of the Lord Jesus Christ and by the Spirit of our God."[45]

Fourth, it means that the message of the Gospel is best communicated with humility rather than ingenuity. As Paul testified, "I came to you in weakness and fear, and with much trembling. My message and my preaching were not with wise and persuasive words, but with a demonstration of the Spirit's power, so that your faith might not rest on human wisdom, but on God's power."[46] Paul did not use cleverness or eloquence or any form of entertainment to win a hearing for the gospel. His method

42. 1 Cor 1:23–24.
43. 1 Cor 1:20.
44. 1 Cor 1:27–29.
45. 1 Cor 6:11.
46. 1 Cor 2:3–5.

of communication was entirely intentional and strictly disciplined. It must not be used as an excuse for lackluster or thoughtless preaching, nor misconstrued as permission to be boring or pedantic. On the contrary, Paul preached with such earnestness and humility that the Spirit's power was revealed.

Nothing but Christ Crucified

The apostle Paul expressed his mission statement in a single sentence: "For I resolved to know nothing while I was with you except Jesus Christ and him crucified."[47] This bedrock conviction parallels and explains what Paul meant when he said, "For no one can lay any foundation other than the one already laid, which is Jesus Christ."[48] Some have felt that Paul's resolve to know nothing but Christ crucified in Corinth was in reaction to his attempt to explain the gospel to the intellectuals in Athens. Instead of debating and dialoguing as he did in Athens, he simply gave the simple plan of salvation to the Corinthians. However, there is no evidence for this conclusion. Paul's letters to the believers at Corinth show that he had no intention of reducing the gospel to an abbreviated form of the plan of salvation.

On the contrary, Paul saw the relevance of the cross in every conceivable sphere of the believer's life. He saw the cross of Jesus as the basis for unity in the Body of Christ. To those who were ready to divide up and follow their favorite leader he asked, "Was Paul crucified for you? Were you baptized into the name of Paul?"[49] To those who were proud of their tolerance of sexual immorality in the church, Paul called for immediate church discipline, because "Christ our Passover lamb has been sacrificed."[50] He commanded, "Flee from sexual immorality," because of the cross. "You are not your own, you were bought at a price. Therefore honor God with your body."[51] He counseled believers to experience their freedom in Christ, regardless of their social circumstances, because of the cross. "You were bought at a price; do not become slaves of men."[52] He advised refraining from eating meat that had been offered to idols if it would cause a new

47. 1 Cor 2:2.
48. 1 Cor 3:11.
49. 1 Cor 1:13.
50. 1 Cor 5:7.
51. 1 Cor 6:19–20.
52. 1 Cor 7:23.

believer to stumble. Or else, "this weak brother, for whom Christ died, is destroyed by your knowledge."[53]

Paul centered the worship life of the church in the cross. "Is not the cup of thanksgiving for which we give thanks a participation in the blood of Christ? And is not the bread that we break a participation in the body of Christ?"[54] He warned believers against using their social positions and income to humiliate other believers. "For anyone who eats and drinks without recognizing the body of the Lord eats and drinks judgment on himself."[55] To those who questioned the reality of the bodily resurrection, Paul affirmed that the saving work of Christ on the cross depended upon the risen Lord Jesus. "For what I received I passed on to you as of the first importance: that Christ died for our sins according to the Scriptures, that he was buried, that he was raised on the third day according to the Scriptures, and that he appeared to Peter, and then to the Twelve."[56] In the midst of every problem, every issue, every conflict impacting the church at Corinth, Paul brought the believers back to the finished work of Christ on the cross. Paul subsumed everything under the cross, even death itself. "The sting of death is sin, and the power of sin is the law. But thanks be to God! He gives us the victory through our Lord Jesus Christ."[57]

As God's children in the household of faith, the qualities we long for cannot be created or controlled by us. We cannot adopt ourselves into the family of God. We don't have a budget that can be compared to the glorious riches of God. We cannot match the power of the indwelling presence of God. No human love or passion can provide the stability and security that comes from being rooted and established in God's love. No racial identity or ethnic group or cultural background or social standing or gender consciousness or generational affiliation or wish dream, can be compared to the unity we are given in Christ. For as the apostle emphasized seven times over, "There is one body and one Spirit—just as you were called to one hope—one Lord, one faith, one baptism; one God and Father of all, who is over all and through all and in all."[58]

53. 1 Cor 8:11.
54. 1 Cor 10:16.
55. 1 Cor 11:29.
56. 1 Cor 15:3–4.
57. 1 Cor 15:56.
58. Eph 4:4–6.

Congregational Life

We cannot follow Jesus apart from being in the body of Christ. It would be like being married without a spouse or employed without a job or being a baseball player without a team or a pastor without a church or a mother without a child. You get my point! We cannot follow Christ and live apart from the people of God. We need to be a part of the household of faith. Many Christians look upon the church as optional, as one of many week-end possibilities. If they're caught up with their work and sleep, and have nothing more pressing to do, they may attend church. Going to church is something optional for many and they feel no compelling reason to really belong to a church.

I compare that attitude to the conviction held by a couple I know, Mary and Jim Brusko. At a time when many young couples decide it's too much trouble to go to church for worship and fellowship, the Bruskos decided they could not face a week without worship. I remember when they dedicated their second child, Michael, to the Lord, and Jim spoke to the congregation welcoming their son into the family. Jim shared how he and Mary believed Michael would play an important role in loving and caring for their oldest child, three-year-old Kimberly. Kimmy had already undergone life-saving heart surgery and was physically and mentally disabled. The prognosis for her development did not look good. She had virtually no muscle control, no ability to speak or feed herself, and her ability to think was severely incapacitated. Jim said, "Mary and I love Kimberly. She is our daughter and we are committed to caring for her."

For nearly eleven years Mary and Jim never wavered in their resolve to parent Kimberly with the love of Christ. For more than a decade they provided total care: lifting, bathing, feeding, loving. Night and day they cared for their oldest child with a persevering love and practical devotion. They accepted God's hand in this and depended upon God to give them the endurance and love that they needed. In spite of this taxing effort, Jim and Mary, along with their young family (which now included another daughter, Sarah) attended church weekly because they were convinced that they needed the rhythm of worship and fellowship. They were surrounded by their own parents, who in turn cared for them in practical, sacrificial ways. Mary and Jim embody what the author of Hebrews meant when he wrote, "Therefore let us leave the elementary teachings about Christ and go on to maturity."[59] They soaked up all that God offered by the grace of

59. Heb 6:1.

Christ and by his Spirit: the blessing of loving parents, faithful Christian friends, a supportive household of faith, and they put their faith to work in loving service to Kimberly, the daughter of Christ. Because of Kimberly, other suffering parents, who shared the same doctors and hospitals, heard about Christ. Because of Kimberly, Mary and Jim matured well beyond their years, experiencing a depth of sorrow and love most young families never reach. It is for the sake of Christ, and couples like the Bruskos, that the household of faith values worship over entertainment and real relationships over superficial encounters. The Bruskos found joy and strength for their journey in the household of faith.

When I think of the importance of the church for sustaining and strengthening our faith in Christ I also think of Mike and Judy Palm. They did something special when their son David turned twelve years old. They hosted a picnic in his honor to celebrate his joining the church. The invitation read:

> *David Palm*
> *is joining the household of faith*
> *of First Presbyterian Church*
> *We invite you to celebrate this occasion*
> *with friends and family . . .*
> *Join us for a picnic, games and a time of sharing*
>
> *Special Request: Please write down any advice and wisdom*
> *you have for David as we recognize his public profession of*
> *faith. We will be keeping a scrapbook of these pages for David as*
> *an encouragement to him in the future.*
> *(You may also share these words of encouragement at the picnic.)*

After we had eaten lunch, we gathered in a large circle and various members of the household of faith shared their thoughts with David. Several of his Sunday school teachers commended him for his Bible memorization and encouraged him to continue to "hide God's word in his heart." One of our oldest and most respected elders shared Proverbs 3:5-6, "Trust in the Lord with all your heart and lean not on your own understanding; in all your ways acknowledge him, and he will direct your paths." Another who had known David since he was a baby quoted from the Westminister Confession, "The chief end of man is to glorify God and enjoy him forever." She sweetly challenged David to *enjoy* God. There was an endearing significance in everything that was said, from the sharing of David's twelve-year-old friends to his eighty-year-old elders. The entire experience was a marked affirmation in David Palm's life of the apostle Paul's words, "He who began a good work in you will carry it on to completion until the day of Christ Jesus."[60] The picnic was a picture of the household of faith at its best.

> For where two or three come together in my name, there I am with them.[61]

Several years ago I had a unique experience of congregational life. Within the downtown church that I pastored, a little church grew up that was formed by my twenty-two-year-old son Andrew, my seventy-eight-year-old mother, and my middle-aged self—a father to my son, a son to my mother, and a pastor to them both. We didn't consciously come together to form a microcosm of the church with Christ at the center, but it happened just the same. Nor were we always expecting the vital presence of Christ, but that too occurred without our efforts. This congregational matrix proved to be the greatest challenge to my pastoral ministry that I had experienced in a long time. It was this little congregation that drew me out of the little trinity of me, myself, and I, and into the holy family of the one and only triune God, Father, Son, and Holy Spirit. Ministers are tempted to spend considerable energy trying to win the favor of people in general, rather than the people they know. Fame is name recognition by the nameless masses, but family is knowing you are loved by those closest to you. For some people it is far more important to be popular than to be loved. They confuse these two and seek a popularity that substitutes for the intimacy of two or three gathered in the name of Christ.

At the start of the year, I remember saying to our ministry team that everything was going so well. We were getting along and enjoying each other, people were positive, ministries were thriving, and life in the church was encouraging. That was before our beloved music and worship director was operated on for a brain tumor, a trusted and faithful associate pastor accepted a call to become a senior pastor, our outwardly happy husband and wife student ministries directors separated, and our servant-hearted, very efficient administrator retired. And just to add to the intensity of it all, I was preaching through the Book of Revelation for the seven weeks leading up to Easter. Yet, even with all that was going on, the real test of my pastoral leadership came in the little church, the congregation of two or three, gathered

60. Phil 1:6.
61. Matt 18:20.

in Christ's name. My mother was in the last months of her earthly life, my son was graduating from San Diego State, and I was in the middle.

There is a lot of living to be learned, living between the generations. Andrew is our middle child, adopted by us when he was seven days old. He has never liked school and like Calvin, as in *Calvin and Hobbes*, he saw the adult world as a conspiracy designed to make him grow up against his will. Of our three children, Andrew and I went head-to-head more frequently and with greater intensity than I ever did with his older brother or younger sister. Our flash points were over attitude, work, and school, not alcohol, drugs, and sex. He never debated about going to church, but he and I argued, sometimes angrily, over how late he should be out on Saturday night. He used to stroll into church pleasantly every Sunday morning for worship in flip-flops and baggy jeans and actually listen to my message. Whenever we invited people over for dinner, he usually complained beforehand, but once our guests arrived he was the most charming and relational person in the family. I love Andrew, even if I can't always understand him, and I know he loves me, even though I'm sure he often can't understand me. Andrew decided to save us money and live at home and go to a state school, because he didn't think it was worth spending any more on college than we had to. For me, it has always been far more important for Andrew to know the Lord—more important than good grades or anything else. When his Bible stayed wrapped in cellophane for several years, I held my tongue. Let's just say, I can empathize with Moses when he struck the rock.

My mother had been a widow since 1972 when my father died at the age of 48. For the last two decades she lived close to my family. We moved her from Bloomington, Indiana, to Denver, and finally to San Diego. I would drop by her one-bedroom apartment for breakfast several times a week. She loved books, read constantly, followed politics and the Chicago Cubs. She wore out several Bibles with her marginal notes, underlining, and penned-in prayer requests. For hours at a time she interceded before God on behalf of my ministry, my family, my brother's family, our extended family, scores of friends, and missionaries, and whatever else the Lord laid on her heart. At times she argued over my sermons vigorously. If she felt an illustration was frivolous, or a point superficial, she did not hesitate to say so. She could be so tenacious in arguing her perspective that sometimes I left our breakfast together vowing to myself that was the last time I was going to share anything with her. But even those hotly contested messages were praised on Sunday after they were preached. Invariably she would say something like, "Well, I guess the Holy Spirit knew best" or "God has called you to do the preaching, not me." A failing heart and diabetes weakened her to the point that even getting to church on Sunday was a major feat for her, but she still insisted on making breakfast for me several times a week.

I felt the irony of these two pushing me to my limit, my son in his last year of college and my mother in her last year of earthly life. Together they formed my congregation in microcosm, my church within a church, reminding me of Jesus' promise: "where two or three come together in my name, there am I with them." The contrasts between them were often humorous. Andrew with his flip-up, picture-taking cell phone and my mother who finally gave in to a cordless phone, after three cell phones had been purchased for her and returned. My mother would have loved a full pastoral prayer every morning. Andrew sighed whenever I said "Let's pray." My mother hardly ate anything in my presence, but insisted on making breakfast for me, while Andrew preferred eating a burrito on the run to sitting down to a family meal. Both of them had weird sleep schedules, especially on Saturday night, when neither of them seemed to get to sleep before two or three in the morning. Andrew was hanging out with his friends and Mom was experiencing chest pains. Of course, I never slept well on Saturday night either, because I was thinking about them and a sermon. Both of them had subjects that they did not want to talk about. For my mother it was her health and for Andrew it was his college courses, two subjects that I was concerned about.

Perhaps the greatest irony of them all was that Andrew and Mom got together every Sunday after the worship service. I never suggested to Andrew that it would be nice if he visited grandmother. He did this on his own, much to his grandmother's delight and mine. She was thrilled with his visits. She could no longer get to a worship service, but she could spend time with Andrew. When we were together, she always insisted that I pray, but when Andrew visited, she prayed, long comprehensive prayers, mainly for him. She got away with giving him all kinds of down-to-earth spiritual direction that he never would have received from me. Andrew kept these conversations between them, but on Monday morning Mom would re-hearse parts of them to me. Sometimes they commiserated together over me—the up-tight father and the over-anxious son, but invariably they discussed the pastor's message. Mom delighted in emphasizing how much Andrew loved and respected his parents.

I found myself re-examining my middle-aged Christian faith through the eyes of my son and my mother. Andrew's emerging faith and my mother's long-standing faith formed a matrix of promise not only for them but for me as well. To accompany them in their journey was to receive the promise of the presence of Christ. Am I willing to step out in faith and trust in Christ for my future just as I hope and pray that Andrew will? Am I willing to come to the end of my life, as my mother did, with only her faith in Christ to show for a lifetime of prayer and service? I pray that I will. They came together in Jesus' name and Christ was there challenging me to grow, testing my love, chastening my hope, pushing my faith to the edge of the abyss.

"Where two or three come together in my name, there am I with them." There I am with Andrew, my mother, and Jesus, our mini congregation. We are like Shadrach, Meshach, and Abednego in the fiery furnace of life, but wait a minute, there are four people "unbound, walking in the middle of the fire, and they are not hurt; and the fourth has the appearance of a god."[62] One of the ironies of our time is that a culture so impressed with numbers could also be so individualistic and self-focused. Perhaps the two are linked, and the more we focus on numbers the more autonomous and isolated we become. Fourth-century theologian Gregory of Nazianzen wrote , "that three gathered together in the Name of the Lord count for more than tens of thousands of those who deny the Godhead."[63] Where two or three are gathered in the name of Christ there is no pretense of a public persona, nor isolation of a private self.

Andrew graduated from State in January and headed to Ghana, West Africa. It was his idea to spend three months in the northern village of Carpenter working alongside African Christian friends engaged in development work. I was to join him after Easter for ten days for a pastors' conference. Just before he went through airport security he handed Virginia and me a letter. It read in part,

> "I believe you two are a perfect example of soul mates. I also believe strongly that I am your soul child and that I was sent to you by God to be in your family. . . . Father, your role as a father and a masterful pastor still exist to awe me. We have bumped our heads a few times, but we are always quick to fix our problems. I think that has to mean something. Mother, I am sure you're crying. You have always been on my back about things and you've had to repeat things to me many times before it sinks in. I thank you for that. You both are awesome. I didn't think I would ever say this, but I hope I can be as great a parent as you have been."

62. Dan 3:25.

63. Nazianzen, "The Last Farewell," 388.

Andrew left knowing that his grandmother probably would not be there to greet him when he returned. When I saw him in Ghana, I thanked the Lord for working in his life. I also came to a deeper understanding of how much more we all need than our earthly fathers can provide. Andrew had a meaningful experience in Ghana and got a taste for the long obedience in the same direction.

My mother was very conscious of dying and she wanted to bring closure to her earthly days with all the courage and trust she could possibly summon. Toward the end she wanted me to talk about heaven. When Virginia and I brought in food and tried to clean her apartment, she would become very agitated, because all she wanted us to do was to sit and talk. She told us old stories about her growing up and how she and my father fell in love. I had never heard some of these stories before and she told them so vividly that it was like they had just happened. I have walked with people up to death's door and I've been present with saints who have taken their last earthly breath, but Mom's dying was different. It was more like my dying. My mother was charting a new course and giving me a taste of what my own dying would be like. I tried to be a good son, but I realized anew, especially in her final days, that she and I both needed the Savior. Pastors are tempted to nurture the self-image of Moses, says Craig Barnes. We think "it's our job to get people into the promised land," but we can't do it.[64] We can be good sons and daughters, good fathers and mothers, but we need the promise of the presence of Christ himself to get us out of the wilderness and into the promised land.

What counts for true intimacy and spiritual nurture is not the smallness of the *small* group, but the One in whom the relationships depend. John Chrysostom said, "What then? Are there not two or three gathered together in His name? There are indeed, but rarely!" It is not the mere "assembling" of ourselves, but the holding to Christ as "the principal ground" of love between us that counts.[65] This truth is beautifully expressed by Jonathan in a vow, "sworn in the name of the Lord," to David, who apart from the Lord would have been his hated rival: "The Lord shall be between me and you, and between my descendants and your descendants, forever."[66]

64. Barnes, *Searching for Home*, 18.
65. Chrysostom, "Homily LX," 10:374.
66. 1 Sam 20:42.

7

Mutual Submission in Christ

*Relationships in the household of faith are based on the trans-
forming work of the Spirit of Christ. The defensive, competitive,
manipulative, and domineering relational strategies of the old nature give way to mutual submission and gift-based, every-member
ministry in Christ. The church is no longer bound but free from
patriarchal and matriarchal control. Nothing the world has to
offer, from traditional male headship to radical feminism, comes
close to expressing the new relational dynamic created in Christ
Jesus.*

WHAT DOES IT MEAN for men and women to serve together in mutual
submission to one another in Christ? The Bible teaches that there are positive differences between men and women that ought to be celebrated, but
do these differences necessarily mean that God built into the created order
a hierarchy of men over women? The twelve disciples, chosen by Jesus,
were all men. Should we interpret this as Jesus' direction that only men
are eligible for church leadership? Some of the apostle Paul's comments on
the subject appear to leave little room for discussion. To the Corinthians,
he sounds emphatic: "Women should remain silent in the churches. They
are not allowed to speak . . ."[1] To the church at Ephesus, Paul comes across
emphatic, if not dogmatic, "A woman should learn in quietness and full
submission. I do not permit a woman to teach or to assume authority over

---

1. 1 Cor 14:34.

a man; she must be quiet."[2] When Paul wrote, "Whoever aspires to be an overseer desires a noble task," did he have only faithful husbands in mind?[3]

How do these statements reconcile with Paul's apparent approval of women praying and prophesying in the church at Corinth?[4] What practical implications did Paul have in mind when he declared that there was neither Jew nor Gentile, neither slave nor free, neither male nor female, for all are one in Christ Jesus?[5] What should we make of Paul's female co-workers, like Priscilla and Lydia? In Romans 16, Paul lists a number of women whom he is comfortable calling co-workers, apostles, and hard workers.

The following themes help to frame the issue of men and women in ministry. They encourage us to explore what the Bible has to say about: (1) God's image-bearers; (2) Spirit-inspired sexuality; (3) the impact of the Fall; (4) the new creation in Christ; (5) the priesthood of all believers; (6) the gifts of the Spirit; (7) church administration; (8) body life; and (9) the Spirit's agenda for the household of faith. In an effort to be faithful to the whole counsel of God, we want to explore mutual submission in Christ from an overarching, canonical biblical perspective. Our aim is to understand the Bible, not perfectly, but better.

We seek to avoid the negative tension that polarizes this discussion into two camps—egalitarian and complementarian—and pits well-meaning Christians against one another in a no-win standoff. Our goal is to be communitarian—to form a true partnership between men and women grounded in Christ. We seek to affirm gender differentiation while emphasizing loving mutual submission in Christ. We believe that recognizing societal gender *norms*, which serve to illustrate the difference between men and women, is healthier than simple compliance with a pre-determined and stereotypical set of societal *roles* for men and women. Faithfulness is an ongoing work of loving discernment. The gospel inspires a relational paradigm shift. Past patriarchal patterns are overcome by a Spirit empowered partnership between women and men. This partnership does not mean that men and women are simply interchangeable or functionally equivalent. Their mutuality in Christ respects their distinctive identity without dictating a hierarchical order. When women cannot teach men, preach, serve as pastors, or offer leadership to men, then the complementarian

2. 1 Tim 2:11–12.

3. 1 Tim 3:1–2.

4. 1 Cor 11:5; 14:31.

5. Gal 3:28.

position is just another name for patriarchy. And a change of heart may only come about when men "feel something of the pain of patriarchy: of being interrupted or ignored in conversation, of being passed over for recognition and promotion, of receiving condescension or suspicion instead of welcome partnership."[6]

Our daughter Kennerly has a Master of Divinity degree from Beeson Divinity School, as does her husband Patrick. Her Monday morning story offers something for us all to think about:

> In the morning service yesterday, a black girl, a sixth grader, thanked the hospitality ministry for always providing refreshments after the service. She said that the children wanted to show their appreciation by providing the treats this morning. After the service, the pastor was talking to Patrick, when a boy, the girl's brother, an eighth grader, came up to the pastor. I overheard him asking if he could talk to the pastor about a friend who wanted to be baptized. Patrick turned to his sister, who was standing right there, and told the little girl that she did a great job in the service. Her brother chimed in agreeing with Patrick. Then, he went on to say that he thought his sister would make a great female priest, adding, "I think she should be a nun."
>
> The pastor explained that the Presbyterian church doesn't have nuns. To which the boy innocently responded, "Then, she could be a pastor." He seemed quite happy with his idea, while his sister stood off to the side smiling bashfully. The pastor then nicely informed the boy that his sister could not be a pastor, to which the boy quizzically wrinkled his forehead and asked, "Why not?" The poor guy didn't know what he was asking. And in all fairness he had just seen women give communion and his teachers in the children's ministry were women. Thankfully, women serve in every facet of the church. The only exceptions are the offices of elder and pastor. Apparently, females can offer communion, the gospel preached visibly, but they cannot preach the gospel verbally. Anyways, the pastor responded to the boy's question by explaining that God had chosen men to lead the church. Women aren't allowed to be pastors because God said so. That ended the conversation and gave the boy something to think about.

6. Stackhouse, "How to Produce An Egalitarian Man," 240.

Image-bearers of God

The Genesis account of creation supports neither individualism (the superiority of the self-actualized person over others) nor subordinationism (the patriarchal superiority of males over females). The focus of the biblical text is on mutuality, not superiority. True personal fulfillment is found in communion with the triune God and in community with one another. The two accounts of creation reinforce equality and differentiation rather than superiority and stratification.

> Then God said, "Let us make man in our image, in our likeness, and let them rule over the fish of the sea and the birds of the air, over the livestock, over all the earth, and over all the creatures that move along the ground." So God created man in his own image, in the image of God he created him; male and female he created them.[7]

These two sentences in Genesis do not make a strong case for hierarchical leadership or a "chain of command" code of conduct prior to the fall. To be faithful to the text we have to be careful not to misconstrue the original meaning and over-interpret it in favor of our cultural traditions. Adam and Eve rule together over the environment. The communitarian character of the triune God forms the basis for the human community and serves as a guide for understanding how men and women ought to live and work together in fellowship with God.

As we discussed in the chapter on self-understanding in the first volume, there is no model or affinity in God our Maker for the self-actualized, autonomous, individual self. There is nothing prior to the triune God. There is no divine reason or thought before the eternal Father, Son, and Holy Spirit. This is different when it comes to humanity. God acknowledged that Adam faced the untenable reality of being alone. The Genesis account focuses on Adam's aloneness and his need for true companionship. Prior to the fall, he does not stand over Eve, he stands in need of Eve.

In God's original blueprint, men and women, image-bearers of God, are engaged in ministry without discrimination and subordination. The idea of women in ministry is not like a homeowner who decides to add on a new kitchen or an extra bedroom on an old home. No matter how well constructed, such additions and renovations always stand out as additions. Women in ministry, unhindered and freely deployed by the Spirit of Christ, are exactly what the triune God had in mind in the original

---

7. Gen 1:26–27.

"footprint" described in Genesis. The truth is not an awkward addition, but true to the blueprint.

Imagine reading Genesis for the first time. Would we conclude that the biblical text makes a case "for the ordering of the sexes that delegates to men the prerogative of leading, initiating and taking responsibility for the well-being of women, and entrusts to women the role of following male leadership, as well as supporting, enabling and helping men"?[8] The trinitarian "us" in "Let *us* make man in *our* image" is free from any speculation on the subject of subordination within the Godhead. What is true of the triune God is true of the human person and the relationship between male and female. There is nothing in the description of either God or the person that necessitates subordination.

Some biblical scholars find in the Trinity a model for female equality of being and subordination of role. They say this establishes a precedent for women being equal with men in their being but subordinate to men in their role. To postulate the eternal subordination of the Son to the Father as a precedent for understanding the being and role of women in relationship to men seems to mount a major theological defense, but where is the biblical case for making this connection between the Son's subordination and female subordination?

In the past, those who argued for female subordination did not feel the need to argue for equality of being, because they assumed that females were mentally and morally inferior (historic patriarchy).

Rebecca Groothuis writes:

> Historically, male superiority was assumed to inhere primarily in a natural male advantage in morality and rationality. But when evangelical patriarchalists today claim that male leadership is natural and fitting given the deeper differences of masculinity and femininity, they accompany this claim with protestations that women are not morally or rationally deficient with respect to men; rather, men and women are "equal in being" but "different" (that is, unequal) in "function" or "role."[9]

Historic orthodoxy has held that the Son voluntarily emptied himself and made himself nothing, out of obedience to the Father and for the sake of our salvation.[10] "But most Christians do not believe that the Son's sub-

8. Grenz, "Biblical Priesthood and Women in Ministry," 272.

9. Groothuis, "Equal in Being, Unequal in Role: Exploring the Logic of Women's Subordination," 302.

10. Phil 2:5–11.

ordination in the incarnation is definitive of the Father-Son relationship in the eternal or immanent Trinity."[11] The notion that the Son has been eternally subordinate to the Father is speculative. We believe that the Bible is clear on all important matters and that we should refrain from going beyond the text. We are aware of the dangers of reading into the biblical text our cultural biases and traditions. The advocates of female equality of being and subordination of role are in danger of imposing traditional hierarchical perspectives on Genesis that are not there in the biblical text.

The Bible states that husbands should sacrifice themselves for the sake of their wives, "just as Christ loved the church and gave himself up for her to make her holy."[12] But the Bible does not make the eternal subordination of the Son to the Father the basis for female subordination to the male. Both sides of this theological equation are speculative.

Those who argue for the permanent subordination of women make 1 Corinthians 11:3 pivotal for the eternal subordination of the Son. New Testament scholar Tony Thiselton concludes that "head" does not denote a relation of subordination or authority over. Paul does not speak of a fourfold hierarchical order (God-Christ-man-woman), but of three paired relationships, Christ-man, man-woman, God-Christ. Paul's concern is not to establish the stratification of the sexes (men over women) but the differentiation of sexes. Paul commends the believers in Corinth for the active inclusion and participation of men and women in public prayer and preaching, but insists that certain cultural clothing customs be followed, such as head-coverings on women, which "generate signals of gender distinctiveness on the basis of the order of creation, which still holds sway even in the gospel era."[13] The apostle Paul emphasized both "a gender-distinctive creation order and a gospel order of reciprocity and mutuality."[14] He did this in the hope of freeing everyone up to use their gifts so that no one should feel demeaned or excluded. No one should say, "I'm a foot, so I don't belong to the body."[15] Thisleton reasons that the apostle Paul is not concerned here about defending male headship, but is making a case for mutuality and reciprocity, leading to self-respect, respect for others, and gender identity in public worship.[16]

11. Giles, "The Subordination of Christ and The Subordination of Women," 335.

12. Eph 5:25

13. Thiselton, *The First Epistle to the Corinthians*, 811.

14. Ibid.

15. See 1 Cor 12:15.

16. Thiselton, *The First Epistle to the Corinthians*, 825.

Hence women use prophetic speech alongside men. However, at Corinth women as well as men tended to place "knowledge" and "freedom" before love in the Christian sense. Paul does not permit their "freedom" as part of the gospel new creation to destroy their proper self-respect and respect in the eyes of others by taking part in worship dressed like an "available" woman. That is not love, for it brings "shame" on themselves, their menfolk, and on God.[17]

The primary issue of individualism lurks behind the symptomatic sins of genderism and subordinationism. Faithfulness and obedience are found neither in structured subordination nor in willful individuality. The social interaction of male and female in community was meant to be modeled after the inter-relationship of the Trinity.

Spirit-inspired Sexuality

Some Christian thinkers have read a great deal into human sexuality, perhaps much more than the biblical text implies. They have implied that there are profound metaphysical differences between the sexes. For example, C. S. Lewis wrote, "We are dealing with male and female not merely as facts of nature but as the live and awful shadows of realities beyond our control and largely beyond our direct knowledge."[18] Professor Thomas Howard argued that all mythologies and Scripture agree that sexuality defines the core of our being.[19] Writer Elizabeth Elliot appeals to "ancient truth which mankind has always recognized. God created male and female, the male to call forth, to lead, to initiate and rule, and the female to respond, follow, adapt, submit. Even if we held to a different theory of origin, the physical structure of the female would tell us that woman was made to receive, to bear, to be acted upon, to complement, to nourish."[20]

On the contrary, a stronger case can be made that the Bible removes mythological and mystical dimensions of sexuality and stratification. The

17. Thiselton, *The First Epistle to the Corinthians*, 821. In agreement with many New Testament scholars, Thiselton defines prophetic speech as "the public proclamation of gospel truth as applied pastorally and contextually to the hearers." It is not limited to spontaneous speech, but "may include applied theological teaching, encouragement, and exhortation to build the church" (826).

18. Lewis, *God in the Dock*, 238.

19. Howard, "A Note from Antiquity on the Question of Women's Ordination," 323.

20. Elliot, *Let Me Be a Woman*, 59–64.

danger in making sexuality the defining determination of one's being is to imply much more about maleness or femaleness than the Bible teaches. Both sexes—male and female, are needed to reflect the image of God, but the Bible never attributes sexuality to God. "Biblical religion stands distinct and apart from pagan fertility religions in its strictly nonsexualized concept of spiritual reality and the nature of God."[21] To speak of God as "Father" is a figurative description and does not imply that God is a male parent nor is Jesus' "maleness" essential to his role as the Incarnate One any more than his Jewishness or singleness. What his incarnation makes absolutely crucial is the inclusiveness of his full humanity.[22] Jesus came as a Jewish man who remained unmarried, but what is important from a redemptive angle is that the Incarnate One assumed our humanity, not necessarily our gender, ethnicity, or marital status. From a prophetic angle, it was important that Jesus was from the chosen people of Israel and from the house of David, but this prophetic fulfillment does not limit his relational identity and redemptive provision for all people.

The argument that hierarchical gender roles are prescribed as permanent facts in creation rest on some misleading assumptions: (1) Adam was created to rule; (2) he was created first; (3) he named the woman and (4) she was designated as "helper." But the question arises, is our reading of the text based on tradition? Anne Atkins reveals some of the biases we may bring to the text by reversing the creation order of Adam and Eve. She illustrates how freely we have read our hierarchical biases into the biblical text. Atkins writes,

> Suppose God had made the woman first, and the man out of her . . . Now who comes over as the helpless, dependent one, the weaker, inferior partner? Why the woman again of course! She could not cope alone; man had to be made to bail her out. Part of her body was taken away to make him; she can never again be complete on her own. The man was made last, after the plants, after the animals, and certainly after the woman; he is the crown of God's creation. He was made out of human flesh; she is nothing but dust. Even her name ("man" now of course) is a diminutive version of his ("woman"). She is to "cleave" to him (and, as it happens, this word is "used almost universally for a weaker cleaving to a stronger"; no doubt a great deal would be made of this if the woman were to cleave to the man!). Most significant of all she is to leave her parents and her way of life

21. Groothuis, *Good News for Women*, 101.
22. John 1:14; Phil 2:7.

to join him and adapt to him; she was clearly found to be inadequate on her own.[23]

The facts are these: that which the man ruled over failed to provide suitable companionship; that which was beneath him did not help him. Only that which God designed to be from him and of him proved equal to him. The man's recognition of this comes in the form of poetry. The designation "woman" does not diminish but distinguishes the helper suitable for him. The man's temporal priority over the woman does not mean he ruled over her. Derivation has nothing to do with the determination of authority and subordination. Paul notes in 1 Corinthians 11:12 that ever since the first man, every man has come from a woman. God created the animals first, but that does not indicate the animals have authority over Adam. The concern of the text is not to establish Adam's authority but his loneliness.

The fact that woman is designated as "helper" implies that the man needs help, not that the woman is his servant. To help is to share in the same tasks and 'help-*meet*' means to do so as 'equal and similar.' Help (Hebrew = *ezer*) is used of God in a number of biblical passages.[24] Theologian Millard Erickson concludes, "The helper envisioned in Genesis 2:18 is not inferior in essence to the one helped. Rather the helper is to be thought of as a coworker or enabler."[25] The notion that the helper is a subordinate must be brought to the text; it is not derived from the text. It may be more logical to argue that man is inferior, because he needed woman's help, than to argue that woman is a subordinate because she is helping him.

Man names the "woman" but to identify something or someone is hardly tantamount to ruling it. "This is now bone of my bones and flesh of my flesh; she shall be called 'woman,' for she was taken out of man."[26] "This is not a statement of power or authority. Rather, the man recognizes the woman as one taken from him (and thus "corresponding to him") by choosing the terms for "man" (*ish*) and "woman" (*ishah*) that are so closely related that the only difference in their pronunciation is the characteristic feminine ending—ah."[27] After the fall, Adam gave woman her name Eve and before the fall they shared the name "Adam." Taken together the two accounts of creation reinforce equality and differentiation rather

23. Atkins, *Split Image*, 20–21.

24. See: Exod 18:4; Deut 33:29; Ps 33:20; 70:5; 115:9–11; 40:17.

25. Erickson, *Christian Theology*, 2:546.

26. Gen 2:23.

27. Hess, "Equality With or Without Innocence: Genesis 1–3," 87.

than hierarchy and stratification. The beautiful description of marriage as a "one flesh" relationship hardly implies husbandly rule and womanly submission.[28] If anything, the metaphor underscores equality and mutuality. The fact that the man leaves his parents and "cleaves" to his wife to become "one flesh" contradicts the notion of male domination and female subordination. If we challenge some of the assumptions we may bring to the biblical text, we see Genesis affirming sexual differentiation and mutuality rather than hierarchy and subordination.

The Impact of the Fall

The consequences of the fall, male dominance and death, are antithetical to God's original design for creation. God's curse reversed God's creation design. Genesis 3:16–17 is a description of the fallen order of things, of how life will be lived as the result of the Fall, rather than how it should be lived. As a result of sin, Adam became subject to the ground and Eve to Adam. "The fall spawned the twin evils of women's suffering in labor and of man's laboring in suffering."[29] The nature of the temptation and the strategy of deception indicates that there was no chain of command in the garden nor hierarchical relationship between Adam and Eve prior to the fall. The blessing of creation and the responsibility of the creation mandate are given to both man and woman.[30] The tree of the knowledge of good and evil was designed by God to serve as a positive reminder to Adam of his humanity and his dependence upon God.

The freedom to eat from every tree of the garden except one underscored God's gracious sovereignty. The gracious permission and the singular prohibition were given specifically to Adam. Eve's vulnerability, when approached by the tempter, was not due to any inherent inferiority but to her lack of direct knowledge of the prohibition. Adam had the advantage of receiving direct communication from God. Eve's weakness was not in her nature but in her relative lack of knowledge of God. Eve was directly confronted by the tempter and fell; Adam was offered the possibility of disobedience by Eve and fell. Who should we judge to be weaker—Adam or Eve? When approached by God, Adam spoke for himself, not Eve. He blamed God for placing Eve *with* him (note, he does not say *under* him) and he blamed Eve for setting him up. "The woman you put here with

28. Gen 2:24.
29. Bilezikian, *Beyond Sex Roles*, 56.
30. Gen 1:28.

me—she gave me some fruit from the tree, and I ate it." If we didn't know the facts to be otherwise, the traditional caricature of women would have had Eve complaining and blaming God, but instead it was Adam who leveled the accusation. For her part, Eve states the facts, "The serpent deceived me, and I ate."[31]

God's curse is poetically brief. Everything is reversed and turned upside down. Sin separates, divides, and destroys. Nature, relationships and work are in conflict. New words are now used to describe life, ugly words, such as, enmity, pain, and toil. God's word is descriptive here, not prescriptive. God takes responsibility, "I will put enmity between you and the woman . . . I will make your pains in childbearing very severe . . . ," but God does not become the enemy, making people dominate one another. Nature and human nature have their own conflicted way of doing things now. Each has a will to power. Genesis 3 and Romans 1 describe the same phenomenon: God gave life over to man's sinful desires. The biblical narrative tracks the tension between God's creation design and God's judgment description. It is tragic when we confuse the curse with the blessing and attribute to creation what came about because of the fall. "When we require women to pay over and over again for Eve's transgression with their silence and submission, we negate the full redemptive power of the gospel."[32]

New Creation in Christ

Faith in Christ means living life the Jesus way. The way to know Christ is for women and men to become like Jesus. The new covenant envisions reconciled and restored relationships. Men and women are forgiven and freed to live the way God intended for humankind to live before the fall.[33] The Jesus way is crucial to our understanding of the relationship between men and women. The upside-down value reversal of the Kingdom of God renegotiates our understanding of power and authority. Instead of taking our cues from the world we need to model our lives after Jesus. All that we said earlier about images of surrender (chapter 6) apply to re-negotiating the gender tension. The Jesus way is a radical reversal of the impact of the fall. No one shows us what it means to be poor in spirit better than Jesus himself. "For you know the grace of our Lord Jesus Christ, that though

31. Gen 3:13.

32. Barton, "How I Changed My Mind About Women in Leadership," 44.

33. 2 Cor 5:16–19; Gal 3:26–28.

he was rich, yet for your sakes he became poor, so that you through his poverty might become rich."[34] This spiritual poverty involves the elimination in us of "selfish ambition" and "vain conceit." It means cultivating the same attitude that was in Christ Jesus, who "made himself nothing, taking the very nature of a servant, being made in human likeness. And being found in appearance as a man, he humbled himself and became obedient to death—even death on a cross!"[35]

Jesus rejected the authoritarian, domineering attitudes of Gentile rulers and one of the ways he did this was by including women in his band of disciples.[36] Jesus chose the Twelve, all males, to symbolize the twelve tribes of Israel and the fulfillment of the Old Covenant. He was not symbolizing the necessity of male-over-female leadership, but rather the necessity of a new called out community representative of the New Covenant. Both men and women were in his traveling team of disciples and women are noted as financial supporters of his movement.[37] When Jesus visited Martha's home, Mary sat at the feet of Jesus, just like the men, to listen to his teaching.[38] The Gospels picture the Twelve abandoning Jesus in his time of crisis, but several women remained at the foot of the cross. Women were the first to come to his tomb, and the first to recognize their risen Lord. Mary Magdalene, Joanna, Mary the mother of James, and the other women with them reported to the apostles that they had met the risen Lord Jesus. The apostles did not believe the women, "because their words seemed to them like nonsense."[39] But it wasn't nonsense; it was the glorious truth.

In a movement marked by the cross, it is not surprising that women should naturally be involved in teaching and leadership, nor was it unusual for women to be targeted, along with men, for persecution.[40] The Christian life is lived under the principle of the cross, "my life for yours." Christian submission does not mean onerous obligation and slavish obedience but a readiness to renounce selfishness. It is not boot-camp obedience nor lock-step conformity but an expression of devotion and ultimate submission

34. 2 Cor 8:9.
35. Phil 2:8.
36. Matt 20:25–28; Mark 10:42–45; Luke 22:25–26.
37. Matt 12:46–50; Luke 8:1–3.
38. Luke 10:38; see Acts 22:3.
39. Luke 24:11.
40. Acts 8:3.

to Christ. Humility and mutual submission are stressed throughout the description of the early church.[41]

Luke drew out the significance of women teachers in his two-volume account of the life of Christ. Mary leads the way with her Magnificat rich in theology, ethics, and social justice, followed by Pentecost's "daughters" prophesying, Philip's daughters preaching and Priscilla's "team teaching" with Aquila.[42] It is apparent from Luke's description in Acts that Paul evidenced particular appreciation and respect for women. He shared in detail Lydia's conversion and subsequent wholehearted commitment to prayer and hospitality.[43] Luke makes special note of "a number of prominent Greek women" turning to Christ.[44] In Corinth, Paul met a like-minded missionary couple, Priscilla and Aquila, and Luke's habit of listing Priscilla's name first would indicate that Paul had special respect for her.

The apostle Paul's way of relating to women co-workers underscores the importance of the priesthood of all believers. He underscores the significance of women in active ministry roles in his letter to the believers at Rome. In his conclusion and greeting, he commends individual women in specific ways. He asks that Phoebe, "our sister, a servant of the church in Cenchrea" be received in the Lord "in a way worthy of the saints and to give her any help she may need from you, for she has been a great help to many people, including me."[45] Phoebe is identified as a deacon (*diakonos*) not a deaconness.

Priscilla and Aquila are referred to as his "fellow workers in Christ Jesus," who "risked their lives" for him. He sends greetings to Mary, "who worked very hard for you" and to Junia, who was imprisoned for the gospel, adding that she was "outstanding among the apostles" and "in Christ" before he was. Tryphena and Tryphosa are commended for working hard in the Lord, as is his "dear friend Persis." He praises the mother of Rufus, "who has been a mother to me, too" and singles out Julia and the sister of Nereus for special mention. One cannot read Paul's personal greetings to the church at Rome without concluding that women and men served side-by-side in leading the church.[46] Paul confirms and commends female leadership and teaching, rather than feeling the need to argue for it and

---

41. Eph 5:21; Rom 12:10; Phil 2:3; 1 Pet 5:5.
42. Bailey, "Women in the New Testament: A Middle Eastern Cultural View," 1–14.
43. Acts 16:11–12.
44. Acts 17:12.
45. Rom 16:2.
46. Rom 16:6–13.

defend it, and as we noted earlier, Paul expressed no reservations about women praying and prophesying alongside men in public worship.[47]

The Priesthood of All Believers: Male and Female

The God-ordained New Covenant made by the sacrifice of Christ provides for the priesthood of all believers—male and female. We are "a holy priesthood, offering spiritual sacrifices acceptable to God through Jesus Christ."[48] This new priesthood offers no privileges based on gender. The argument has already been made in volume one that the Old Testament male priesthood is not the model for the New Testament pastor. Both C. S. Lewis and J. I. Packer reasoned that Christ is represented best through the male. Lewis argued that the role of the male priest is to "represent us to God and God to us," and Packer wrote, "Since the Son of God was incarnate as a male, it will always be easier, other things being equal, to realize and remember that Christ is ministering in person if his human agent and representational function most readily displayed as ordained ministers represent Christ at the Eucharist."[49] However these perspectives do not seem to take into account that gender stipulation has been removed in the New Testament understanding of the priesthood and that it was Jesus' humanity, not his maleness, that is stressed in the Bible and the Nicene Creed.[50]

Many remain convinced that "headship" can mean nothing other than a person in authority over another person or persons. So that when Paul says, "the head of the woman is man," he is referring specifically to a chain of command or a hierarchy of authority that requires the woman to yield to the authority of the male.[51] By virtue of his gender the man is in authority over the woman. So strident are the proponents of this view that any discussion of Jesus' repudiation of authoritarian rule, the priesthood of all believers, the New Testament description of female leaders and teachers, and the gifts of the Spirit, and even the exegesis of 1 Corinthians 11, are all perceived as beside the point. One word,

---

47. 1 Cor 11:5, 13.

48. 1 Pet 2:5.

49. Lewis, *God in the Dock*, 236; Packer, "Let's Stop Making Women Presbyters," 20.

50. John 1:14; Phil 2:7.

51. 1 Cor 11:3.

"*kephalē*" decides the outcome of how men and women relate and who is permitted to teach and lead.

For the moment, let us assume that "head" means simply "authority over" and that Paul could not possibly have meant "origin of," which some scholars claim is a legitimate interpretation. Paul begins by praising the Corinthian believers "for holding to the traditions just as I passed them on to you."[52] What traditions are these? Are they not rooted in the principle of the cross? Do they not include the priesthood of all believers, Christ-like humility, personal self-sacrifice, contentment with our place in life, and great freedom in Christ? He was hardly speaking like an Old Testament priest or Pharisee, one who was intent on preserving the authority structure of the church. Clearly, Paul's traditional values were different from Jewish, Gentile, and American traditional values. The traditions commended here by Paul contradict the traditionalism of sexism and selfism.

Paul says, "I want you to realize that the head of every man is Christ . . ." What does it mean for me as a man to have Christ's authority over me? Does it mean that my wife does not have Christ's authority over her and that I am to represent Christ's authority over her? Am I placed in the role of mediating Christ to my wife as if she does not have direct access to God? Does she need to wait for me, for my instruction and guidance, like Saul needed to wait for Samuel?[53] This strikes me as reading way too much into the passage and making Paul say something he never intended to say.

We can look at the meaning of the text another way. Because I am under Christ's authority I must serve others the way Jesus did. "Greater love has no one than this: to lay down one's life for one's friends."[54] My contribution to the body life of the believers will be governed by the principle of the cross—"my life for yours." Thus in the second paired relationship, "the head of the woman is man" the woman benefits from the Christ-like, sacrificial headship of the man. Since this relationship is patterned on Christ's leadership, it would have to be a radical reversal of what the world understands headship to mean. For even if we interpret "head" as "authority over" it could never mean the kind of authoritarian rule that smacks of male chauvinism. It could never mean anything remotely sexist or self-serving. Nor could it mean that the husband is the king of his castle.

We would expect that a "headship" modeled after Jesus, who empowered women and was supported by women, would call women to use their

52. 1 Cor 11:2.
53. 1 Sam 13:7–14.
54. John 15:13.

Spirit-gifts to serve and teach men and women. The distinction between a life-giving headship and a ruling headship strikes me as an important distinction to be made. We want to affirm the sacrificial responsibility of the man to lay down his life for the woman. We want to celebrate the differences between men and women, but we do not want to impose on the biblical text a hierarchy of men over women.

In the third paired relationship, "the head of Christ is God," we have the ultimate relational model—the inter-trinitarian communion of the Godhead. Is this a hierarchical relationship? Certainly not in the sense of a master/servant relationship. It is a familial relationship on the order of a loving father/son relationship. How can God be over God, but in love and self-surrender? Here, God is the head of Christ, but elsewhere Christ has been appointed by God "to be head over everything for the church."[55] Everyone in these three relational pairs gives away authority freely! Christ who has been given all authority commissions men and women to fulfill his mission. In the end it is not so much a matter of authority over others as authority given away for the sake of others. If we examine these three paired relationships closely we are inclined to conclude that the difference between "head" meaning "authority over" and "head" meaning "origin of" is rather inconsequential. If Paul's intention was to stress a hierarchal order, he would have begun with God as the head of Christ, and then Christ as the head of man, and then man as the head of women. "But instead, the 'head' relationships are listed in chronological order of origin. First man originated from Christ, by whom all things were created.[56] Then, woman came from man, according to Genesis 2:21–22. And in the incarnation, Christ came from God the Father.[57] Paul preaches a life-giving model of headship, not a chain-of-command model.

After stating that "God has given men a certain 'headship' (1 Cor 11:3; Eph 5:22)," John Stott asks, "how can women teach men without infringing masculine headship?" His answer: "Perhaps by remembering that 'headship' means responsibility rather than authority (Eph 5:25–30); that what Paul forbids is not so much an office as an attitude (pride); that what is regarded as inappropriate in the behavior and ministry of women varies from culture to culture; and finally, that the team ministry should be the

---

55. Eph 1:22.
56. John 1:3; Col 1:16.
57. John 1:1, 14; 8:14, 42.

norm, in which all members including women, contribute their particular gifts to the common good."[58]

As we said earlier, Paul's main point in 1 Corinthians 11:1–16 is not male headship nor the cultural necessity of women wearing head coverings in worship. His spiritual direction is about men and women preserving their God-given sexual identity in culturally appropriate ways for the sake of the gospel of Christ. In Paul's day it meant that a man led worship without a head-covering and with relatively short hair and a woman led worship with a head-covering and relatively long hair. In other words in dress and decorum there was nothing among women or men that suggested sexual appeal, gender confusion, or self-glorification.

Paul based his case for gender differences on the interpersonal reality of the Triune God, the Genesis description of the creation of woman from man and for man and the social norms of the day. The differentiation and ordering between the sexes that Paul had in mind, was consistent with the equality and differentiation within the Godhead between the Father and the Son. These gender differences did not imply inferiority nor suggest rank and privilege nor diminish the opportunity for ministry.

Gender differentiation called for self-discipline, restraint, and respect for others. Paul's encouragement for men to be men and women to be women in humble, self-effacing ways is imperative for the worship life of the church. It should be noted that the distinction he calls for is not found in ministry responsibilities but in dress and demeanor. Are we flaunting our ego and trying to make a self-serving statement about our importance? Or are we clothed with humility toward one another and willing to serve Christ and his church with the nature and gifts that God has given to us?[59]

Dallas Willard underscores the humble obligation women and men have to serve. He writes, "Women and men are indeed very different, and those differences are essential to how God empowers each to induce the kingdom of God into their specific life setting and ministry. What we lose by excluding the distinctively feminine from 'official' ministries of teaching and preaching is of incalculable value. That loss is one of a few fundamental factors that account for the astonishing weakness of 'the church' in the contemporary context."[60]

---

58. Stott, *The Living Church*, 78.

59. 1 Pet 5:5.

60. Quoted in Johnson, *How I Changed My Mind About Women in Leadership*, 10.

Paul's concern for humility is consistent with God's design for worship from the beginning. You recall God's warning to Israel that when they built an altar they were not to use "dressed stones" or turn it into a work of art. Their worship was not to call attention to themselves, but to their need for the mercy of God. It was not a medium for self-expression, but an act of repentance. Neither were they to raise up the altar on steps, "lest your nakedness be exposed."[61] When we take pride in our performance and assert our own rights we are actually bringing shame upon ourselves. Theologian Paul Stevens observes:

> Men who serve in public ministry often seem to develop an unnatural femininity in order fully to encompass the complete ministry of the church. Some women who have successfully broken into the male world of public ministry have succeeded only by adopting a masculine bearing. Is it not better for men to be men and women to be women in ministry and leadership? The church has been neutered by the restriction of ministry roles to given genders, and by the resulting androgyny of her ministers . . . What is needed is a ministry that prizes the shared contribution of both sexes. There is a divine synergy in this. The whole is more than the sum of the parts. This is also true in marriage.[62]

Jesus honored gender differences throughout his earthly ministry. Far from using his masculinity to distance himself from women, Jesus related to women in ways that underscored their significance and self-respect. His strength and sensitivity appealed to both women and men. Luke tells us that Jesus was supported by a number of women, including several who, like Mary Magdalene, had been healed of evil spirits or diseases, as well as others who appear to have been financially well-off, such as Joanna, who was married to the manager of Herod's household.[63] People found in Jesus a composure and confidence that both genders could appreciate and learn from. He provoked deep passions among his followers that found expression in ways unique to each gender. Mary showed her devotion by taking a pint of expensive perfume and pouring it on Jesus' feet and wiping his feet with her hair; Peter showed his devotion by leaving his fishing boat behind and following Jesus.

---

61. Exod 20:24–26.
62. Stevens, "Breaking the Gender Impasse," 31.
63. Luke 8:2–3.

Gifting over Gender

The Spirit's ministry includes both fruit and gifts. Christ's nature and ministry must be recreated in character (fruit) and in service (gifts) and both are intended for the benefit of the believing community. Under the New Covenant, gifted service and ordained leadership are "fruit" and "gift" based, rather than gender based. The Spirit is manifest throughout the priesthood of all believers without limitation according to gender. The fruit of the Spirit makes mutuality in Christ practically and personally possible. The essential nature of the fruit of the Spirit is the reproduction of the life of Christ in the believer and the believing community.

Gifts embody manifestations of the Spirit for the sake of service. Any reference to the Holy Spirit that distances the gifts of the Spirit from Christ-likeness or fails to grasp the God-centeredness of the Spirit's gifts has not understood the truth about the Holy Spirit. This is why Paul wrote, "There are different kinds of gifts, but the same *Spirit* distributes them. There are different kinds of service, but the same *Lord*. There are different kinds of working, but in all of them and in everyone it is the same *God* at work."[64] Paul's trinitarian emphasis prevents any twisted spirituality from driving a wedge between the Spirit's work and following Jesus as Lord or glorifying the Father in heaven. For Paul, sharing the Spirit's gifts, offering Christ-like service, and engaging in God-honoring work are three ways of saying the same thing. Let no one pull apart what God the Father, Son, and Holy Spirit have joined together.

Against any form of spirituality that caused believers to boast of their gifts and accomplishments, Paul stressed "the manifestation of the Spirit" for "the common good." He referred repeatedly to "the same Spirit" and concluded by saying, "All these are the work of one and the same Spirit, and he distributes them to each one, just as he determines."[65] It may be our tendency to belabor the identification and explanation of each individual gift, but it wasn't Paul's, who insisted on emphasizing the Spirit's distribution and determination of the gifts. Believers often stress the importance of discovering their own spiritual gift(s), but Paul stressed the singular source of all spiritual gifts, the common purpose of all spiritual gifts and the inherent value of all spiritual gifts. There should be no pride of ownership for what we did not deserve, nor sense of personal achievement for

64. 1 Cor 12:4–6.
65. 1 Cor 12:7–11.

what we did not accomplish. Paul's earlier admonition bears repeating, "Let those who boast boast in the Lord."[66]

Paul's main point is that the Spirit empowers the church in many ways to confess that Jesus is Lord. We do not all have same gifts, but we are all part of the same body, because "we were baptized by one Spirit so as to form one body—whether Jews or Greeks, slave or free—we were all given the one Spirit to drink."[67] There was to be no "inner circle" of giftedness, nor "advanced status" attributed to certain gifts. If anything Paul plays down the gifts that may seem more experiential and spectacular, and prioritizes the gifts that focus on the message of the gospel. There was plenty of opportunity for Paul to say that some gifts are better suited to men and some to women, but he didn't. The thrust of Paul's spiritual direction was that all believers have been gifted by the Spirit for the common good in the body of Christ. These gifts do not set us apart from one another but unite us in Christ. His stress was not on our diversity but our unity. We need one another and together we declare, "Jesus is Lord." There are marked parallels between this passage and Jesus' upper room discourse and prayer.[68]

The early church fathers emphasized the indispensable role that the weaker members serve in the body of Christ. The church needs "those to whom they can show active care, protection, support, and love; otherwise they cannot serve as Christ served 'for others.'" Thiselton continues, "The Reformers, especially Luther and Calvin, further expound the Pauline theme that only through human weakness can the people of God fully 'glory' in God alone." The church that is made up of a "self-styled 'gifted' elite would not be the church of Christ."[69]

When the apostle Paul examined the gifts of the Spirit he did not see a discovery problem, as if the primary issue was identifying our spiritual gift. Nor did he see the subject of gifts as a recruitment opportunity, as if the challenge was how to put believers to work. Instead, he saw the real issue to be the body of Christ working together in unity to witness through its words and actions that Jesus is Lord. "It is not so much a matter of *having* a gift, as of *being* a gift."[70]

What biblical precedent do we have for driving a wedge between spiritual gifts and the ordained office of pastor? What is the theological

66. 1 Cor 1:31.

67. 1 Cor 12:13.

68. John 14–17.

69. Thiselton, *The First Epistle of Corinthians*, 1008.

70. Suurmond, "A Fresh Look at Spirit-Baptism and the Charisms," 105.

basis for separating *gift* and *role*? Paul's vision for the church and his Spirit inspired understanding of gifts contradicts the conventional wisdom of church leadership. Gifting is more important than gender for service in the church. Gordon Fee writes, "I for one have as much resistance to the notion that women *ought to be* in leadership along with men as to the notion that *only* males are gifted to lead. The former notion also assumes a gender-based, not gift-based, model for leadership; and both Scripture and common experience give the lie to the second notion."[71]

The Spirit's priority on gifting over gender for ministry, means ministry is less authority driven and more ministry driven; it alleviates the problem of men thinking they are gifted for ministry just because they are men; it opens the door to the possibility that ministry is a two-way street. "Official" ministry does not come from just half of the community of faith. The Holy Spirit is gender inclusive. The gifts of the Spirit help us to distinguish between going through the motions for the sake of the institution or engaging in ministry for the sake of others for whom Christ died. Spirit gifts help us to fulfill the Lord's calling in our lives rather than meeting people's expectations. They highlight the difference between church work and the work of the church. The church is tempted to perpetuate itself through its traditions, budgets, and bureaucracy, but the apostle saw the church dependent upon the life and breath of the Spirit of Christ for her vitality and health. The gifts of the Spirit are given to the living body of Christ, men and women, so that people might come to know that Jesus is Lord and be transformed by the message of the cross.

Church Administration

Church leadership in the New Testament was more relational than legal and more personal than bureaucratic. It was gift-based rather than institutionally oriented. The working analogy for the early church was a household of faith instead of an organization with governing bylaws and operational strategies. None of the churches described in the New Testament would have been accused of having an "old boys' network" running the show. The New Testament shows little interest in how churches arranged and organized their leadership offices. "The net result is that we know very little about the 'organization' of the early church."[72]

71. Fee, "The Priority of Spirit Gifting for Church Ministry," 249.
72. Ibid., 242; see 1 Tim 3:1–13; Titus 1:5–9.

Professor emeritus of New Testament at Trinity Evangelical Seminary Walter Liefeld makes the following observations on the organization and structure of the early church: (1) house churches with plural leadership by elders kept the organization relatively simple; (2) there is no evidence in the New Testament that one person with special authorization "presided" at the Lord's Supper; (3) the interdependence of ministry and leadership was stressed (each needs the other); (4) no provision was made in the New Testament for apostolic succession; (5) pastors functioned within congregations not above them; (6) there were no certain definitions of their role or rank; (7) elders were shepherds, not a board of directors; (8) ordination as we know it was not practiced in the early church. The laying on of hands conferred a "gift," not a status.[73] It was not an "office" or "position" but a gift "in" the person to enable them to minister; (9) Jesus discouraged the use of titles to portray superiority or authority.[74]

By contrast, today's organizational complexity has tended to exclude women from positions "on the basis of modern perceptions of organizational leadership." Liefeld observes: (1) ministry responsibilities are formalized into "offices" and ordination "elevates the individual and bestows privileges not envisioned in the New Testament;" (2) the authority of the apostles has been transferred to today's pastors; (3) healthy, servant leadership teaching and guidance is not sufficiently distinguished from unhealthy, domineering teaching and leadership; (4) women have been marginalized and their ministry role downplayed.[75]

Ironically, the modern church is much more male oriented than the early church. Michael Green observes in *Evangelism in the Early Church* that Christianity "was from its inception a lay movement, and so it continued for a remarkably long time." When the believers were evicted from Jerusalem as a result of persecution that followed Stephen's martyrdom, men and women "went everywhere gossiping the gospel; they did it naturally, enthusiastically, and with the conviction of those who are not paid to say that sort of thing. Consequently, they were taken seriously, and the movement spread, notably among the lower classes." The absence of a distinction between "full-time ministers and laymen in this responsibility to spread the gospel by every means possible," meant that "there was equally no distinction between the sexes in the matter. . . . Everyone was to be an apologist, at least to the extent of being ready to give a good account of the

---

73. 1 Tim 4:14; 2 Tim 1:6.

74. Matt 23:8.

75. Liefeld, "The Nature of Authority in the New Testament," 260–70.

hope that was within them. And this emphatically included women. They had a very large part to play in the advance of Christianity."[76]

Body Life

Paul intended his spiritual direction in Ephesians 5 to bridge the gender divide, not reinforce it. He was seeking to heal the fracture between belief and behavior, not make it worse. The verb "submit" is missing in verse 22 and needs to be supplied from verse 21, but that is not the only thing that needs to be supplied to make sense of Paul's admonition. If reverence for Christ is missing then nothing Paul says about marriage is going to make sense. The key to everything is mutual submission in Christ and under Christ. We have often failed to see just how carefully balanced and nuanced Paul's description of marriage is. Theologian Sarah Sumner identifies three couplets in this passage, designed by Paul to bring out the meaning of marriage:

1. submission is coupled with sacrifice;

2. the body is joined to the head to form one flesh;

3. and a wife's respect for her husband is matched by a husband's love for his wife.[77]

Interpreters tend to jump to the wrong conclusions here. They have contrasted submission with headship and debated the difference between love and respect. They have ignored Paul's emphasis on "one flesh" and concentrated instead on what they see as the hierarchal implications of the text. But this is not what Paul had in mind. Paul's challenge to make the most of every opportunity calls for husbands and wives to model in the home what Christ has done in the church. Precisely because love can be romanticized, sentimentalized, or spiritualized, Paul uses the verb *submit*. Marital love depends not on romantic or pious feelings but on covenant and commitment. The shared work of marriage has to do with forgiveness, truthfulness, self-control, and compassion.[78] Fidelity does not depend upon feelings, but feelings depend upon fidelity. Romance does not create love; it is love that creates romance.

---

76. Green, *Evangelism in the Early Church*, 173–75.

77. Sumner, "Bridging the Ephesians 5 Divide," 61.

78. Col 3:12–17.

The focus in this passage is on the everyday opportunity *in Christ* for husbands to sacrifice for their wives and for wives to submit to their husbands. The truth of this passage is not limited to extreme situations, such as when a wife's life is endangered or when a husband and wife are at a serious impasse. The very remote possibility of a husband being called upon to give up his life for his wife only serves to fuel the chivalrous fantasy of a macho husband acting heroically. The more likely possibility of husband and wife being at loggerheads implies that there are many more occasions for a wife to submit than a husband to sacrifice. Sarah Sumner writes, "The problem with this model of *emergency-time sacrifice*, and *impasse-time submission* is that it fails to meet the scriptural standards. The Bible says that wives are to be subject to their husbands 'in everything.' Likewise, the sacrifice of husbands is a full-time relational posture."[79]

Mutual submission "out of reverence for Christ" applies the principle of the cross to the marriage relationship in a million ways. The reason Paul's spiritual direction has caused such debate is because of our sinful tendency to confuse humility with humiliation. The humility Paul has in mind has nothing to do with passivity or subservience, but rather with obedience and faithfulness. A wife's life is not subject to the whim of her husband but is defined in Christ, even as a husband's love is patterned after Christ's love for the church. Husbands are not explicitly told to submit to their wives, but all Christians are called to "serve one another humbly in love," to be "like-minded, having the same love, being one in spirit and of one mind," "to be devoted to one another in love," and to clothe themselves "with humility toward one another."[80]

In Ephesians 5:21-33, believers are given "the spirit, the shape, and the reason for mutual submission of husband and wife," but not the roles. Paul Stevens writes, "I believe there is an inspired reason for the silence of Scripture on the question of marriage roles. We are invited to write our own play."

> The deepest issues of our life in Christ resist reduction to manageable ideas or stereotyped roles. Biblical teaching is often ambiguous in just these areas. Hence we find ourselves living with tensions individually, maritally, and in the church. These tensions can generate friction and frustration. Or they can be resolved by an artificial choice to live out only one side of the biblical witness. Alternatively, the tension can be embraced in

79. Sumner, "Bridging the Ephesians 5 Divide," 61.
80. Gal 5:13; Phil 2:2; Rom 12:10; 1 Pet 5:5.

a contemplative manner. The ambiguity can be seen as pointing to a God-sized issue. The tension can be lived out experientially, incarnationally, by a joyous attention and submission to the triune God who uniquely loves and addresses each individual, marriage, and church, while remaining "one God and Father of all, who is above all and through all and in all" (Ephesians 4:6).[81]

These three paired references, submission and sacrifice, body and head, respect and love, raise an interesting question: Can what is said to the husband be also said to the wife? Can what is said to the wife be also said to the husband? Is there a unique and distinctive way that submission, body, and respect, apply to the wife, and sacrifice, head, and love, apply to the husband? To answer that question, we have to examine the two-fold thrust of Paul's message. His overarching stress is on mutuality in marriage. It is, as we have said, hard to distinguish between submission and sacrifice, body and head, respect and love. But with that said, Paul places the weight of responsibility for this one-flesh sacrificial mutuality in marriage squarely on the husband. He is meant to take the lead in this cruciform life. The husband is not the king of his castle, lording it over his wife. He is like his Lord and Savior, willing and ready to lay down his life for his wife. The tradition Paul had in mind is radically Christ-centered, like no other cultural tradition known to humanity.

Trouble-Shooting Gender Issues

We are not forced to choose between the stark extremes of sexless sameness and sexist subordination. We are asked to embrace a God-centered understanding of sexuality that presents both women and men as a social metaphor for God himself. Paul's encouragement for men to be men and women to be women in humble, self-effacing ways is imperative for the worship life of the church. It should be noted that the distinction he calls for is not found in ministry responsibilities but in dress and demeanor. This leads us to examine two sentences in Scripture that have been especially problematic for those who advocate women in ministry. The first comes from Paul's letter to the church at Corinth.

Women should remain silent in the churches.[82]

---

81. Stevens, "Breaking the Gender Impasse," 31.

82. 1 Cor 14:34.

Everything depends upon what Paul meant by speaking up in church. No one, as far as I know, has ever thought Paul literally meant that women should not say anything in church. So even those who say they follow a strict literal meaning qualify Paul's admonition in some way. Women may not speak from the pulpit, but they sing solos, lead in prayers, read Scripture, and teach Sunday school classes. We should remember that in this same letter Paul expressed no reservations about women praying and prophesying alongside men in public worship.[83] Remember, he sought to preserve gender differences between men and women in how they were dressed, but not in the nature of ministry. Paul encouraged everyone to share in the worship life of the congregation. He made no distinction between men and women when he said "each one of you has a hymn, or a word of instruction, a revelation, a tongue or an interpretation."[84] Nor did he preclude women when he said, "For you can all prophesy in turn so that everyone may be instructed and encouraged."[85]

Judging from Paul's earlier concern for mutual respect and gender differentiation, it is certain that some women were aggressively flaunting their self-styled spiritual freedom in sexually provocative ways. Could it be that there was a feisty feminist element in the church at Corinth that used public worship as an opportunity to monopolize the service, ask disruptive questions and cross-examine their own husbands? It is more reasonable to conclude that Paul was prohibiting some form of provocative and disruptive speech than it is to believe that he is directly contradicting his earlier acceptance of women praying and prophesying. What he was silencing was not prayer and prophecy, but a negative interrogation that resulted in humiliation and disgrace. Nor did he permit men to engage in this kind of speech, as if it was acceptable for them but unacceptable for women. What was shameful was not women praying and prophesying but women engaging in abusive speech which was hostile, egotistical, and disruptive.

Paul stresses four truths:

1. As in Genesis, the co-humanity of women and men is underscored in their relationship with God and with one another.

2. Paul uses the same words to state that both men and women pray and prophesy, and in so doing, he underscores their equality in ministry. Prophecy does not mean ad hoc, spontaneous, emotional messages,

83. 1 Cor 11:5, 11.
84. 1 Cor 14:26.
85. 1 Cor 14:31.

but "applied theological teaching, encouragement, and exhortation to build the church."[86]

3. Both men and women are equally responsible for maintaining the distinctiveness of their sexuality. Neither women nor men should blur the distinction that is rooted in creation, culture and the church.

4. Both men and women are mutually interdependent as well as equally dependent on God. "Nevertheless, in the Lord, woman is not independent of man, nor is man independent of woman. For as woman came from man, so also man is born of woman. But everything comes from God."[87]

Instead of ending this section by appealing to his own authority, Paul chose to stress their mutual commitment to the Word of God. Neither he nor the believers at Corinth were meant to be innovators trying to shape the church according to their likes and dislikes. Paul anticipated a rebuttal to his plea for intelligible worship, meaningful evangelism, and edifying fellowship, which prompted him to ask, "Or did the word of God originate with you? Or are you the only people it has reached?"[88] He felt compelled to repeatedly remind the believers that it was not about them, their wish dreams, spiritual experiences, and quests for success. It was and is about God's great salvation history story. Paul saw himself under the command of the Lord, striving to faithfully teach and practice the Word of God. Obedience was not a matter of speculation but of submission. That same challenge, to be faithful disciples following the way of the cross, still stands today.

The second biblical sentence that has caused so much difficulty comes from Paul's letter to Timothy.

> I do not permit a woman to teach or to assume authority over a man.[89]

On the face of it this passage seems to contradict the whole thrust of what we have been saying. Is this a universal and normative description of the role of women in the church for all time or a prohibition relevant only for women in a historically specific circumstance? This biblical text, like any other, ought to be interpreted in the light of the whole counsel of God.

---

86. Thiselton, *The First Epistle to the Corinthians*, 826.

87. 1 Cor 11:11–12.

88. 1 Cor 14:36.

89. 1 Tim 2:12.

Biblical interpretation requires that we consider the context and the specific situation. In this situation, Paul was dealing with those who were teaching "false doctrines" and turning to "meaningless talk." The false teaching included meaningless distractions—"myths and endless genealogies," and over-scrupulous behavior, such as forbidding marriage and instituting dietary laws. It appears that there was plenty of contention in the Ephesian church. Paul warns against some women who are "busybodies who talk nonsense" and at the end of his letter, he warns Timothy, "Turn away from godless chatter and the opposing ideas of what is falsely called knowledge, which some have professed and in so doing have departed from the faith." The problem seems to persist into the second epistle, where Paul references "gullible women, who are loaded down with sins and are swayed by all kinds of evil desires, always learning but never coming to acknowledge the truth."[90]

Paul's first piece of spiritual direction had to do with dressing modestly, without elaborate hairstyles or expensive clothes. Instead of copying the attention grabbing styles of the culture, women were to focus on good deeds. In other words, instead of a shallow and superficial fixation with appearance, women were to engage in good deeds, "appropriate for women who profess to worship God."[91] The specifics may be culturally relative, but the principle is applicable universally. Learning in quietness and full submission implied that women should receive theological instruction which was in itself unique among Christians. We may think nothing of this, but in Paul's day this was a radical initiative. For women to study and learn, like men, was not a common practice. Learning "in quietness and full submission" does not mean that women were docile, passive learners, kowtowing to their husbands' authority. It means that Paul intended for women to be humbly receptive and submissive to the Word of God, just as the men were supposed to be. "Submission" may have been to their husbands, but it may also have been to God and his Word.

Ephesus was a hotbed of female spiritual agitation generated by the fertility goddess cult of Artemis, also called Diana. Female priests served in the largest temple in Ephesus, proclaiming the superiority of women over men and offering their bodies for "sacred" prostitution. Given the circumstances, Paul's spiritual direction countered the radical feminist agenda that threatened the church and demeaned women. Who are these women Paul commanded not to teach? Instead of concluding that Paul

90. 1 Tim 1:3, 6; 4:3; 5:13; 6:20; 2 Tim 3:6–7.
91. 1 Tim 2:9–10.

laid down a principle that contradicts all the times that he encouraged women to teach and preach, is it not reasonable to conclude that Paul has in mind here women who are uninformed and ignorant of the truth?

The apostle confronted the specific danger of perpetuating false doctrine through women teachers. Paul used the word *authentein*, not *exousia*, for authority. "We should notice that Paul did not employ his usual term for 'the normal exercise of authority' (*exousia*). He chose an unusual word (*authenteo*) that could carry negative connotations such as 'to usurp or misappropriate authority' or 'to domineer.' The unusual term probably signifies an unusual situation."[92]

> "A woman should learn in quietness and full submission. I do not permit a woman to teach or to assume authority over a man; she must be quiet" (TNIV).

> "I don't let women take over and tell the men what to do. They should study to be quiet and obedient along with everyone else" (The Message).

> "I do not permit a woman to teach a man in a dominating way but to have a quiet demeanor [literally, 'to be in calmness']."[93]

Paul was as angry and as forceful for the truth as his female opponents were for false doctrine. Misguided, arrogant women must not be allowed to dominate the church. Paul was writing into a conflicted, emotionally charged situation. He was exhorting women to exercise humility and submit to the orthodox teaching of the church. He was certainly not making a case for male only teachers, who felt it was their right to exercise authority over women.

Does Paul establish male authority and female subordination by referencing Adam and Eve, or does he use Eve's deception to illustrate the deception of Ephesian women by false teachers? Rebecca Groothius offers an explanation:

> If the women in Ephesus were teaching the heretical doctrine that woman was the originator of man, and were retelling the story of woman's deception so as to make Eve the hero who brought knowledge and enlightenment to Adam, then Paul's statement that Adam was created first and Eve was deceived

---

92. Towner, *1–2 Timothy & Titus*, 77.

93. Belleville, "Teaching and Usurping Authority: 1 Timothy 2:11–15," 219.

would serve simply to refute as a direct refutation of this heresy—which Paul does not permit women to teach.[94]

Another possible heresy impacting the church at Ephesus was that women should not get married and have children. Paul refuted this false teaching by saying in effect, "Childbearing is not an evil act! It is an act blessed by God. A woman can prosper through childbearing, if they (the husband and the wife) continue in faith and love and holiness with good judgment."[95]

The Spirit's Agenda for the Household of Faith

The Holy Spirit brings a new, forward-looking orientation to the church, empowering believers to live into the future in the present age. "Christ established the church not merely to be a mirror of original creation but to be the eschatological new community, living in accordance with the principles of God's new creation and thereby reflecting the mutuality that lies at the heart of the triune God."[96] The dividing wall of hostility has been brought down in Christ. The negative tensions, which resulted from the fall, have been reversed. A history of demeaning allegations of inferiority and dominating ways of oppression and subjection have been overcome by the blood of Christ. The old, debilitating negative tension of gender hostility has been transformed into an empowering and endearing positive tension. Mutual submission in Christ between men and women means a full deployment of the gifts of the Spirit throughout the body life of the church and into the world. Sexual differentiation is clear and celebrated. Sacrifice and submission demonstrate the character of the body of believers. No one is lording it over anyone else and no one is a law unto themselves.

One fundamental feature of the 'Spirit-life' is absent in the church today. That key feature is the sense that heaven (not a spatial sense but understood as a foretaste of a promised future), in all its wholeness, fullness, and beauty, has invaded planet Earth by means of the Spirit. New Testament scholar Gordon Fee encourages believers to see the church as the arena in which that "heavenly invasion" plays itself out. Because the Spirit has "invaded" and a brought a new, forward-looking orientation to

94. Groothius, *Good News for Women*, 217–18.
95. Bailey, "Women in the New Testament: A Middle Eastern Cultural View," 10.
96. Grenz, "Biblical Priesthood and Women in Ministry," 286.

the empowered church, because its redemption is sealed and guaranteed, because God's nature has "infected" human hearts, and because the very power that raised Jesus from the dead is accessible, the church should live differently—as "a colony of heaven." We throw ourselves into the present, precisely because the future is already secured. Living righteously before one another is not a matter of doing duties but of living the life of heaven now. The Holy Spirit helps us grasp the already and the not yet reality of our life in Christ. "Empowered by the Spirit, we now live the life of the future in the present age, the life that characterizes God himself."[97]

The late theologian Stan Grenz observed,

> In the end, the case against women in the pastorate rests on a supposed divinely intended hierarchical ordering present within creation. Yet even if God had so ordered the sexes from the beginning (which he did not), this would not necessarily require that the church continue to be governed by structures that perpetuate male leadership and female subordination. Christ established the church not merely to be a mirror of original creation but to be the eschatological new community, living in accordance with the principles of God's new creation and thereby reflecting the mutuality that lies at the heart of the triune God.[98]

The church lives within a "wonderful tension" of two contradictory realities—heaven and fallen earth. If this tension is strung too tightly, warns Gordon Fee, the church goes into heavenly overdrive, claiming too much, too fast, and usually for the wrong reasons (triumphalism, experientialism). When this tension is too loose, however, the church's vibrant witness falls flat. Rather than reflecting the rule of heaven, it resembles the reality of the world. That, says Fee, is what typically afflicts the contemporary Western church. The world, not heaven, "is too much with us."

The coming of the Spirit is God's promise fulfilled: his presence returned to his people. The gift of the Spirit is received by the entire church and universalizes the mission of the church to the entire world.[99] "For we were all baptized by one Spirit into one body—whether Jews or Greeks, slave or free—and we were all given the one Spirit to drink."[100] The Spirit makes "the many" one. Salvation in Christ can only be realized on an individual basis, but it is not individualistic. Paul's key images for the church

97. Fee, *God's Empowering Presence*, 804.

98. Grenz, "Biblical Priesthood and Women in Ministry," 286.

99. Joel 2:28–30.

100. 1 Cor 12:13.

embody relationally interdependent constructs: temple, family, body. The temple was God's new dwelling place in the corporate life of the individual members of his church, the "living stones," to borrow Peter's imagery. A theology of ministry and organic church growth depend upon the Spirit of Christ animating the entire body of Christ, men and women in meaningful service, empowered and gifted by the Spirit. The whole counsel of God liberates the whole body of Christ to serve together in mutual respect and humble service.

8

Organic Church Growth

Jesus' church growth strategy contradicts the conventional wisdom promoted by church growth experts. Churches can be either seeker-sensitive or consumer-oriented but they can't be both. A church known for costly disciple-making will be marked by the cross and filled with the Spirit. A church known for attracting the consumer may stay on the cutting edge of innovation and excitement, but lose its soul. Both the disciple-making church and the market-driven church pay a high cost for success. One pays the high cost in obedience and faithfulness, the other pays the high cost in money and burnout.

WHEN OUR FAMILY MOVED from a large suburban evangelical church in Denver to an old downtown mainline church in San Diego, we left an upscale, homogenous neighborhood and a relatively wealthy congregation for a highly diverse, struggling urban congregation. We went from ministering to a target audience of baby boomers to being the target in a conflicted church that was struggling with its identity and fighting over the homosexual issue. The church in San Diego was a diverse congregation made up of blue-blood Presbyterians, a social gospel soup kitchen for the poor, a religion and arts concert series for the highbrow, and a core group of believers who wanted biblical preaching. The church was divided over the gay issue with a sizeable group of members wanting the church to publicly bless and embrace the gay lifestyle. With the Lord's help and a decade of ministry we gradually moved from being a fragmented, polarized congregation into becoming a Christ-centered household of faith.

We ministered to the flip-flop, board-shorts crowd as well as to downtown professionals. Every Sunday afternoon we fed several hundred needy people a hot meal in the church dining room and distributed bags of food through the week. We witnessed conversions in Christ and lives transformed. Young families joined us and the average age of the congregation became younger. The most exciting thing was that lost, searching people joined our worship services and came to Christ. We had the privilege of proclaiming the gospel of Christ and being the church amidst young professionals, pagan new-agers, the poor, postmodern secularists, downtown condo retirees, students, the homeless, and suburban families.

We endeavored to be a nurturing, loving, serving, joyful, intergenerational, cross-cultural, mission-focused congregation, open to the powerful work of the Holy Spirit. I am sure we failed many times. I know I failed many times to live up to that high calling, but the Lord showed us his mercy and worked through us nevertheless. We understood that to be a growing church we needed to be compassionate to all, especially to the poor. We needed to faithfully proclaim the Word of God, engage in meaningful worship, and use our Spirit-gifts to serve others. The ministries the Lord called us to were clear: Christ-honoring worship and evangelism, effective Christian education for all ages, an urban Christian elementary school, a ministry to the homeless, and a partnership with cross-cultural missionaries.

Jesus' Church Growth Strategy

If we look to Jesus on the subject of church growth we come away with a decidedly different message than the one we receive from modern church growth experts. Jesus' images of growth do not transpose well into today's fascination with modern marketing, powerful personalities, entertaining "worship," and a full range of felt-need programs. His images of growth point away from humanistic techniques to God's hidden work of grace. Jesus never even came close to prescribing *Ten Steps to Church Growth*. Instead, he drew on analogies that insisted on a natural, organic growth process that remained a mystery to the harvester. In the parable of the growing seed, the farmer scatters the seed on the ground and, miraculously, it grows! Jesus seems to relish telling us that the growth process is out of the farmer's hands. "Night and day, whether he sleeps or gets up, the seed sprouts and grows, *though he does not know how.* All by itself the soil produces grain—first the stalk, then the head, then the full kernel in the head."[1] Jesus' organic models of growth clearly suggest that kingdom growth cannot be manufactured by human strategies. Jesus wants us to respect the mustard seed reality of the kingdom of God. What the world deems small and insignificant has the potential of growing great, not because of anything we do, but because of what God will do. In the parable of the seed and soils, God is sovereign and the good seed reproduces abundantly. Entrepreneurial church growth replaces a vision of Christ with human ambition and seeks to explain the mystery of God by man-made methodologies.

Jesus' growth strategy is no excuse for sloth. As planters and harvesters we are part of the process, but the real growth remains a divine mystery rather than a human endeavor. If anything, Jesus' models of growth cause us to pray. He commanded, "Ask the Lord of the harvest . . . to send out workers into *his* harvest field."[2] He also reminded us that the cost for such growth is high, but not in the cost-effective ways we are in the habit of measuring today. The truth of the matter is that "unless a kernel of wheat falls to the ground and dies, it remains only a single seed. But if it dies, it produces many seeds." Jesus said this not only to explain his death, but our ministry. "The person who loves his life in the world will lose it, while the person who hates his life in this world will keep it for eternal life. Whoever serves me must follow me; and where I am, my servant also will be."[3] If we look to Jesus, the founder and finisher of our faith, we will not be tempted to feel that the kingdom lies in our initiatives, methodologies and budgets. We pray for people who are called by the Lord to come alongside us and participate in this labor of love for Christ and his kingdom.

Seeker-sensitive does not mean Consumer-oriented

Understanding cultural trends in order to engage our culture with the gospel is different from framing the gospel to fit the expectations and dreams of "spiritual" consumers. Consumer-oriented church growth experts claim that they are not altering the gospel, but striving to make it relevant enough to attract people. In some circles, consumer-oriented church growth involves selecting a market niche, focusing on a target audience, meeting a wide range of felt needs, pursuing corporate excellence, identifying dynamic and personable leaders, and creating a positive,

1. Mark 4:27–38.
2. Matt 9:38.
3. John 12:24–26.

upbeat, exciting atmosphere. Consumer-oriented evangelism asks, "What does it take to make Christianity relevant, cool, exciting, and attractive?" But when do our efforts to make Christianity more appealing to the un-churched end up altering the gospel and distorting the message of Christ? Cultural observers such as Marshall McLuhan, Neil Postman, and Jacques Ellul have made us aware that the methods and media we use to commu-nicate can significantly alter the message. When evangelism takes its cues from polling consumers and focus groups we may be manipulating and massaging the message to please the spiritual consumer.

The problem of altering the gospel to make it more appealing is not new to this generation. The logic that supports this consumer-orientation is based on the failure of the "traditional" church and the success of mar-keting in American culture. In this context, marketing refers to product promotion in a competitive commercial arena. Marketing seeks to sell the consumer something. Marketing should not be confused with effective communication. There is a difference between selling a product and com-municating good news.

For church marketers the traditional church represents a low-energy, repetitive, irrelevant, preachy presentation of the gospel, with doctri-nal squabbles, boring services, and a legalistic morality. The traditional church can be insensitive, unintelligible, impractical, inflexible, and in-grown. Hiding behind a spiritual facade the church becomes stuck in a maintenance mode. Sermons are pedantic, doctrinaire, boring, repetitive, and predictable. Preachers become insensitive when it comes to using re-ligious jargon, and are uncreative in finding meaningful starting points that connect with their listeners for the sake of the gospel. In the past such a church would have been criticized for succumbing to dead orthodoxy and being out of step with the Spirit of Christ, but today, church growth experts criticize the traditional church for not adapting to a changing cul-ture, appealing to consumers, and marketing the church. Church market-ers claim that innovation will lead the church to success. John Maxwell writes, "When churches run out of new ideas or new programs, they stop growing."[4]

The book of Hebrews is the New Testament's longest sustained ar-gument against traditional religion. The author addressed believers who were pressured to diminish the sufficiency and supremacy of Christ be-cause they clung to the religious forms and legal codes of Judaism. They were tempted to put their trust in obsolete spiritual practices and rituals

4. Quoted in Elmer L. Towns, *10 of Today's Most Innovative Churches*, 29.

and become "semi-believers" in Christ. They were hedging their religious commitment by returning to their deeply rooted traditions, the very traditions that were designed to point to Christ. They were in danger of substituting a religious tradition for a personal relationship with the living Lord.

The author of Hebrews responds to this heretical challenge, which was both a doctrinal and a practical distortion of authentic Christian living, with a bold, multifaceted reaffirmation of the total redemptive sufficiency of Christ. His corrective to a church stuck in the past, fixating on religious forms, was a serious reminder to fix their eyes on Jesus.[5] The church growth consultant proposes a different solution to solve the problem of the traditional church than the one given by the author of Hebrews. The church growth expert does not criticize the traditional church so much for its spiritual weakness as for its market insensitivity. He attributes the problems of the traditional church to a generation frozen in time and he claims the solution is a new vision—a willingness to change with the times. The church-growth expert calls for new leadership, not for spiritual renewal. The fatal flaw in the traditional church, according to the consultant, is an older generation's paradigm paralysis and market insensitivity, rather than biblical disobedience and a spiritual weakness. The proposed solution is found in shifting from the maintenance mode to the marketing mode. Their prescription for a church stuck in the past and muddling through the present is not spiritual transformation: repentance, forgiveness, prayer, and deeper insight into the Word of God, but a practical sociological transformation: exciting facilities, market-savvy communication, high-energy programs, and enviable personalities.

Market-driven churches accept rather than resist the obvious fact that we are a consumer-oriented culture. Since we are immersed in a highly competitive, materialistic, secular marketplace that vies for our attention, we need to accept the fact that we live in an image-conscious consumer culture and we need to find ways to appeal to the consumer. Today's theory is that churches need to keep up with the latest trends in music, communications, technology, architecture and leadership if they expect to compete effectively in today's marketplace. In our rapidly changing world, churches that don't keep up will be left behind. Years ago, George Barna, one of America's most respected forecasters of church trends, said,

> My contention, based on careful study of data and the activities
> of American churches, is that the major problem plaguing the

5. Heb 12:2.

Church is its failure to embrace a marketing orientation in what has become a market-driven environment.[6]

Can you imagine the prophets concluding that the reason the church was weak and anemic was because the people of God had failed to copy the Canaanites or the Babylonians in building up their community? As far as I know, George Barna has never retracted this assertion or ceased to determine his church growth strategy by polling the culture. Marketing assumptions are preoccupying many in the church today. These are the ideas that many seminars and conferences seek to promote. It has become old-fashioned and almost cynically pietistic to speak about keeping our eyes on Jesus. Modern Christians seem to assume that they know all they need to know about Jesus; all that remains is for them to make the church attractive and relevant so the unchurched will attend and share their assumption that they know Jesus, too. The net effect has been to develop churches that promote Christianity without Christ. Church marketers argue that the choice is between entertaining worship or boring worship, both of which are a contradiction in terms. They argue that the choice is between how-to, feel-good, fix-it sermons or take-it-or-leave-it, don't ask any questions, info-sermons. But a growing church finds an alternative to both the market-driven church and the boring traditional church.

Market-driven churches believe that there are two sets of tactics: one to grow the church numerically and another to grow it spiritually. They advise the church to combine a biblical approach to spiritual growth and a marketing approach to church growth. George Barna writes, "The tactics required to develop strong spiritual character . . . are very different from the tactics required to generate numerical growth. Failure to pursue and achieve balance between those competing but complementary interests leads to an unhealthy church."[7] When marketers quote the proverb "Where there is no vision the people perish," they have in mind a marketing vision, not a ministry vision. They redefine the original intent of the proverb— "Where there is no prophecy [revelation], the people cast off restraint, but happy are those who keep the law"—in favor of a marketing vision for consumer sensitivity, meeting felt needs, excitement, and excellence.[8] If every generation deserves an innovative re-framing of the gospel, and if every target audience has to be appealed to in unique ways, then should the church start from scratch with each new generation and subculture?

6. Barna, *Marketing the Church*, 23.
7. Barna, *User Friendly Churches*, 23.
8. Prov 29:18.

Would the church be better off without heritage and tradition? But in that case, wouldn't the church lack wisdom, depth, and staying power?

The consummate consumer is looking for professional child care, fully staffed Christian education departments, exciting youth programs, a dynamic singles ministry, plenty of parking. and convenient service times. The modern consumer is conditioned to look for the best possible deal for the lowest possible price. Given this pervasive consumer orientation, the critical question is, how materialistic does the church have to become to be spiritually effective? Put conversely, to what degree is the church to be counter cultural, bucking consumerism for the sake of the kingdom of God? Should we not challenge the dehumanizing power of consumerism. The church that tries to impress the world falls into the temptation of trying to prove its identity by changing stones to bread. It bows before a secular standard and forfeits its true character. Are we catering to connoisseurs of religious experience who value their freedom of choice and personal tastes at the expense of long-term commitment to the Body of Christ? Are we reaching the unchurched or unchurching the churched.[9] Sarah Hinlicky, writing in *First Things*, criticizes efforts to reach her over-stereotyped generation X:

> We know you've tried to get us to church. That's part of the problem. Many of your appeals have been carefully calculated for success, and that turns our collective stomach. Take worship for instance. You may think that fashionably cutting-edge liturgies relate to us on our level, but the fact is, we can find better entertainment elsewhere. The same goes for anything else you term 'contemporary.' We see right through it: it's up-to-date for the sake of being up-to-date, and we're not impressed by the results. ... We know intuitively that, in the cosmic scheme of things, the stakes are too high for that. ... On the other hand, you shouldn't be excessively medieval and mysterious, either. Mystery works up to a point, but it's addictive, and once we get hooked on it, the Church won't be able to provide enough to support our habit. We'll turn instead (many of us already have) to Eastern gurus and ancient pagan spiritualities. ... The Church has fought against that Gnostic impulse from the start: Christianity is explosively non-secretive, God en-fleshed for everyone to see, the light shining the darkness. We're much too comfortable alone in the dark; we need light to shake us up.[10]

9. Horton, "Seekers or Tourists?," 14.

10. Hinlicky, "Talking to Generation X," 30.

A church may do a great job focusing on their target audience (the upwardly mobile, success-driven, child-centered baby boomer or the laid-back, hi-tech, fun-loving, present-moment, Gen-Xer, Buster, or Millennial) and miss their mission. I recall a conversation with a ballerina who danced in the San Diego Ballet and her fiancée who was the lead singer in a rock group that had just returned from touring in Europe. I said, "What drew you to our church? I would have thought that you would have found this old stone church and traditional worship unappealing?" Josh answered, "You know, we have visited a lot of churches, and it always seems like we are being worked. We wanted to come to a place that was serious about the Bible and lifted Jesus Christ up."

Keith Phillips, president of World Impact, believes that how a church treats the poor is the most accurate indicator of church health. Limiting outreach to people who understand your sense of humor, live in similar homes, earn the same income, shop in the same stores, share the same family concerns and eat in the same restaurants may create a comfort zone for evangelism, but it may also limit our spiritual growth and our dependence upon God. The rich young ruler represented an appealing market niche but Jesus did not accommodate the gospel to meet his felt needs. When a pastor defines his target audience as the people he would like to spend a vacation with, he has exalted personal preference over Christian mission and has confused discernment with discrimination. Tailoring the gospel to fit the consumer distorts the gospel, discounts the work of the Holy Spirit and dehumanizes men and women made in the image of God.

A number of related issues are embedded in consumer oriented Christianity, such as the surrender of the church to heterodoxy and the surrender of the culture to technology. Consumer orientation is not just a symptom of the spirit of the times, but the controlling force, working to compromise theology and ethics. Marketing the church fosters moral ambiguity and a tacit approval of pre-martial sex, marital infidelity, and a sentimental spirituality. It exalts in "youthfulness" at the expense of children and the elderly. The issue runs deeper than a strategy for church growth. Consumerism is the primary malignancy with a host of secondary symptoms.

The High Cost of Attracting the Consumer

Both a consumer-oriented church and a seeker-sensitive church pay a high cost for effectiveness, but the nature of the cost is radically different. One church pays the high cost of non-discipleship and the other church pays the high cost of discipleship. Consider the following comparative costs:

1. The expenditure of emotional energy, material resources, and personal commitment to meet the high expectations of affluent, self-focused people diverts resources from global missions and social justice concerns. Does it jeopardize obedience to the Great Commission?

2. Market-driven strategies depend upon time-pressured, family-focused, career-centered baby boomers to meet the consumer's demand. Is it a recipe for "religious" burnout? Does it violate Jesus' principle of the "easy yoke"?

3. The marketing medium is not a value-neutral medium and when it is employed by the church it is in danger of sacrificing substance for the sake of strategy. In this sense, the market-driven church minimizes theology in a way reminiscent of the old social gospel and modern liberation theology's "magisterium of the people." The relationship between strategy and substance is an important one. Is theology driving church growth strategy or are the needs of the consumer dictating strategy? Has the church lost out when worshipers can choose from six worship styles (edgy alternative, acoustical, contemplative, exuberant praise, traditional, classical)? Are we becoming a church of diverse tastes united around a video presentation of our favorite Christian speaker? Will this satisfy or frustrate the longing for community?

4. By catering to self-interests and felt needs the church is held hostage to the tyranny of desire. The consumer culture has great material and relational expectations, but little commitment to anything beyond immediate personal pleasure. Instead of showing people "a road right out of the self," the market-driven church is providing spiritual strokes. It's not surprising that in a consumer-oriented culture the deep-seated spiritual longing to worship God is scaled back to a Starbucks enhanced spiritual experience. How do we satisfy the longing for something real without catering to narcissistic desires?

5. The market-driven church justifies its strategy with numbers. Large numbers are impressive and bigness legitimizes effort. Yet as Einstein reportedly said, "Not everything that counts can be counted and not everything that can be counted counts."

   Consumers are captivated by easily visualized formulas. We like a world defined by winners and losers. We would be pleased if life were like a baseball game where errors are judged and performance applauded on the spot. People want their religion the way they get their baseball: simple, obvious, unambiguous, and by the numbers.

The High Cost of Obedience and Faithfulness

Now consider the high-cost of discipleship:

1. Need-meeting Jesus' style involves compassion, not competition; proclamation, not performance; and fellowship instead of excitement. A true transformation of felt needs moves people from self-centeredness to Christ-centeredness. It is consistent with Jesus' invitation, "If anyone would come after me, he must deny himself and take up his cross daily and follow me. For whoever wants to save his life will lose it, but whoever loses his life for me will save it."[11] The responsibility of the household of faith is not to compete for the consumer's attention in the spirit of the marketplace, but to provide a Christ-centered alternative. People come to church expecting to be taken seriously. They are looking for community. Sometimes they are even half-conscious of a deep-seated longing for God. But the big-event orientation and the entertainment mode of large market-driven churches leave these longings unfulfilled.

    There is no secluded place for a private, individualized, spiritualized religious faith that lets *me* focus on *my* self and *my* religious tastes and spiritual preferences. Jesus says, "Come follow me," and we know that he is heading toward the cross. This is why Jesus said, "Do not suppose that I have come to bring peace to the earth. I did not come to bring peace, but a sword. For I have come to turn 'a man against his father, a daughter against her mother, a daughter-in-law against her mother-in-law—a man's enemies will be the members of his own household.'"[12] This is disturbing news for people who thought Christ would simply make life go a little better. There is far more to following Christ than we bargained for. "Whoever finds his life will lose it, and whoever loses his life for my sake will find it."[13] Alan Kreider writes, "Early Christian conversions produced people whose approach to the addictions of their time was transformed

11. Luke 9:23–24.
12. Matt 10:35.
13. Matt 10:39.

whereas programs of evangelistic teaching in our time leave people 'converted' but unchanged."[14]

2. Modernity boxes people into cluster categories, but Jesus intentionally de-categorized people. Instead of artificially limiting his ministry to a so-called "target audience" he broadened the scope of his outreach to include everyone, especially the poor, the despised, and the oppressed. He was sensitive to people's differences, but he was neither selective nor discriminatory. A cursory survey of the Gospels shows that Jesus reached out to those who were demonized, sick, diseased, moral outcasts, foreigners, widows, and prostitutes. If he targeted anyone it was the lost, a "category" that he focused on in the parables of the lost sheep, the lost coin, and the lost son. His encounters with Nicodemus, the Samaritan woman, Zacchaeus, and the Roman Centurion, reveal the scope of his ministry and the depth of his cultural awareness. Jesus exemplified what the apostle Paul aspired for, when he said, "From now on, therefore, we regard no one from a human point of view."[15]

3. Jesus used metaphors and analogies, such as the "little flock" and the vine and the branches to picture the emerging church.[16] The apostles spoke of God's chosen people and members of God's household.[17] Peter emphasized, "But you are a chosen people, a royal priesthood, a holy nation, a people belonging to God, that you may declare the praises of him who called you out of darkness into his wonderful light. Once you were not a people, but now you are the people of God; once you had not received mercy, but now you have received mercy."[18] The apostle Peter certainly spoke the truth when he said we were called out of darkness. He did not exaggerate when he said that we were once not a people.

4. Today's concern to reinvent the church so it will compete more effectively for people's attention contradicts the blueprint for church growth found in the New Testament. The metaphor of "new wineskins" applies to the gospel of grace. It does not mean that the church should be redesigned to meet the changing expectations of

14. Kreider, *The Change of Conversion and the Origin of Christendom*, 103.

15. 2 Cor 5:16.

16. Luke 12:32; John 15.

17. Col 3:12; Eph 2:19.

18. 1 Pet 2:9–10.

consumers and re-envisioned for each generation. The real test for an authentic church remains outlined for us in the second chapter of Acts. Herein lies the key to turning a crowd into disciples, an audience into a congregation, and isolated individuals into the family of God. In Acts 2 we find the nexus between God's work and our work, rendering everything else superfluous and extraneous. If we don't pay serious attention to these basic functions which are universally necessary for all churches everywhere, we will never experience authentic growth.

The apostle Paul's approach to future ministry flies in the face of today's church growth visionaries. Paul refused to be tied down to a definite timetable, much less a long-range plan (or a marketing strategy!). He hoped someday to witness for Christ in Rome; but seeing that he risked his life on a regular basis, that was entirely in the Lord's hands. When Paul spoke of his plans, he did so tentatively and humbly: "Perhaps I will stay with you awhile, or even spend the winter, so that you can help me on my journey, wherever I go. For I do not want to see you now and make only a passing visit; I hope to spend some time with you, if the Lord permits."[19] Pastor Ray Stedman observed, "How gloriously indefinite! How unsettled the apostle is in this!" Taking his cue from Paul, Stedman used to respond to inquiries about his ten-year plan for Peninsula Bible Church, by saying, "We don't have any. We are committed to doing consistently, year after year, the principles that God has taught us from the Word, and we plan to keep on doing that until the Lord returns."[20] Stedman's view is refreshingly New Testament: "Do not feel the necessity to try and project interminably into the future, and make definite plans about where you are going to be five or ten years from now. How do you know where you will be?"[21]

Practical Suggestions for Church Growth

For churches guided by the Word of God and independent of focus groups, the latest polls, and church growth consultants, there are a number of things that can be done to help encourage growth.

1. Focus on the basics: teaching the Word, building relationships, engaging in worship, and learning to pray. Prioritize multi-generational

19. Acts 16:6–7.
20. Stedman, "Giving and Living," 5.
21. Jas 4:13–17.

worship and cross-cultural mission. In an effort to take God more seriously than budgets and buildings, build the leadership team on the foundation of prayer and Bible study.

2. Discover how God-centered worship is the most effective tool in evangelism, fellowship, disciplemaking, and mission. Make worship the chief goal of God's mission in your congregation. Learn to pray the Psalms and cultivate a comprehensive vision of life that proclaims Jesus is Lord. Use the Psalms to focus meditation, to guide the call to worship and to give depth to corporate worship. Bring all those involved in directing the worship services together for monthly prayer and planning sessions.

3. Emphasize the importance of the sabbath principle for the rhythm and pattern of family and personal life. Reclaim Sunday from sport and shopping for the sake of spiritual growth, fellowship and worship. This can be done positively through teaching and personal example, rather than dogmatically and legalistically. Do not fill Sunday with church meetings.

4. Nurture a congregation of worshipers by weaning people from a spectator mentality and a performance expectation. Move away from entertaining, crowd-pleasing performances. Look at worship as an integrated whole, rather than component parts. Diminish the master-of-ceremonies role in favor of a liturgy that focuses on God through great hymns, songs of praise, prayer, preaching, and holy communion. Begin worship with a call to worship, include prayers of confession and intercession. Identify the Lord as the audience of your worship, not the religious consumer.

5. Restore to preaching its true purpose of guiding people in the whole counsel of God. Overcome the unwarranted distinction between preaching and teaching and edification and evangelism. The Bible is far more than a starting point for a series of illustrations and anecdotes. Preaching should be biblical teaching that moves, comforts, instructs, and challenges the body of believers. Authentic preaching will also be effective in answering questions and concerns of earnest seekers. Solid preaching that edifies and inspires believers is the best form of evangelism. Feeding a congregation a constant diet of entry-level-evangelism neither builds up believers nor wins true converts.

6. Permit seekers and strangers easy access to information about the church. Designate key people, who are gifted in building relationships,

to help befriend newcomers. Create a nonpressured approach to new people that will avoid both forced friendliness and uncaring anonymity. Personally invite visitors to a home fellowship group or a special gathering where they can meet the leadership team. Show people love, but do not chase them or cling to them.

7. Integrate the proclamation of the Word of God on Sunday morning with small-group ministries and youth programs. Not only is good preaching shaped by the Word of God from beginning to end, it also shapes the biblical community. The Bible ought to shape the leadership and administrative culture of the church. Real preaching enlivens the whole church to God's mission in the world.

8. Start early in training children to hear and interact with the Word of God. Move away from amusing young people and socializing adults. Encourage young people and adults to prepare for Sunday school and small group fellowships by working through a Bible-study lesson. This will increase thoughtful participation and deepen the church's appreciation for the Word of God. Mentor parents to become their children's primary spiritual directors. Pastoral care begins in the home.

9. Use the sacraments of the church, baptism and holy communion, in a theologically thoughtful way. Whether a particular church adheres to believer's baptism by immersion or covenantal infant baptism, the church has the opportunity and the responsibility of affirming the meaning and integrity of personal commitment to Christ. The sacraments should be preserved from a perfunctory administration. Leaders should meet with individuals and families who desire baptism and use this as an occasion to strengthen faith in Christ.

10. Educate people in a disciple-making process that begins early and extends through life. Show practical interest in how the Christian life is worked out in the home and at work. Special studies for Christians in business, retail sales, law, science, medicine, education, law enforcement, and the arts will help people think Christianly about their vocations.

11. Prepare high school students to understand their culture from a Christian worldview. Using the Word of God, interact with the events, philosophies, music, personalities of the culture. Students should have at least a basic understanding of God and humanity, good and evil, pain and suffering, salvation and death. Carefully work through

one of the Gospel accounts to develop a clear understanding of the life and purpose of Jesus.

12. Encourage mission trips. Begin close to home. These may include inner city soup-kitchens, nursing homes, hospitals, and day-care centers. Before students and adults go on African and Asian mission trips they ought to become involved in local ministries. There are many opportunities to minister in the name of Christ without going far from home.

13. Network with believers from other cultures and with missionaries. Develop a direct relationship with a church or churches in another culture. This may mean a close-relationship with an inner-city church, where members of a suburban church teach tutorials and help meet physical needs, while members of the urban church teach Sunday school classes at the suburban church. Build genuine friendships across cultural and ethnic boundaries for the sake of the kingdom. This will change the way we pray and use the Lord's money.

14. Pray to the Holy Spirit for an openness and sensitivity to the dynamic of God's work in your church. Ask the Lord to lead you to people in need: single parents, widows, international students, young parents with disabled children, foster parents, and the unemployed. The un-evanglized are everywhere, but it is often at the point of obvious need where people are most receptive to the gospel of Christ.

15. Expect the household of faith to evangelize through its counter-cultural distinctiveness, rather than through cultural accommodation. Remember, it is God's called out, visible community, set apart to be salt and light in a dark world. Quietly refuse to accommodate by catering to the world's expectations. When the church gathers, it is for the purpose of glorifying and praising God. Weddings and funerals are not social services to the community; they are God-centered worship services. If they cannot be done in integrity, they should not be done.

16. Reverse the trend that makes the pastor more a manager than a theologian, more an administrator that a spiritual director, more a master of ceremonies than a worship leader. Under the auspices of the leadership team, delegate administrative responsibilities to gifted, capable people. Develop a team ministry approach that relies on the spiritual gifts and commitments of mature believers. Encourage

the priesthood of all believers while maintaining the authority of the pastoral team.

17. Offer training for prospective leaders based on the biblical rationale, description, and expectation of leadership in the household of faith. Develop a mentoring relationship between mature, gifted leaders and potential leaders. In all areas of church life, appoint leaders who are holy in character and spiritually wise. Constituency representation should not be a primary qualification for leadership in the household of faith.

18. Encourage membership in the body of Christ through a nurturing fellowship, rather than an informational program. Inclusion in the church is on the basis of a clear confession of faith in Christ and baptism. Membership classes stress personal commitment and responsibility to the church and its mission. Spiritual direction emphasizes the priesthood of all believers, every-member ministry, and the immense value of ministry outside the four walls of the church in the "secular" arena.

19. Practice preventative and corrective church discipline. Encourage nonthreatening conversations with church members about their walk with God, their growth in Christ, and their ministry responsibilities. Confront, rather than overlook, sinful behavior. Do this in a manner and spirit true to the counsel of the Word of God. Express a genuine concern for individual believers and the integrity of the household of faith, so that Christians will not be left in their sin and the witness of Christ will not be distorted.

20. Remember that the life of the church and the growth of the body are under God's sovereign care. It is our responsibility to actively participate in the divine patience—waiting, watching, working in the tradition and example of our Lord Jesus Christ. We make it our goal to do everything the Jesus way.

These practical suggestions are not offered as an exhaustive checklist. They are a New Testament guide to church growth, designed to encourage believers to apply themselves in ways that are both meaningful and purposeful. There is nothing trendy and innovative about this agenda. Implementation is more a matter of spiritual discipline than financial resources. It is a team effort, best executed by mature women and men in Christ, rather than by a charismatic leader. Genuine church growth cannot be bought or programmed. It is organic growth arising from the vital life of Christ in the household of faith and numbered in people transformed by the Spirit of Christ.

9

God's Mission Is Our Mission

Our theology of ministry is founded on God's mission. We have been called to reveal the manifold wisdom of God to everyone from the "the rulers and authorities in the heavenly realms" to "every family in heaven and on earth." At the center of his missionary letter to the church at Ephesus, the apostle Paul articulated the purpose, power, and prayer of missions. His theology of mission is like a tightly compressed atom, packed with truth that is as personal as it is all-encompassing.

FOR NEARLY TWENTY YEARS we received "missionary letters" from Steve and Sue Befus. These one-page letters to family and friends, describing their work in Liberia, were similar in style and substance to Paul's letters. Their unembellished account of their work always conveyed a deep compassion for their brothers and sisters in Christ. They accepted their responsibility as a privilege instead of a burden. Their stories were free from either "look-at-me" heroism or "woe-is-me" pity. And they were always sensitive to the fact that those who received their letters were also engaged in ministry. Reading their letters, you had a sense that we were partners together in the work that the Lord has called us to do. Sue and Steve took the tough times and real emergencies in stride. In addition to a sense of freedom and joy, they conveyed a sense of patience with the church and a perseverance with the work. These are the truths that a missionary letter should communicate.

Missions is best presented as a personal story inspired by the Spirit of Christ. In his letter to the church at Ephesus, Paul asked nothing from them except that they not be ashamed of his suffering, but it is safe to assume that he hoped they would be *inspired by his example* to embrace the mission mandate of the gospel. Roland Allen was an Anglican missionary to China from 1895 to 1903. He spent the next forty years writing on the mission of God and applying the way of Christ and his apostles to missionary principles. In his classic study of Paul's missionary methods, Allen writes, "It seems strange to us that there should be no exhortations to missionary zeal in the Epistles of St Paul. There is one sentence of approval, 'The Lord's message rang out from you,' but there is no insistence upon the command of Christ to preach the gospel."[1] Missionary statesman Leslie Newbigin agrees, when he writes,

> There has been a long tradition which sees the mission of the Church primarily as obedience to a command. It has been customary to speak of "the missionary mandate." This way of putting the matter is certainly not without justification, and yet it seems to me that it misses the point. It tends to make mission a burden rather than a joy, to make it part of the law rather than part of the gospel. If one looks at the New Testament evidence one gets another impression. Mission begins with a kind of explosion of joy. The news that the rejected and crucified Jesus is alive is something that cannot possibly be suppressed. It must be told. Who could be silent about such a fact?[2]

In post-World War II America, a generation of believers was highly motivated to carry the gospel to the nations. Wars fought in Europe and the Pacific opened the eyes of the church in the West to the tremendous global need for spreading the gospel. In the 1940s and 50s many saw the Great Commission as a spiritual call to arms. Their strong sense of duty and sacrifice may have waned in subsequent generations, but in the Spirit, the freedom and privilege of partnership in the mission of God can be recovered and embraced. The sacrifice involved in proclaiming and living out the gospel is no less real today than it was in their day.

The mission mandate to make disciples of all nations has been given to the global church and in the providence of God, missionaries are being sent cross-culturally from every direction. But even more significantly, is the truth that all disciples everywhere are meant to be missionaries. Christopher Wright defines our mission: "Fundamentally, our mission (if it is biblically informed and validated) means our committed participation as

---

1. Allen, *Missionary Methods: St. Paul's Or Ours?*, 93.
2. Newbigin, *The Gospel in a Pluralistic Society*, 116.

God's people, at God's invitation and command, in God's own mission within the history of God's world for the redemption of God's creation."[3]

Our Mission Purpose

Halfway through his carefully reasoned letter to the Ephesians, Paul had what my daughter and her college friends call an RDT with the saints at Ephesus. In case that acronym is unfamiliar to you, as it was to me, RDT stands for a *Relationship Defining Talk*. Paul turned *emphatically* personal, not because he had something to get off his chest or because he wanted to defend himself, but because he wanted to lead by example. He embraced the mission of the gospel of grace with a palpable sense of privilege and passion. He made no attempt to cajole, berate, or browbeat people into the work of missions. What he sought to do was compel them by his infectious joy, his profound gratitude, and his sense of great honor. He was truly grateful for the responsibility of administering the gospel of grace.

> For this reason I, Paul, the prisoner of Christ Jesus for the sake of you Gentiles . . . . [4]

His opening phrase, "For this reason," gathers up all that Paul has said about worship and salvation as the foundation for what he is about to say about missions. Paul knew the incomparable riches of God's grace. He understood that we have been chosen, predestined, adopted, and redeemed in Christ. He knew the power of God to overcome humanity's depravity and alienation; to raise up those who were dead in their transgressions and sins; and to destroy the dividing wall of hostility. He knew what it meant to be God's workmanship created in Christ Jesus to do good works. Paul believed in the importance of being citizens of God's kingdom and members of God's family. He was convinced "that the whole building is joined together and rises to become a holy temple in the Lord." This theology of grace formed the foundation for what Paul was about to say about the mission of the church. If we are not truly convinced of the truth laid out in the first two chapters (1:1—2:22), there will be no basis for accepting what Paul says about missions.

The Bible is all about mission and mission is the reason for the Bible. It is not just that there is a biblical basis for missions, but that without

---

3. Wright, *The Mission of God*, 38.
4. Eph 3:1.

mission there would be no Bible.[5] "The whole Bible renders to us the story of God's mission through God's people in their engagement with God's world for the sake of the whole of God's creation."[6] If we expect to stay in the story, that "grand narrative that constitutes truth for all," we have to join in on God's mission. There is no believing in the Bible or being filled with the Spirit and not participating in the work of God whose mission it is to transform the old creation into a new creation. There are no other options. To be a believer is to be a follower of the Lord Jesus. To be a disciple is to be a missionary. All these terms: believer, disciple, and missionary, describe the same person and can be used interchangeably. A theology of ministry is a theology of mission. Oswald Chambers wrote,

> Whenever the call of God is realized, there is the feeling, "I am called to be a missionary." It is a universal feeling because the Holy Spirit sheds abroad the love of God in our hearts, and "God so loved the world." . . . We make a blunder when we fix on the particular location for a service and say, "God called me there."[7]

Paul begins, "I, Paul, the prisoner of Christ Jesus for the sake of you Gentiles." This unique missionary introduction sets up a series of powerful paradoxes. Although Paul was literally a political prisoner of Caesar, most likely under house arrest in Rome, he saw himself as a prisoner *of* and *for* Christ.[8] In the eyes of the world, Paul was either a victim of Roman injustice or a troublemaker who deserved to be imprisoned by the authorities. However, in the eyes of the Lord, Paul was a steward of the mystery made known to him by the revelation of God. He was entrusted with the responsibility of administering the gospel of grace. Others may have despised and pitied him, but he saw himself as an ambassador for Christ, albeit in chains.[9] Instead of languishing in prison, Paul possessed the freedom to approach God with confidence.[10] This paradox of worldly shame and heavenly glory seems to often characterize believers engaged in the mission of the gospel.

5. Wright, *The Mission of God*, 29.

6. Ibid., 51.

7. Chambers, *So Send I You*, 16.

8. Eph 3:1; 4:1.

9. Eph 6:20.

10. Eph 3:12.

Administrating the Mystery

> This grace was given to me: to preach to the Gentiles the bound-
> less riches of Christ, and to make plain to everyone the admin-
> istration of this mystery, which for ages past was kept hidden in
> God, who created all things.[11]

The second paradox is "the administration of this mystery." To the modern reader the idea of managing a mystery doesn't make sense. The concepts of "administration" and "mystery" don't belong together. How can anyone comprehend, let alone control, what by definition is unknown, insoluble and incomprehensible? That which is "mysterious" is vague, inscrutable, and puzzling, definitely not something that can be managed. Commentators are quick to say that the word "mystery" (μυστήριον) refers to the revelation of God, previously hidden, but now made known. This is true, but it doesn't answer why Paul used the word "mystery" instead of "gospel." Why use a word that reminded his readers of the various mystery cults?

Paul did this to drive home a very important truth. The mystery cults kept secrets that were made known only to initiates, "giving them great spiritual privileges unavailable to others without this knowledge."[12] These secret societies were more or less religious clubs, spiritual fraternities, with their own little elite in-groups. They were proud of their exclusivity. Paul took over the word "mystery" intentionally, to distance the gospel of Jesus Christ from the exclusivity of the mystery cults with their esoteric knowledge. He did this to make clear that the truth disclosed in the revelation of the gospel was meant to be proclaimed to everyone. By suggesting a comparison to the mystery cults Paul was reinforcing the missional character of the gospel. In the mystery cults "administration" meant keeping secrets, but in the church it meant making the gospel of Jesus Christ known to both Jews and Gentiles. The church today that keeps the mystery to itself is more like the ancient mystery cults than the open-bordered kingdom of God, or the ever-welcoming household of God, or the organically growing temple of the Lord—a dwelling in which God lives by his Spirit. The word for administration (οἰκονομίαν) is the seventh word Paul used in the "house" word group. The thrust of Paul's artful presentation underscores the inclusiveness of the missionary challenge. Missions belongs to the household of God—to everyone in the church, and not to a select group of "missionaries" set aside for this purpose.

11. Eph 3:8–9.
12. Lincoln, *Ephesians*, 31.

Of course, the problem of restricting missions to "professionals" does not lie with the "missionary" but with us and how we view missions. We are often guilty of acting like we belong to a mystery cult. Only in our case, we may not be proud of our "secret" as much as embarrassed and intimidated by it. Christopher Wright reminds us, "Mission is not ours; mission is God's . . . It is not so much the case that God has a mission for his church in the world but that God has a church for his mission in the world. Mission was not made for the church; the church was made for mission—God's mission . . . The marvel is that God invites us to join in."[13]

The third paradox implied in this passage has to do with the relationship between truth and mystery. Skeptics grab hold of this term, *mystery*, and exploit it for their own purposes. It becomes a convenient way to distance themselves from the truth. This is proof, they say, that Paul did not have a corner on the truth. Mystery implies that God surpasses our human understanding and that no one can know the truth with any degree of confidence. God is simply beyond our human capacity to understand. British-American journalist Andrew Sullivan claims, "We cannot know with the kind of surety that allows us to proclaim truth with a capital T. There will always be something that eludes us. If there weren't, it would not be God."[14] Of course, there will always be something that eludes us, but the Christian truth claim is that God is perfectly capable of communicating Truth to human beings.

Sullivan's perspective turns truth into a liability. The skeptic argues that only the arrogant claim to know the truth, because the truth by definition must be unimaginable, ineffable and incomprehensible. The skeptic is not willing to entertain the notion that God is capable of revelation. In a sense the skeptics are right, Paul would never have claimed to have had a corner on the truth. This is one of the reasons why he used the word *mystery*, so as to underscore the fact that the truth did not come from him but from God. The only reason he knows the truth of the gospel is because of the revelation of God. Knowing the truth was not a matter of Paul's genius but of God's grace, and it was not for Paul's sake but for the benefit of others. The reason this was a knowable mystery and an open secret was because God had made it known.

The administration of God's grace was *given* to Paul, not achieved by Paul. It was a mystery made known by revelation. Paul's Spirit-led insight into the mystery of Christ was not something so ineffable and

13. Wright, *The Mission of God*, 62, 67.
14. Sullivan, "When Not Seeing Is Believing," 60.

incomprehensible that people couldn't understand it. Paul had not imbibed the modern spirit of "humility" with its refusal in principle to accept the revelation of God. He administered the mystery confidently. Roland Allen comments on Paul's forthright proclamation of the gospel:

> There is no attempt to keep the door open by partial statements, no concealment of the real issue and all that it involves, no timid fear of giving offence, no suggestion of possible compromise, no attempt to make things really difficult appear easy. . . . There is an unhesitating confidence in the truth of his message, and in its power to meet and satisfy the spiritual needs of people.[15]

Paul was confident about the gospel but humble about himself. "Although I am less than the least of all the Lord's people, this grace was given me: to preach to the Gentiles the boundless riches of Christ, and to make plain to everyone the administration of this mystery, which for ages past was kept hidden in God, who created all things."[16] Paul was fully impressed with his own littleness in contrast to the immensity of this universal truth that no one could truly know and then hesitate to proclaim.

The Manifold Wisdom of God

The fourth paradox, implied in Paul's theology of mission, is the contrast between the largeness of the full-orbed gospel preached by Paul and the smallness of the gospel we often preach. Our thoughts about personal salvation often clash with the promise of the gospel to work for justice and overcome social alienation. Note carefully the way Paul expressed the meaning of the mystery, when he said, "This mystery is that through the gospel the Gentiles are heirs together with Israel, members together of one body, and sharers together in the promise in Christ Jesus."[17] The gospel of grace is the culmination of salvation history, "which for ages past was kept hidden in God, who created all things."[18] The purpose of the gospel is nothing less than "to bring unity to all things in heaven and on earth under Christ."[19]

---

15. Allen, *Missionary Methods*, 64.
16. Eph 3:8–9.
17. Eph 3:6.
18. Eph 3:9.
19. Eph 1:10.

That which was hidden, "what neither the Old Testament nor Jesus revealed was the radical nature of God's plan, which was that the theocracy (the Jewish nation under God's rule) would be terminated, and replaced by a new international community, the church."[20] This is why Paul said, "And God placed all things under his feet and appointed him to be head over everything for the church, which is his body . . ." The scope of salvation is well beyond the personal salvation of the individual, as important as that is. The church encompasses "the fullness of him who fills everything in every way."[21] God's plan is "to bring unity to all things in heaven and on earth under Christ."[22]

The administration of this mystery is far from a simple strategy of getting people to say "yes" to Jesus. Stewards of the gospel of grace preach "the boundless riches of Christ" across all barriers, whether they are ethnic, racial, linguistic, cultural, political, religious, ideological, gender, or generational. We seek Christ and his kingdom in every aspect of life and in every culture. That which was hidden has now been revealed by God. "His intent was that now, through the church, the manifold wisdom of God should be made known to the rulers and authorities in the heavenly realms, according to his eternal purpose that he accomplished in Christ Jesus our Lord."[23]

Paul's theology of missions is not about sending somebody else to a far away place to share the gospel nor is it about building a church to entertain the masses. The mission of the church is to make known everywhere *the manifold wisdom of God* to the principalities and powers in the heavenly realms. The ministry is much greater than we imagined. The call to action is more intense and demanding than we expected. The unity is far deeper and more complex than we thought possible. It is not only a conversion of the heart and mind, but it is a *sociological* conversion. We cannot be a new creation in Christ without belonging to the new community in Christ. As a concrete, sociological body, the church was meant to be "a sign and proof of a change that affects the institutions and structures, patterns and spans of the bodily and spiritual, social and individual existence of all humanity."[24] We were meant to bear witness to all of creation, and even to the cosmic spiritual powers, that Jesus Christ is Lord.

20. Stott, *God's New Society: Ephesians*, 118.
21. Eph 1:23.
22. Eph 1:10.
23. Eph 3:10–11.
24. Barth, *Ephesians*, 365.

If we embrace the mission of the gospel, we will be placed in an extraordinary position to see "the manifold witness of God." When I think of the manifold wisdom of God I think of my friends, David and Brenda Mensah, who I wrote about earlier. Their work, along with many others, in northern Ghana, is a solid testimony to the multi-faceted nature of God's wisdom. We have seen firsthand the effectiveness of their mission work. By God's grace arid land has been turned into usable farm land, new schools and medical clinics have been built and staffed, and thousands of Ghanians are participating in food co-ops. Thirty-three churches have been planted in surrounding villages and lay pastors have been trained. A fish hatchery is producing tilapia and farmers are growing acres and acres of tomato plants. Hundreds of people have come to Christ from villages once in bondage to witchcraft and shamanism. What a wonderful witness to the manifold wisdom of God!

The testimony of the church is not enhanced by becoming impressive in the eyes of the world. Suffering rather than success is the key to revealing the manifold wisdom of God. Like Paul, prisoners for Christ often end up prisoners of Caesar. Leslie Newbigin describes the impact of the missional church:

> It follows that the visible embodiment of this new reality is not a movement which will take control of history and shape the future according to its own vision, not a new imperialism, not a victorious crusade. Its visible embodiment will be a community that lives by this story, a community whose existence is visibly defined in the regular rehearsing and reenactment of the story which has given it birth, the story of the self-emptying of God in the ministry, life, death, and resurrection of Jesus.[25]

The great paradox confronting the church is that this gospel of peace in Christ that is designed to destroy the walls of hostility actually provokes hostility. The old paganisms and the new messianisms fight against the church with everything they have. Newbigin writes,

> Wherever the gospel is preached, new ideologies appear—secular humanism, nationalism, Marxism—movements which offer the vision of new age, an age freed from all the ills that beset human life, freed from hunger and disease and war—on other terms. . . . Once the gospel is preached and there is a community which lives by the gospel, then the question of the ultimate meaning of history is posed and other messiahs appear. So the

25. Newbigin, *The Gospel in a Pluralistic Society*, 120.

crisis of history is deepened. Even more significant as an example of this development than the rise of Marxism is the rise of Islam. Islam, which means simply submission, is the mightiest of all the post-Christian movements which claim to offer the kingdom of God without the cross. The denial of the crucifixion is and must always be central to Islamic teaching.[26]

If the church expects to reveal the manifold wisdom of God to "the rulers and authorities in the heavenly realms," the church, like the apostle, will have to be marked by the cross. Once again, Newbigin, insists that the church shape its expectations according to the life of Jesus and his apostles rather than an entrepreneurial or evolutionary model of development. He writes,

> The gospel calls us back again and again to the real clue, the crucified and risen Jesus, so that we learn that the meaning of history is not immanent in history itself, that history cannot find its meaning at the end of a process of development, but that history is given its meaning by what God has done in Jesus Christ and by what he has promised to do; and that the true horizon is not at the successful end of our projects but in his coming to reign. One may say, therefore, that missions are the test of our faith.[27]

The manifold wisdom of God is a beautiful way of articulating the all-encompassing work of Christ's cross through the priesthood of all believers in the body of Christ, the church. God intends for all believers to bear witness to the saving power of Christ and to demonstrate the manifold wisdom of God in all that they do. Christopher Wright affirms the centrality of the cross:

> We need a holistic gospel because the world is in a holistic mess. And by God's incredible grace we have a gospel big enough to redeem all that sin and evil has touched . . . Ultimately all that will be there in the new, redeemed creation will be there because of the cross. And conversely, all that will not be there (suffering, tears, sin, Satan, sickness, oppression, corruption, decay and death) will not be there because they will have been defeated and destroyed by the cross. That is the length, breadth, height and depth of God's idea of redemption.[28]

---

26. Ibid., 122.
27. Ibid., 126.
28. Wright, *The Mission of God*, 315.

We need the whole church to manifest the manifold wisdom of God. We need mothers, dentists, homebuilders, politicians, educators, engineers, evangelists—you name it; we need the whole vocational range of *real* missionaries who bear witness to Christ and his cross in their daily lives and work. This is why we emphasized the priesthood of all believers and every-member ministry and the shared gifts of the Spirit. This is why we have said that all believers are called to salvation, service, sacrifice and simplicity.

The Lord used one particular incident to impress upon me the meaning of the manifold wisdom of God. David and Brenda Mensah were visiting from Ghana and we had gathered at a friend's home for dinner. We had a great conversation about their holistic ministry in Ghana, but I was feeling anxious. Andrew, our son who had spent three months in Ghana working alongside David, was a no-show. At the time, Andrew was working as an ocean lifeguard off the coast of California and usually finished his shift at 6 p.m. Knowing how much he was looking forward to seeing David and Brenda again, I thought that something must be wrong. When he arrived at 9 p.m., he said very little. His demeanor was subdued. His eyes were bloodshot and he looked exhausted. I pulled him aside and asked him if he was okay. He explained,

> Just before sundown we got a distress call from a boat about a mile offshore. I took off on the jet ski, praying, 'Lord help me find this boat.' It was getting really dark. Then there was a break in the clouds, some moonlight came through and it reflected off the boat. The guy on board was unconscious, lying on the deck with his guts hanging out. He was a bloody mess. I think he was leaning over the boat engine when it exploded. I took off my shirt and wrapped it around him and duct-taped his chest and stomach to stop the bleeding. Loaded him on the jet ski and radioed for an ambulance. By the time I got to shore the ambulance was waiting for us.

Andrew didn't think the man would live, but the next day he got a call from his captain congratulating him and telling him that the man had survived surgery and was expected to recover. By God's grace, Andrew saved a life. The juxtaposition of the Mensah's ministry in Ghana and Andrew's ministry as a lifeguard reflects something of the range of God's mission. The manifold wisdom of God, made known through the church, calls each and every follower of the Lord Jesus to a life of obedience, witness, and mission.

Christopher Wright raises the question we should be asking,

> Is *the church as a whole* reflecting the wholeness of God's re-
> demption? Is the church (thinking here of the local church as
> the organism effectively and strategically placed for God's mis-
> sion in any given community) aware of all that God's mission
> summons them to participate in? Is the church through the
> combined engagement of *all* its members, applying the redemp-
> tive power of the cross of Christ to *all* the effects of sin and evil
> in the surrounding lives, society and environment?[29]

Two final thoughts: First, the beauty and humility of the church, marked by the cross and revealing the manifold wisdom of God "to the rulers and authorities in the heavenly realms," eliminates triumphalism. God's mission is fulfilled without fanfare and publicity. For the most part, money, power, and status are not prerequisites for success, but liabilities. Entrepreneurial church leaders who talk big and show off to the world frequently end up backtracking. Their grand schemes often have more to do with their oversized egos than with the mission of the church and they end up doing more harm than good.

Second, Paul never conceived of missions as a burden or a duty to be imposed on believers. He didn't go around thinking of himself as God's public relations chief, trying to urge lackadaisical believers to get excited about missions. It wasn't his job to lay on the church at Ephesus a guilt trip about missions. On the contrary, he challenged the believers to renegoti-ate their understanding of success. True success, the kind marked by the cross, involved suffering for the sake of the gospel. Paul didn't want them discouraged because of his imprisonment and suffering. He wanted them to see his effort and their partnership as God's "eternal purpose." This was the missionary purpose he embraced with every fiber of his being.

Our Mission Prayer

> I pray that out of his glorious riches he may strengthen you with
> power through his Spirit in your inner being, so that Christ may
> dwell in your hearts through faith.[30]

Given Paul's perspective on missions it would be hard to imagine any other posture than on our knees before God the Father, Son, and Holy

29. Ibid., 322.
30. Eph 3:16–17.

Spirit. *Prayer*—communion with God, is central to following Jesus and being the church. The administration of God's grace presents a missions agenda so weighty and significant that prayer is a natural response for all who are in Christ. Paul's parenthetical thought on missions is not a digression, but an inspiration. If our aim is to become enveloped by the purposes of God as Paul was, prayer is the natural response.

Paul prays to the Father (πατέρα) "from whom all families (πατριὰ) in heaven and on earth derive their name." The God and Father of the Lord Jesus Christ is the God and Father of all the families in the cosmos.[31] Paul's mission-minded prayer is for everyone to come to the realization that their Heavenly Father has made himself known through Christ. All relationships in heaven and on earth have their roots in God the Father. Within the created order there is no ground for racism. "The built-in arrogance of every race, nationality and clan has no ultimate basis."[32] There is "one God and Father of all, who is over all and through all and in all."[33] Paul begins his prayer by stressing the inclusiveness of the gospel of grace. This conviction was not any more acceptable in Paul's day than our own, but the power of the gospel is dependent on this relationship. Whether men and women acknowledge their God and Father or not, all of us derive our name, our very being, from the Father. It is the defining relationship for all people in a personal universe.

Paul was in prison but he prayed for the saints at Ephesus. He was weak, but he prayed for their strengthening. He was in poverty but his mind was on their glorious riches in Christ.[34] Paul felt that his outer being was wasting away but his concern was for their inner being. He prayed that God the Father would strengthen them "with power through his Spirit in [their] inner being, so that Christ may dwell in [their] hearts through faith."[35] In this prayer, the work of the Father, Son, and Holy Spirit is simultaneous and symphonic; everything is in perfect harmony. The enriching, empowering, and indwelling work of God leads to a well-rooted and well-established believer. Paul's previous description of the church parallels this description of the individual believer. His prayer highlights what is most important for us to pray for one another. Let the redundant list-making

31. Eph 1:3, 17.
32. Snodgrass, *Ephesians*, 186.
33. Eph 4:6.
34. Eph 1:7; 2:4, 7: 3:8, 16.
35. Eph 3:16–17.

prayers cease and the worshipful, selfless prayers commence! Paul prayed for one thing four different ways.

First, he prayed that we would be rooted and established in love, just like a well-rooted tree or a well-built home.

Second, he prayed that we would "have power, together with all the Lord's people, to grasp how wide and long and high and deep is the love of Christ." What better prayer for missions can there be, but to grasp "the extravagant dimensions of Christ's love." Paul's outlook was anything but pessimistic. It was not a question of whether he could find glimpses of God's love here or there, but whether he could keep up with the full range of God's love. Paul's prayer was a call to action: "Reach out and experience the breadth! Test its length! Plumb the depths! Rise to the heights!"[36]

Third, he prayed that we would "know this love that surpasses knowledge." This reminds us of Paul's prayer for the peace of God that passes all understanding and the love that abounds more and more in knowledge and depth of insight.[37] God's loving ways are beyond our ways. His thoughts are so much greater than our thoughts. Thankfully, God's love is not limited by our knowledge or controlled by our understanding.

Fourth, Paul prayed that we would "be filled to the measure of all the fullness of God." This is what it means to live life to the full. Jesus said, "I have come that you might have life and have it to the full."[38]

God's Multi-dimensional Love

Like a good pastor/missionary, Paul worked to integrate theology and life. Prayer is one of the main tools we have for building a relationship with the Lord and with one another.

When Paul prayed for the believers to be well-rooted and built up in love, he used planting and building metaphors to bring home the truth of the body of Christ. To be rooted and established in love connects with being citizens of God's Kingdom, members of God's household, and worshipers in God's temple. The two themes are inseparable. In Paul's mind the metaphors for the church connect with the botanical and architectural metaphors he used for the individual believer. When he prayed this way he expected believers to make the connection. For Paul it would be

36. Eph 3:18, *The Message.*
37. Phil 4:7; 1:9.
38. John 10:10.

inconceivable for any believer to think they were well-rooted and well-established in love, yet remain out of fellowship with the body of Christ.

To have power, *together with all the Lord's people,* emphasizes the believer's personal experience of the love of Christ in solidarity with the people of God. The power to *grasp* this love involves an ability to lay hold of it—a capacity that requires a certain kind of strength. An ocean lifeguard works out regularly to build up his forearm and strengthen his grasp. There are more than eight muscles in the forearm that wrap around the bone and give it strength. For most of us, these muscles are like rope, but in lifeguards and carpenters they seem more like steel cables. Any fisherman or fireman can identify with Paul's metaphor of the strength to grasp the love of God. Paul prayed that we would have the power to grasp the multi-dimensional character of God's love.

The key to interpreting what Paul meant by the width, length, height, and depth of God's love, can be found in the spatial analogies that Paul has already used in his letter. The *width* reminds us of the inclusiveness of God's love and grace that encompasses all people. Jew and Gentile alike are included in the breadth of God's love. The *length* recalls the spatial analogy of "near" and "far." God has gone to great lengths to bring Gentiles into his fellowship and to break down the dividing wall of hostility. "But now in Christ Jesus," Paul wrote, "you who once were far away have been brought near by the blood of Christ."[39] The *height* suggests the distance between being dead in our transgressions and sins and being raised up with Christ and seated in the heavenly realms. This vertical dimension captures well the height of God's love. The *depth* suggests the extent to which God will go to redeem us from our depravity and despair. As death camp survivor Corrie ten Boom said so well, "No pit is so deep, but that God's love is not deeper still."[40] If we apply Paul's prayer to the spatial analogies and themes he has already developed we may come closest to understanding his intentions.

This interpretation encourages further reflection and meditation on the multi-dimensional character of God's love. Paul's prayer inspires doxology. We cannot think of the breadth of God's love without thinking of "members of every tribe and language and people and nation" that have been purchased by the blood of Christ.[41] "For God so loved the world that he gave his one and only Son, that whoever believes in him shall not perish

39. Eph 2:13.
40. Corrie ten Boom, *The Hiding Place,* 227.
41. Rev 5:9.

but have eternal life."[42] Nor can we contemplate the height and length of God's love without echoing the psalmist: "For as high as the heavens are above the earth, so great is his love for those who fear him; as far as the east is from the west, so far as he removed our transgressions from us."[43] The love of God is long enough to last forever. The great preacher Charles Spurgeon said that God's love is "so long that our old age cannot wear it out, our continued tribulations cannot exhaust it, our successive temptations cannot drain it dry, and like eternity itself it knows no bounds."[44]

The faithful have contemplated the love of God in spatial language throughout salvation history. David prayed, "If I go up to the heavens, you are there; if I make my bed in the depths, you are there. If I rise on the wings of the dawn, if I settle on the far side of the sea, even there your hand will guide me, your right hand will hold me fast."[45] There is no limit to the love of God. "Surely goodness and love will pursue me all the days and I will dwell in the house of the Lord forever."[46]

The multi-dimensional character of God's love has special relevance to Paul's theology of mission and the church's responsibility to make known "the manifold wisdom of God." God's love is manifested through the broadest range of vocational pursuits from the arts to architecture and from music to medicine; from the factory worker to the flight attendant and from education to farming. The manifestation of God's love through the performing arts or the building trades or the health care industry or the financial world always leaves the testimony that there is much more to this work than "performing" or "building" or "earning." If we work well, as unto the glory of God, there will be a palpable sense of the reality of God. People will come to realize that we do not love money or music or medicine as ends unto themselves, but we love God. In this sense, our work ought to become a devotional expression of our love for God.

God's love spans the difference between old and young, rich and poor, educated and uneducated, black and white, and male and female. God's love is intended for everyone, everywhere. God's love raises up the sinner to salvation and heals the broken-hearted. God brings "down rulers from their thrones but lifts up the humble."[47] We should acknowledge

42. John 3:16.

43. Ps 103:11–12.

44. Spurgeon, *The Metropolitan Tabernacle Pulpit,* vol. 12, 478.

45. Ps 139:8–10.

46. Ps 23:6.

47. Luke 1:52.

that such love makes our lives more complex and difficult. If we were to love only ourselves, only are own little group, then we would never know the kind of love Paul so earnestly prays for. We would have simplified our lives, but at the expense of our impoverishment.

In the household of faith there is bound to be a built in tension with this expansive love. If the eyes of our heart are enlightened, we will be able to look the homeless and the elderly in the eye. If we know something of the power of God we will be able to overcome our insecurities and reach out to others. We should anticipate generational and societal tensions when we embrace the love that embraces all others with the love of Christ. Given the multi-dimensional love of God it should be difficult for those who are rooted and established in love to be narrow minded, short-sighted, low-energy, and shallow. God's love and wisdom are marked by depth and meaning. Paul sums it up well when he writes, "Oh, the depth of the riches of the wisdom and knowledge of God! How unsearchable his judgments, and his paths beyond tracing out!"[48]

The nineteenth-century pastor of Trinity Church, Cambridge, Charles Simeon spoke of *the four magnitudes of God's love*. By definition, *magnitude* is the quality of being great: great in rank or position; great in size or sound, great in significance or importance. The seismologist measures the force of earthquakes in magnitudes and the astronomer measures the brightness of stars in magnitudes. It is a fitting word to use for the size, scope, significance, and the strength of God's love. Given the magnitude of God's love how can all those who are in Christ, be anything but magnanimous, that is to say, great in courage, superior to petty resentment, generous in disregard to injuries, and confident in the love of God.

Another way that Paul's prayer unites theology and mission is the paradox of love and knowledge. He prayed for the believers "to know this love that surpasses knowledge." Recalling what was said earlier about paradox, we might see this as the fifth and final paradox in his theology of mission or the fitting summation of the previous four. To recap the four paradoxes discussed earlier:

1. Paul looked like he was a prisoner of Caesar, but in fact he was really a prisoner of and for Christ.

2. Paul spoke of administering the mystery of the gospel, but not in the exclusive manner of the mystery cults but under the divine mandate of an inclusive gospel.

48. Rom 11:33.

3. Paul used the word *mystery* to convey with confidence the certainty of the revelation of God in Christ. He did not use *mystery* to obfuscate the truth but to proclaim the truth.

4. Paul presented a full-orbed gospel that reflected the manifold wisdom of God rather than an individualistic and truncated gospel. In each one of these paradoxes, the love of Christ transcends circumstances, exceeds expectations, and surpasses knowledge.

Paul's prayer for believers to know the love that surpasses knowledge in no way diminishes the importance of knowing God. Paul prayed in his eucharistic prayer for believers to have the Spirit of wisdom and revelation so that they might know the Lord better.[49] Knowing God through God's revelation could not have been more important to Paul. His point was not to disparage knowledge but to point "to the immensity and incomprehensibility of Christ's love."[50] The love of Christ is so all-encompassing and longsuffering, so far beyond us and in-depth, that we will never be able to fully comprehend it, much less begin to exhaust it. Paul would have gladly said with Job, "I know that you can do all things; no purpose of yours can be thwarted. . . Surely I spoke of things I did not understand, things too wonderful for me to know."[51] Knowing what we do know of the love of Christ, how could we think otherwise?

Does this prayer request have special implications for doctrinal disputes? Those who want to distance themselves from doctrinal orthodoxy might use this verse to justify their errant ways. They reason that since God's love surpasses knowledge there is no need to take doctrine seriously. The love of God, they claim, always trumps doctrinal differences. Take for example a pastor who claims that he fully depends on the love of God but cannot accept the doctrine of the atoning sacrifice of Christ on the cross. He argues that it is a barbaric doctrine that may have made sense in the first century among people acquainted with sacrificial rituals but in the twenty-first century it is nonsense. He claims that Jesus illustrated the highest degree of sacrificial love, but he was not the atoning sacrifice demanded by God and confessed by the church through the centuries. The love that surpasses knowledge is not the love that disputes the revelation of God. It is, rather, the love that embraces God's revelation, knowing that

49. Eph 1:17.
50. Lincoln, *Ephesians*, 213.
51. Job 42:3.

we will never know the full extent of God's love, but we accept what God has revealed about his love. Earlier Paul wrote,

> In love he predestined us for adoption to sonship through Jesus Christ, in accordance with his pleasure and will—to the praise of his glorious grace, which he has freely given us in the One he loves. In him we have redemption through his blood, the forgiveness of sins, in accordance with the riches of God's grace that he lavished on us.[52]

The love that surpasses knowledge is more like the covenantal love between a husband and wife than the contractual agreement between two business partners. Covenantal love pledges our all. It is grandly inclusive of all we are and have. A business contract, on the other hand, is all about limiting obligation and liability. It is guarded and calculated. Doctrinal affirmations are more like a covenant than a contract. Knowing the love that surpasses knowledge means that there is always more to our relationship with God than we can possibly express, but never less than the truth clearly revealed in the Bible. Sometimes teachers frustrate thoughtful students by demanding rote memorization in order to pass their tests. But pity the husband or wife who cannot bring themselves to say, "I love you."

Paul's prayer for believers to "be filled to the measure of all the fullness of God" is a final way that he connected his theology of worship, salvation, and missions with practical Christian living. Paul was anything but conservative when he contemplated the believer's utmost for God's highest! No prayer request could ever be bolder. But this is consistent with what Paul has been saying from the beginning of his letter. He began by saying, "Praise be to the God and Father of our Lord Jesus Christ, who has blessed us in the heavenly realms with every spiritual blessing in Christ."[53] It made perfect sense for Paul to expect great things from those who had been chosen, predestined, and redeemed, all in accordance with the riches of God's grace.

The fullness of God is a theme that runs through the letter. Paul ended his eucharistic prayer by referring to the church, "which is [Christ's] body, the fullness of him who fills everything in every way."[54] He spoke of the body of Christ "attaining to the whole measure of the fullness of

---

52. Eph 1:4–8.
53. Eph 1:3.
54. Eph 1:23.

Christ."[55] He challenged believers to "be filled with the Spirit."[56] There is an obvious tension here between what the church is in principle and what she is in actual practice. The gap between expectation and realization can be explained, at least in part, in the tension between the "already" and the "not yet." We will not have realized our goal for being the people of God until Christ returns. Nevertheless, Paul expected believers to live up to their God-given potential and to realize the fullness of God in ever increasing ways. The rest of the letter will help to explain and visualize what the fullness of God looks like in practical day-to-day living.

If the church is going to make known "the manifold wisdom of God" to the rulers and authorities in the heavenly realms, it has to have a real experience of the love and power of God. Paul had no concept of the church as a beleaguered and fearful minority fighting for its life. He saw the church, which the world saw as nothing, as the concrete expression of the love and power of God in the world. Reflecting on the truth that Jesus Christ will come again to rule and reign, Karl Barth commented on how Christians ought to speak to non-Christians:

> We must not sit among them like melancholy owls, but in a certainty about our goal, which surpasses all other certainty. Yet how often we stand ashamed beside the children of the world, and how we must understand them if our message will not satisfy them. He who knows that "my times are in your hands" (Psalm 31:15) will not haughtily regard the [people] of the world, who, in a definite hope that often shames us, go their way; but he will understand them better than they understand themselves. He will see their hope as a parable, a sign that the world is not abandoned, but has a beginning and a goal. We Christians have to put the right Alpha and Omega into the heart of this secular thought and hope. But we can only do so if we surpass the world in confidence.[57]

The apostle Paul exudes confidence in God, and so should we, but not in any worldly way or by some secular means or in a proud spirit of triumphalism. Make no mistake, the mission of the church, in so far as it is the mission of the crucified and risen Lord, will be accomplished, only through the power of the cross. Doxology completely overshadowed any lament that Paul might have felt over his circumstances.

55. Eph 4:13.
56. Eph 5:18.
57. Barth, *Dogmatics in Outline*, 132.

Now to him who is able to do immeasurably more than all we
ask or imagine, according to his power that is at work within us,
to him be the glory in the church and in Christ Jesus throughout
all generations, for ever and ever! Amen.[58]

58. Eph 3:20–21.

10

Resilient Saints

Faithfulness to the end subscribes to humility and hope. The long obedience to the end aspires for the Lord's commendation, "Well done good and faithful servant, enter into the joy of your reward." Self-betrayal is the danger to be resisted and littleness of soul the enemy. Each of us has our own passion narrative to endure for Christ and his kingdom.

SHORTLY AFTER GRADUATION FROM Ontario Theological Seminary in Toronto, Hernando Hernandez and Laura Binkley were killed. Laura was stabbed to death in her Russian apartment. She was serving in an orphanage in Moscow and the police suspected that one of her assailants was a girl she had befriended and with whom she had shared Christ. Hernando was coming home from a student conference in Colombia with a car load of young Christian leaders. Their car was struck on a narrow mountain road by a speeding bus and sent careening over a cliff into a deep ravine. Everybody in the car was killed. Both Hernando and Laura came from solid, supportive Christ-centered families that had offered them up to the Lord. It was a crushing blow. They were two of the seminary's best students, marked by selfless love and kingdom focus. No sooner had they graduated than they were gone.

Laura was a home-grown Canadian. Hernando was a Latin American Colombian. They both had a profound impact on me. I was a young seminary teacher, fresh out of the school, and they were my teaching assistants in Theology 101. Their passion for Christ, coupled with their compassion for the poor and their global sensitivity, raised the excitement level exponentially in our introductory theology class. Their tutorials went way beyond processing information. Laura embraced theology with tears of compassion for the lost and needy. Hernando, dressed in green fatigues and a black t-shirt, was a bold, fiery, yet friendly prophet. He was determined to unsettle our bland complacency and focus our attention on Christ's social justice. Hernando accomplished this the Jesus way—with humility.

These two young disciples taught me that there are no heroes, only saints who have gone before. Sometimes our time is short, and without much notice we join that "great cloud of witnesses" who have run the race with their eyes fixed on Jesus, the pioneer and perfecter of faith. The emphasis in Hebrews 11 is on momentum, not memorials; faithfulness, not heroics. The race continues. The saints cheer us on. What is important is that we remain faithful to the end.

No Heroes

Faithfulness to the end runs contrary to cultural expectations. No memorials. No shrines. No heroes. No celebrities. As it was with Abel so may it be with us. The testimony of God's first sacrificial lamb runs true. "By faith Abel still speaks, even though he is dead."[1] The biblical call narratives are not matched by exit interviews and the discipline of surrender continues unabated to the end.

Have you noticed that the Bible does not enshrine the saints who have gone before? There is a difference between idolizing and remembering. Abraham lived 175 years before he was "gathered to his people." His effort to buy a burial plot from the Hittites near Mamre in order to bury his wife Sarah receives detailed attention. Nomadic wanderers like Abraham who were "looking forward to the city with foundations, whose architect and builder is God," had to make special arrangements to bury their dead.[2] Abraham died "at a good old age" and Isaac buried him next to Sarah, but I doubt that there was much of a eulogy that day, at least not a eulogy commensurate with his stature in salvation history. Did Isaac recall that defining moment when by faith his father Abraham offered him up as a sacrifice? That moment of faithfulness became a movement of divine promise, because "Abraham reasoned that God could even raise the dead, and so in a manner of speaking he did receive Isaac back from death."[3]

1. Heb 11:4.
2. Gen 23; Heb 11:10.
3. Heb 11:19.

The author of Hebrews celebrated Isaac, Jacob, and Joseph's faithfulness to the end by highlighting their last act of faithfulness. Our attention is focused on their faith and trust in Yahweh's promise right up to the end. Jacob, "when he was dying, blessed each of Joseph's sons, and worshiped as he leaned on the top of his staff."[4] By faith, Joseph spoke about the exodus. Their "death-bed" faithfulness pointed forward, because they were "longing for a better country—a heavenly one."[5]

If anyone qualified for hero status, it was Moses, but Moses died unheroically and in one sense prematurely.[6] He was buried by God in an unmarked grave in Moab outside of the Promised Land. God made sure that there was no possibility of erecting a shrine or creating a memorial. Even though Moses was faithful to the end, preaching God's Word, warning the people of their sinful propensity to rebellion and disobedience, and establishing Joshua's leadership, God held Moses accountable for his willful act of disobedience. Obedience was never optional and Yahweh's verdict was certain, "because you broke faith with me in the presence of the Israelites . . . and because you did not uphold my holiness among the Israelites . . . you will see the land only from a distance; you will not enter the land I am giving to the people of Israel."[7] If God treated Moses as a servant whose work was done, what business do we have setting up leaders on pedestals, lionizing their achievements and building memorials to them? What is it about human nature that worships the leader, but ignores the Lord? Have you ever wondered why God didn't allow Israel to conduct a memorial service for Moses?

The prophets ended their ministries in silence. Hardly a word is spoken of their deaths. Elijah was taken up to heaven in a tornado and Elisha "died and was buried."[8] Samuel's story is eclipsed by David's story. We are not even told of the prophets, as we are with the patriarchs, that they were "gathered to their people." Isaiah passes from the scene without a trace. Jeremiah's forty-year career ends without notice. The closest we come to Jeremiah's last will and testament are his words to Baruch, his administrative assistant, "Should you seek great things for yourself? Seek them not!"[9] The prophets are empowered by God's Word and personally expendable.

4. Heb 11:21.
5. Heb 11:16.
6. Deut 34:7.
7. Deut 32:51–52.
8. 2 Kgs 13:20.
9. Jer 45:5.

They come and go quietly without fanfare and a praise band. Their lives are engulfed by the picture of salvation. That's all they can think about and that's all God wanted us to think about. Since God saw fit to reveal his Word without artistic sketches of the prophets and the apostles we have no idea what these key figures in salvation history even looked like. No tombs to visit. No pictures to honor. The Bible's absolute indifference to images and appearance curbs our appetite for hero worship and starves our bent toward personality cults and idolatry.

After Daniel had completed his ministry and proclaimed his God-revealing word, the Lord told him, "Go your way. . . As for you, go your way till the end. You will rest, and then at the end of the days you will rise to receive your allotted inheritance."[10] As if to say, "Daniel, your work is finished, get on with life and death, and in the end you will have your inheritance." The big climax is not about us, but about the Lord God. Life is not about what we have done, but what God is doing. Our ministry comes to an end, and by divine design, only modest attention is drawn to that end. The penultimate end in our faithfulness to the end is always overshadowed by the ultimate end. Until then we wait. We wait for the Lord's coming.

Prayer is one of the better ways to end a ministry. Nehemiah's closing prayer exemplifies how we should think about life and ministry. His prayed out refrain "Remember me" is pivotal. He didn't ask to be remembered as a great leader of Israel or as a strategic risk-taker in salvation history. He was not a hero in his own eyes, but a humble servant who tried to do what the Lord wanted him to do. His prayer recalled the nagging issues of disobedience afflicting the people of God—Sabbath desecration, sexual defilement, and priestly perversion. Nehemiah made himself unpopular among some by attempting to tackle these thorny issues, but that didn't matter. He wasn't out to win the people's approval. His theology of ministry was shaped by the Word of God.

Nehemiah's prayer sounds more like the prayer of the repentant tax collector in Jesus' parable than the prayer of the Pharisee. The accent falls on humility in his three-fold refrain "Remember me."

> Remember me for this, my God, and do not blot out what I have
> so faithfully done for the house of my God and its service . . .
> Remember me for this also, my God, and show mercy to me

10. Dan 12:9, 13.

according to your great love . . .Remember me with favor, my God.[11]

The Bible's intentional avoidance of dramatizing the death of the Old Testament patriarchs and prophets continues in the New Testament. John the Baptist was murdered. James, the brother of Jesus and leader of the Jerusalem church, was executed. Stephen was stoned, but beyond that nothing is said in the Bible about the death of Christ's apostles. They pass from the scene like the tide swept out to sea by a new wave of believers. The absence of biographical detail that we moderns crave is remarkable. We are compelled to see that the real story is not in their deaths, but in God's mission. Nothing dies with their passing. Each played a crucial role in proclaiming the gospel but, having completed their assignment, they move on without shrines and memorials. Apparently, funerals were not a big deal on God's agenda.

When I was in my forties two close friends died. Steve Befus, whom I spoke of earlier, died after a twenty-year calling in medical missions in Liberia. And Dan Lam, a businessman, was killed after decades of sacrificial service on behalf of unreached people groups. Dan's passion was for nationals to reach nationals. He set up disciple-making training centers in Mongolia, Cambodia, Myanmar, and Vietnam. His death in a plane crash in Siberia was a blow to thousands of Christians of all nationalities. At his memorial service I read Jesus' words, "Very truly I tell you, unless a kernel of wheat falls to the ground and dies, it remains only a single seed. But if it dies, it produces many seeds. Those who love their life will lose it, while those who hate their life in this world will keep it for eternal life. Whoever serves me must follow me; and where I am, my servant also will be. My Father will honor the one who serves me."[12] At the time, I reflected on the image of organic growth and Christ's kingdom work. We celebrated the impact of Dan's witness on believers around the world.

But now in retrospect I think about that last line, "My Father will honor the one who serves me." How did God honor his servant Dan Lam? Certainly not with fame and a long life on earth, but with God's friendship and eternal life. Perhaps the key to understanding how the Father honors Dan and all the saints who have gone before is in the previous sentence: "And where I am, my servant also will be." As the apostle said, "to be absent from the body is to be present to the Lord."[13] In the end, it

11. Neh 13:14, 22, 31.
12. John 12:24–26.
13. 2 Cor 5:8.

matters little whether we pass from this earthly scene quietly or violently, quickly or slowly, if we can say with Paul, "For me to live is Christ and to die is gain."[14] And in the end, it is not about what we have done, but what God is doing.

"For all the saints who from their labors rest," to borrow a phrase from a great hymn, teaches us that the *experience* of loss is not our defining moment. What is crucial is how we *respond* to loss. Jerry Sittser in his wonderful book, *A Grace Disguised*, writes, "Loss requires that we live in *a delicate tension*."[15] Sittser articulates this profound tension for those who have not only suffered loss but experienced the grace of Christ:

> Never have I felt so broken; yet never have I been so whole. Never have I been so aware of my weakness and vulnerability; yet never have I been so content and felt so strong. Never has my soul been more dead; yet never has my soul been more alive. What I once considered mutually exclusive—sorrow and joy, pain and pleasure, grief and gratitude—have become parts of a greater whole. My soul has been stretched. Above all, I have become aware of the power of God's grace and my need for it.[16]

There are no heroes, only the saints who have gone before. In the Book of Revelation the saints who have died are eager for the consummation of the end of the age. They are pictured in blood-cleansed white robes praising God. They are waiting for us, praying for us, and calling out in a loud voice, "How long, Sovereign Lord, holy and true, until you judge the inhabitants of the earth and avenge our blood?"[17] In the Book of Hebrews they surround us like a great cloud of witnesses or like a stadium of fans cheering us on, giving us home-field advantage. Their lives inspire us to "throw off everything that hinders and the sin that so easily entangles," so that we "run with perseverance the race marked out for us, fixing our eyes on Jesus . . ."[18]

14. Phil 1:21.
15. Sittser, *A Grace Disguised*, 41 (emphasis his).
16. Ibid., 179–80.
17. Rev 6:10.
18. Heb 12:1–2.

Faithfulness to the End

The author of Hebrews weans us away from our preoccupation with the start of the Christian life and focuses our attention on the perseverance of faith. Life is not a sprint but a marathon. It's not over until it's over. Faithfulness to the end affirms our faith from the beginning. And the end in faithfulness to the end may be a long way off, but it is the only end worth pursuing. "Today we emphasize the New Birth," writes Peter Gillquist, while "the ancients emphasized being faithful to the end. We moderns talk of wholeness and purposeful living; they spoke of the glories of the eternal kingdom . . . the emphasis in our attention has shifted from the completing of the Christian life to the beginning of it."[19]

Three stories put faithfulness-to-the-end in perspective for me: a wedding, a graduation, and a farewell. Several years ago I was asked by Elizabeth Befus, Steve and Sue's oldest daughter, to officiate at her wedding to Billy Byerly. Twenty-five years earlier I was Steve's best man in his wedding to Sue. These two Befus weddings bookended more than two decades of ministry. In my twenties I remember thinking that people in their forties and fifties had it all together. But what impressed me as I stood before Elizabeth and Billy on their wedding day to give the meditation and lead them in their marriage vows was that I was in many respects the very same person that I was in my twenties. Hopefully a little more experienced and mature, but essentially the same person. We never outgrow our need to trust and grow in the grace and knowledge of the Lord Jesus Christ. We may expect life to get easier and more put-together, but it doesn't. Our life and testimony in our twenties are just as important to God as they are in our fifties. My ministry did not get more or less valuable as I grew older.

When the Psalmist says, "Teach us to number our days so we may gain a heart of wisdom," we know two things: our days are valuable and our time is limited.[20] Our worth is not measured by what we achieve, but by what we receive in Christ. Our joy is measured by how faithful and obedient we have been to what we have received. We were never meant to become less dependent upon the Lord; only more dependent. "As for mortals, their days are like grass, they flourish like a flower of the field; the wind blows over it and it is gone, and its place remembers it no more."[21] Life is short and often hard. The goal is being faithful, not making a name

19. Gillquist, "A Marathon We Are Meant to Win," 22.

20. Ps 90:12.

21. Ps 103:15.

for ourselves or building a reputation. We identify with Paul: "I haven't arrived, but I press on to take hold of that for which Christ Jesus took hold of me."[22]

The second story that puts faithfulness-to-the-end in perspective involves my good friend David Mensah, who is still alive and continuing to run the marathon of faith. In 2006 David spoke at the graduation service of the Tamale Baptist College in northern Ghana. His text was Hebrews 12 and his wife Brenda reminded me that I spoke from that same text at David's graduation from Ontario Bible College in 1981. The time lag between graduation services was twenty-five years. Brenda said that as the first student in his cap and gown passed across the stage for his diploma, she recalled David being in that same place twenty-five years ago. Then she started to think about all that she and David had witnessed God do, just in their little corner of the globe where the Lord had placed them. She reflected on how meaningful their lives have been because the Lord had kept them in His race. Memory after memory flooded back and she just couldn't stop weeping. Brenda said, "I wondered what it would be like to meet with all the graduates who had walked across that stage twenty-five years ago and to hear their stories of God's grace over the years. And then I wondered what great plans God has for these young pastors that are running up behind us to take the baton."

Twenty-five years ago, at David's graduation, I illustrated the metaphor of the race by comparing two runners. In the movie *Chariots of Fire*, which was popular at the time, Eric Liddell expressed his reason for entering the 1924 Olympics with the famous line, "God made me fast, and when I run I feel his favor." The movie captured that moment of exhilaration when Liddell crossed the finish line winning gold. He had committed several years of his life to preparing for the Paris games. All of his time and energy were poured into running the Olympic race and when he won, the race was over. Eric Liddell knew what he had to do, and he did it. He achieved his goal. In life we long for that moment of exhilarating release when we have accomplished the long sought-after goal—when we can finally say it is finished. But Christ's followers face the challenge of a long obedience in the same direction, not a 400-meter race. Discipleship requires more than a quick burst of spiritual energy for a few years. The race God has called us to is not a sprint but a marathon.

The second image that I used to illustrate the metaphor of the race came closer to capturing the essence of the Christian race. Terry Fox died

---

22. Phil 3:12.

from cancer in 1981, but not before inspiring a nation with his personal courage. Setting out to jog across Canada on an artificial limb, he became a symbol of hope and perseverance. His quest came to be called the Marathon of Hope. His trek across Canada received nightly news coverage and he captured the attention of the nation. Terry Fox succeeded in raising millions of dollars for cancer research but even more importantly, and impossible to measure, was the impact of his courage and determination on millions of Canadians. Terry Fox's marathon was not over until his life was over. This is how it is for those who "run with perseverance the race marked out for us, fixing our eyes on Jesus . . ."[23]

Although Terry Fox's Marathon of Hope may be a better analogy of the Christian life than Eric Liddell's 400-meter Olympic race, Liddell's life proved to be an outstanding example of spiritual stamina and Christ-centered endurance. He obeyed the call of God to go to China as a missionary where he served until his death. His life did not peak at the 1924 Olympics. He saw Jesus leading him to China for a life of service and hardship far more demanding than the Olympics. Eric Liddell put behind him the events that made him famous, and ran the marathon of faith with his eyes fixed on Jesus. A friend of mine, David Michell (former Canadian director of Overseas Missionary Fellowship), remembered Eric Liddell from his experience as a young boy when he, along with 174 other children of missionary parents, were imprisoned in a Japanese Internment Camp in China during WWII. Eric Liddell was a prisoner at the same camp and became known for his Christ-like presence and his selfless devotion to helping the children in the camp. Liddell died of a brain tumor three days before the Allies arrived, but right up to the end, Liddell's reputation as a follower of Jesus was evident to all.

The third story that puts faithfulness-to-the-end in perspective for me comes out of this same Hebrews 12 text. For several years I was under considerable pressure. We had three small children and I was teaching full-time in a seminary and serving as a pastor in a small urban church, just east of the Beaches, in Toronto. After eleven years of studying, teaching, and pastoring in Canada we were led by the Lord to accept an invitation to pastor a church in the United States. The leaders in the Toronto church scheduled a weekend retreat as a special time for us to say goodbye and pass the leadership baton to a new pastor. Hebrews 12 was the key text for the retreat and the whole church participated. It was a great time for

23. Heb 12:1–2.

the church family to worship together. We rededicated ourselves to Christ and his ministry.

I remember longing for that moment when I would be released from the burden of pastoral ministry and full-time teaching. Those who knew me well agreed that I had carried a heavy load for a long time. I was spent. I had hit the wall. I felt like I had worked flat out for several years and I was eager for that moment when my ministry would be officially done. I had the finish line in view and I was ready to break the tape. Then something happened in that final farewell meeting that I had not anticipated. It hit me hard. I desperately wanted closure, a palpable sense of finish-line exhilaration, but what I got was anything but. Instead of "Well done, good and faithful servant," I sensed in my soul God saying, "You have only just begun. Get going." I can't explain how or why I felt this way. It was like I had sprinted a 50-yard dash only to be told that I was running a 26-mile marathon. I broke down and started to cry. Normally I'm not a very emotional person. I'm sure everyone thought I was upset because I was leaving them and that I was going to miss them (and I did). But what I found overwhelming was the burden of the work ahead. In that awe-ful moment, the Lord impressed upon me that I was not anywhere near the finish line. The Lord was saying to me what he said to Jeremiah, "If you have raced with people on foot and they have worn you out, how can you compete with horses? If you stumble in safe country, how will you manage in the thickets by the Jordan?"[24]

One of Jesus' parables comes to mind. His no-big-deal-work-ethic parable offsets any pity party we are inclined to throw.[25] Disciples who respond to the call of God—the call to salvation, service, and sacrifice— do not put God in their debt. Disciples are not accruing credit through their faithful service, they're simply doing what is expected of them—what God's grace has equipped and empowered them to do. Jesus told the story this way: "Suppose one of you has a servant plowing or looking after his sheep. Will he say to the servant when he comes in from the field, 'Come along now and sit down to eat'? Won't he rather say, 'Prepare my supper, get yourself ready and wait on me while I eat and drink; after that you may eat and drink'? Will he thank the servant because he did what he was told to do? So you also, when you have done everything you were told to do, should say, 'We are unworthy servants; we have only done our duty.'"

24. Jer 12:5.
25. Luke 17:7–10.

There is a positive tension between being the adopted children of God—chosen in Christ before the creation of the world, and being "servants" who respond to the call of duty without questioning and complaining. This parable takes nothing away from friendship with Jesus. As he said to his disciples then, he says to his disciples today: "I no longer call you servants, because servants do not know their master's business. Instead, I have called you friends, for everything that I learned from my Father I have made known to you. You did not choose me, but I chose you and appointed you so that you might go and bear fruit—fruit that will last."[26] Neither does this parable take away from the reward Jesus promises for faithful service, but it does underscore what the disciple's attitude should be.[27] Jesus is our friend and brother, but he is also our Lord, and we were meant to shoulder the burden of ministry without making a big deal of it. The apostle Paul spoke not only of himself but for all of us who follow the Lord Jesus when he said,

> We proclaim him, admonishing and teaching everyone with all wisdom, so that we may present everyone fully mature in Christ. To this end I strenuously contend with all the energy Christ so powerfully works in me.[28]

Self-Betrayal

One of the greatest preachers in the early church, John Chrysostom, provides a powerful example of how to end our earthly ministry, no matter what our gift and responsibility may be. He died in 407, but not before leaving a compelling testimony of faithfulness to the end. His letters and treatises from exile are strong, uncompromising epistles, written by a resilient saint, who steeled himself against the world, the flesh, and the devil. John's controlling thought was simple: nothing can destroy you but yourself. Your own worst enemy is not the devil or disease, but your sinful self. Your greatest danger is self-betrayal. Your greatest weakness, littleness of soul.

John's counter-cultural prophetic message and his passion for Christ worked well in Antioch—a pagan, pluralistic city. But his reputation for outstanding preaching got him into trouble. In 397, he was literally

26. John 15:15–16.
27. See Luke 12:35–38.
28. Col 1:28–29.

kidnapped by armed guards, escorted 800 miles to Constantinople and forcibly consecrated as archbishop. The emperor's chief advisor Eutropias thought the church in the capital city ought to have the best orator in Christianity.[29] John accepted this twist of political fate as the providence of God. He believed he was being called to deliver his message of renewal and reform at the very center of religious and secular power. But if anyone thought that success and privilege would mellow John, they were wrong. In spite of the pressure to become a political super-pastor, John dug in his heels and drove his message home against money, sex, and power. He preached and lived like a prophet. He had a passion for the poor and he made it a habit of offending ecclesiastical dignitaries. He made sure funds given for the poor got to the poor. He set up a leper colony next door to an upscale neighborhood. He preached against the high and mighty, and in due course they determined to bring him down. No matter how good the preaching may be, implying that the emperor's wife was a "Jezebel" jeopardizes the preacher. John preached with passion, exposed corruption, and made enemies. By 404, John was driven into exile and by 407 he was dead.[30]

John was arrested and deported, exiled to Cucusos, a remote mountainous town in Armenia. In fragile health, he suffered a seventy-day journey lying on a litter pulled by a mule. The trip nearly killed him. Destitute and abandoned, he suffered loneliness and inactivity. Everything had been taken from him— health, church, friends, ministry, and preaching. Everything, but the one thing— the truth that this exhausted fifty-six-year-old prophet pastor never tired of repeating either in lecture or by letter—his devotion to Christ. "Have you been carried into exile?" John asks. If you are wise, he insists, "you will regard the whole world as a strange country."[31] No one in Christ is at home in this world. We are all sojourners.[32]

Faced with every reason to quit and with every excuse to become bitter, John contended that "no one who is wronged is wronged by another, but experiences this injury at his or her own hands."[33] Nothing can ruin our virtue or destroy our soul, that is not self-inflicted. John argued that poverty cannot impoverish the soul. Malignancy cannot malign the char-

29. Krupp, "Golden Tongue & Iron Will," 8.

30. Brown, *The Body and Society*, 317–18.

31. Chrysostom, "To Prove That No One Can Harm The Man Who Does Not Injure Himself," 274.

32. Ps 119:19.

33. Chrysostom, "To Prove," 272.

acter. The lack of health care cannot destroy a healthy soul. Famine cannot famish one who hungers and thirsts for righteousness. No! Not even the devil and death can destroy those who live sober and vigilant lives. The devil robbed Job of everything but could not rob Job of his virtue. Cain took Abel's life, but could not take away his greater gain. Only those who injure themselves are injured. "Don't confuse the argument," John insists, "I did not say that no one injures, but that no one is injured."[34]

The truth of John's argument can be found everywhere in the Bible. He cites Joseph in Egypt, John the Baptist before Herod, and Shadrach, Meschach, and Abednego in Nebuchadnezzar's fiery furnace. He celebrates Paul's many trials and afflictions. His bottom line is clear: none are harmed; all are honored. In the parable of the rich man and Lazarus, John elaborates on the liability of luxury and the blessing of lowliness. It is the rich man that is impoverished and Lazarus who is rich in eternal reward. John delights in the broad sweep of "that wonderful history of the Holy Scriptures, as in some lofty, large, and broad picture . . . from Adam to the coming of Christ," all of which makes his case:

> No one will be able to injure one who is not injured by himself, even if all the world were to kindle a fierce war against him. For it is not stress . . . nor circumstances . . . nor insults . . . nor intrigues . . . nor catastrophes . . . nor any number of ills to which humankind is subject, which can disturb even slightly the person who is brave, and disciplined, and watchful.[35]

Educator Parker Palmer offers a similar insight when he writes, "No punishment anyone lays on you could possibly be worse than the punishment you lay on yourself by conspiring in your own diminishment."[36] Theologian Jerry Sittser describes the challenge we face this way:

> The difference between despair and hope, bitterness and forgiveness, hatred and love, and stagnation and vitality lies in the decisions we make about what to do in the face of regrets over an unchanging and painful past. We cannot change the situation, but we can allow the situation to change us. We exacerbate our suffering needlessly when we allow one loss to lead to another. That causes gradual destruction of the soul. . . . The death that comes through loss of spouse, children, parents, health, job, marriage, childhood, or any other kind is not the worst kind of

34. Ibid., 273.
35. Ibid., 279.
36. Palmer, *The Courage to Teach*, 171.

death there is. Worse still is the death of the spirit, the death that comes through guilt, regret, bitterness, hatred, immorality, and despair. The first kind of death happens to us; the second kind of death happens in us. It is a death we bring upon ourselves if we refuse to be transformed by the first death.[37]

Self-betrayal is the danger, littleness of soul the problem. "Those who do not injure themselves become stronger," wrote John, "even if they receive innumerable blows; but they who betray themselves, even if there is no one to harass them, fall of themselves, and collapse and perish."[38] The best preachers are those who preach first to themselves and then to others. The herald hears the Word in the soul before it is spoken in the sanctuary. This was true of John. His "prison epistles" are free from lament and bitterness. He modeled the spiritual direction he sought to give.

John's own life was the unspoken metaphor behind the message. He was the hidden parable in the proclamation. The messenger and the message were one. He was the illustration illuminating the text. This is the John I want to walk beside and draw strength from. I need to learn from him how to live and how to die. The end in faithfulness to the end may be a long way off, but it is the only end worth pursuing. I agree with my brother, Saint John, the golden mouth and stalwart contender for the faith, when he writes,

> Let us then, I encourage you, be sober and vigilant at all times, and let us endure all painful things bravely that we may obtain those everlasting and pure blessings in Christ Jesus our Lord, to whom be glory and power, now and ever throughout all ages. Amen.[39]

The Long Obedience

One of the severest shocks to hit David Livingstone, the renown nineteenth-century missionary to Africa, was when the London Missionary Society withdrew their support for his missionary activity. They determined that his geographical exploration, which Livingstone saw as the necessary first step in the missionary effort, was only remotely connected to the spread of the gospel. Besides, they stated, "your reports make it

---

37. Sittser, *A Grace Disguised*, 86–87.
38. Chrysostom, "To Prove," 280.
39. Ibid., 284.

sufficiently obvious that the nature of the country, the unhealthfulness of the climate, the prevalence of poisonous insects, and other adverse influences, constitute a serious array of obstacles to missionary effort, and even were there a reasonable prospect of their being surmounted—and we by no means assume they are insurmountable—yet, in that event, the financial circumstances of the Society are not such as to afford any ground of hope that it would be in a position, within any definite period, to enter upon untried, remote, and difficult fields of labor."[40]

Livingstone responded respectfully. He acknowledged the practical rationale of the directors of the London Missionary Society and the purity of their motives, but he reaffirmed his resolve to focus on *the untried, remote and difficult fields* to which, he writes, "I humbly yet firmly believe God has directed my steps." His conviction was based on "the simple continuance of an old determination to devote my life and my all to the services of Christ in whatever way He may lead me in Intertropical Africa."[41] As Livingstone explained, his decision to work in Africa was rooted in the will of God and was not dependent on the Society's support and approval. His definition of a missionary may have been out of touch with the London Missionary Society but it impresses us today as faithful to the New Testament vision and in keeping with the best of contemporary mission perspectives. Livingstone wrote,

Nowhere have I appeared as anything else but a servant of God, who has simply followed the leadings of His hand. My views of what is missionary duty are not so contracted as those whose ideal is a dumpy sort of man with a Bible under his arm. I have labored in bricks and mortar, at the forge and carpenter's bench, as well as in preaching and medical practice. I feel that I am 'not my own.' I am serving Christ when shooting a buffalo for my men, or taking an astronomical observation, or writing to one of His children who forget, during the little moment of penning a note, that charity which is eulogized as "thinking no evil"; and after by His help having got information, which I hope will lead to more abundant blessing being bestowed on Africa than heretofore, am I to hide the light under a bushel merely because some will consider it not sufficiently, or even at all, *missionary*? Knowing that some persons do believe that opening up a new country to the sympathies of Christendom was not a proper work for an agent of a Missionary Society to engage in, I now

40. Seaver, *David Livingstone*, 269.
41. Ibid., 270–71.

refrain from taking any salary from the Society with which I
was connected; so no pecuniary [monetary] loss is sustained by
anyone.[42]

   Livingstone's biographer George Seaver argues that if we evaluate
Livingstone's life from a secular perspective we would likely conclude that
he was a failure. "In everything he had failed: he had failed as a husband;
he had failed as a father; he had failed as a missionary; he had failed as a
geographer; he had failed most of all as a liberator." But if we judge his life
by eternal values and the will of God that he so tenaciously sought to follow, Livingstone stands "as one of the moral giants of our race."[43] Like the
resilient saints described in Hebrews 11, he was one for whom the world
was not worthy. He was commended for his faith, but he did not receive
in this life what he had been promised, for God has planned something
better for him.[44]

   Dietrich Bonhoeffer agonized over his decision to return to Germany
in 1939. He had been invited to the United States to teach and preach, just
as the church struggle was intensifying in Germany. Martin Niemoller,
a leading pastor in the Confessing Church movement, had already been
sent to a concentration camp. German Christians were being manipulated
to support Hitler's racial policy of maintaining the purity of the Aryan
nation. Aboard the ship on June 8 he wrote in his journal, "We ought to be
found only where God is. We can no longer, in fact, be anywhere else than
where God is. He takes us with him. Or have I after all, avoided the place
where he is?"[45] By the time Bonhoeffer's ship docked in New York City he
was in agony over his decision to come in the first place. The Americans
treated him with generosity and affection, but he was not at peace. Theologian Paul Lehmann begged him to stay, citing the powerful influence he
would have on theology in America, not to mention the loss he would feel
personally if Bonhoeffer returned too quickly to Germany. But Bonhoeffer
within weeks made up his mind that he must return to Germany. He wrote
to Reinhold Niebuhr:

> I have made a mistake in coming to America. I must live through
> this difficult period of our national history with the Christian
> people of Germany. I will have no right to participate in the re-
> construction of Christian life in Germany after the war if I do

42. Ibid., 285.
43. Ibid., 629–31.
44. Heb 11:38–40.
45. Bethge, *Dietrich Bonhoeffer*, 650.

> not share the trials of this time with my people. . . . Christians in Germany will face the terrible alternative of either willing the defeat of their nation in order that Christian civilization may survive, or willing the victory of their nation and thereby destroying our civilization. I know which of these alternatives I must choose; but I cannot make the choice in security.[46]

Paul's Passion Narrative and Ours

In the final chapters of the book of Acts, Paul is brought to trial because of his faith in Jesus Christ.[47] Luke's account is similar to the passion narratives in the gospels. As the religious and secular authorities converge against him, Paul, like the Lord Jesus, is under attack on all sides. The Jews and the Romans, and the even the forces of nature, are arrayed against him. He is charged with heresy and treason as he goes from one trial to another, until he ends up under house arrest in Rome awaiting his final trial. Luke's chronicle of Paul's final chapter parallels not only Jesus' passion narrative but ours. Life is filled with trials and storms, injustices and shipwrecks, and we need an example to follow. We find it in Paul, not as a hero, but as a fellow traveler "pressing on to take hold of that for which Christ Jesus took hold [of us]."[48]

Paul's passion narrative promises to shape our expectations of the life of discipleship, instruct us in how to defend God's truth, and inspire our courage in the face of opposition. Luke says in effect, "This is how you pull off a long obedience in the same direction. This is how you do faithfulness to the end." Through sacrifice, sensitivity, and courage, Paul transformed the trials of life into the trials of faith for the sake of the gospel.

The trials of life are not necessarily the trials of faith. Many of our trials are brought on because of our sin and disobedience. We are placed on the defensive because of something we did wrong, but Paul was placed on the defensive because of something he did right. The trials he faced were brought on because of his obedience to the Spirit of Christ. He was *falsely* accused of heresy and treason. Luke's theme was not that life is full of trials, "woe is me," but that life is full of costly opportunities to represent Christ, and "Do I have the courage to stand up for Christ?"

---

46. Ibid., 655.
47. See Acts 23:11.
48. Phil 3:12.

Paul might have easily avoided these trials by refusing to go to Jerusalem, but he chose to take them on because he was convinced of the will of God. From his perspective these trials were unavoidable, as he said to the elders of Ephesus,

> And now, compelled by the Spirit, I am going to Jerusalem, not knowing what will happen to me there. I only know that in every city the Holy Spirit warns me that prison and hardships are facing me. However, I consider my life worth nothing to me, if only I may finish the race and complete the task the Lord Jesus has given me—the task of testifying to the gospel of God's grace.[49]

We have the freedom to pursue God's call with boldness, in spite of how it may look to others. When we try to become all things to all people for the sake of the gospel, we should be prepared for criticism from not only those we seek to lead to Christ, but even from our fellow Christians. I imagine some of the believers who tried to persuade Paul from going to Jerusalem were tempted to say, "We told you this would happen!" or "You are such a strong-willed, stubborn person that you bring these trials and problems on yourself." Famed Bible expositor and former pastor of Tenth Presbyterian Church of Philadelphia, Donald Barnhouse, wrote in his commentary on this passage that Paul was insistent on asserting his own willful plan. "It's sad that [Paul] could be such an ardent, devoted follower of the Lord Jesus Christ, but then would go off on a tangent of his own stubbornness."[50]

Barnhouse calls Paul, "an opinionated, stubborn man, determined to have his own way" and claims this is one of the saddest sections in the Bible.[51] For Barnhouse, Paul lost his spiritual discernment and compromised the faith. "How horrible that the apostle Paul should have come to this!"[52] But what Barnhouse saw as stubbornness, Luke saw as humility; what Barnhouse saw as obstinacy, Luke saw as graciousness. If you are going to reach out to people for the cause of Christ and become all things to all people so that by all possible means you might win some, you have to be prepared for well-intentioned Christians who will misread your intentions and judge your actions.

Twenty-five years or so after the first Pentecost, Paul arrived in Jerusalem to begin his own passion narrative. But there was no fresh

49. Acts 20:22–24.
50. Barnhouse, *Acts*, 189.
51. Ibid., 190.
52. Ibid., 193–94.

outpouring of the Holy Spirit. There was no sound of a rushing wind or tongues of fire or declarations of praise to God in a multitude of languages. On this Pentecost, the Spirit was manifest in the courage of a single dissident, who insisted on delivering his message to the crowd. The Roman commander thought Paul was an Egyptian terrorist, but when Paul spoke in Greek and assured him that he was a Jew and a citizen of Tarsus in Cilicia, the commander allowed him to speak to the crowd in Aramaic. As far as we know, no one spoke in tongues that day, but the Holy Spirit spoke through Paul in the vernacular of the people. Nor did thousands place their faith in Christ that day and join the church, but Christ was honored by Paul's defense of the gospel. When Paul had finished telling the story of his conversion and explaining his call to proclaim Christ to the Gentiles, the crowd shouted, "Rid the earth of him! He's not fit to live!"[53]

The next night, Paul was reminded of the continuing work of the Lord Jesus through him. He was neither alone nor fighting for himself, but the Lord was with him and for him all the way. After two days of life-threatening violence and brave-hearted witness, Paul might have wondered how he would ever get out of Jerusalem alive. In the night, "the Lord stood near Paul and said, 'Take courage! As you have testified about me in Jerusalem, so you must also testify in Rome.'"[54] The challenge to rise up and be courageous came with the assurance that Paul would make it to Rome safely for the sake of the gospel. To turn life trials into faith trials we need what Paul had, a personal story of salvation, a compassion for the lost, a conviction of the soul, and the courage to stand up for Christ.

The Storms of Life

Paul's journey to Rome serves as a case study in how the followers of Christ can persevere. Epic sea journeys and stories of shipwrecks were common in Luke's day. Homer's *Odyssey*, the heroic tale of Odysseus' quest for home, written during the time of the prophet Isaiah, continued to capture the popular imagination in the first century. Homer's epic story used larger-than-life characters against the backdrop of the Mediterranean culture and the mythical world of his own imagination to accentuate the inherent conflicts of life between order and chaos, good and evil, love and hatred, life and death, destiny and decision. Homer's hero Odysseus is portrayed as a strong, independent character who survives by his wits against human

53. Acts 22:22.
54. Acts 23:11.

treachery, the forces of nature, and the fate of the gods. Odysseus is an ancient version of the modern, independent, self-reliant individual who rises to meet life's challenges with heroic effort and good luck. Odysseus in *The Odyssey* is like Tom Hanks in *Castaway*, Brad Pitt in *Troy*, or Mel Gibson in *Braveheart*. In contrast, Luke's report on Paul in Rome reminds us of Joseph in Egypt, Jeremiah in Jerusalem, Daniel in Babylon, and John on the island of Patmos.

Perhaps one of the reasons Luke described the voyage and the ship-wreck in such detail was precisely because he felt Paul provided the perfect example of how to weather the storms of life. In particular, Luke was sensitive to the blessings of life that persisted in the midst of hardships. This is a theme that runs throughout Luke's narrative. It is easy to add up what had gone wrong for Paul. He was nearly killed by a mob, attacked and condemned by the Sanhedrin, targeted in an assassination plot, unjustly imprisoned for two years in Caesarea, forced to appeal to Caesar or face trial in Jerusalem, and subject to a life-threatening sea voyage.[55]

When life is difficult, human nature is inclined to concentrate only on the negative, but Luke, Paul's traveling companion, records not only the difficulties but the blessings. Luke was aware of both sides of the story. Paul and his companions were warmly received by the believers in Jerusalem. Paul's Roman citizenship afforded him significant legal rights and the plot against his life was exposed. Roman soldiers protected his life and permitted him access to his friends. He was able to enjoy the companionship of Aristarchus and Luke. On board ship, Julius, the Roman centurion, might have made Paul's life very difficult, but instead he granted Paul special privileges, including access to friends who cared for his needs. Julius' respect and regard for Paul extended to saving his life.[56] The hardships were great, but so were the blessings. Paul remained unhurt by a poisonous snakebite in Malta and was the beneficiary of Publius' hospitality. Paul was encouraged by believers in Puteoli and met by a delegation of believers from Rome who walked over forty miles to meet him and welcome him to the city. Luke's honesty in reporting the blessings along with the hardships ought to encourage the followers of Christ to keep a balanced perspective in their own lives.[57]

Luke was especially attuned to Paul's role as a servant-leader. Paul fulfilled Jesus' Sermon on the Mount mandate to be "salt and light" in a

55. Acts 21:30; 23:2, 14; 24:27; 25:9; 27:1.

56. Acts 21:17; 22:29; 23:16; 24:23; 27:3.

57. Acts 28:5, 7, 15.

pagan setting. Even though Paul was a prisoner, he emerged as a leader, whose practical knowledge and spirituality was a benefit to everyone on board. Oftentimes, it seems Christians impress the world as eccentric and peculiar, but not Paul. He spoke from personal experience as a veteran sea traveler. On three previous voyages Paul had been shipwrecked. He had even experienced a night and day in the open sea before he was rescued.[58] Paul's confidence was evident, not only in his practical knowledge of the sea and the seasons, but also in his perception of God's guidance.

After days of fighting for their lives against a raging sea, Luke reports, "we finally gave up all hope of being saved." Everyone, that is, but Paul who "stood up before them" with just as much courage and conviction as ever and shouted above the storm, "I urge you to keep up your courage, because not one of you will be lost; only the ship will be destroyed." Paul went on to make it clear that this hope rested not in his personal opinion, but in the very revelation of God. "Last night an angel of the God whose I am and whom I serve stood before me and said, 'Do not be afraid, Paul, you must stand trial before Caesar; and God has graciously given you the lives of all who sail with you.' So keep up your courage, men, for I have faith in God that it will happen just as he told me. Nevertheless, we must run aground on some island."[59] Paul is still turning the trials of life into trials of faith.

After fourteen days of going without food Paul urged them all to eat. He reiterated the incredible promise, "Not one of you will lose a single hair from his head." And then, "he took some bread and gave thanks to God in front of them all. Then he broke it and began to eat." Luke tells us that they were all encouraged and ate some food themselves. Paul was not celebrating the eucharist with these pagan soldiers, sailors and prisoners, but the scene appears to have impressed Luke as reminiscent of the Lord, when he took break and broke it and gave it to the disciples. Can there be a eucharistic feel to a common meal among pagans, when God is thanked and his name is lifted up? In the midst of the storm, Paul broke bread and gave thanks to God and they were all encouraged.

When the ship finally ran aground and began to break up, the soldiers intended to kill the prisoners to prevent them from escaping. But in order to spare Paul's life, Julius kept them from carrying out their planned execution of the prisoners. For the sake of one man, all the prisoners were saved. This too, makes us think of Jesus, who gave his life so that we might

58. 2 Cor 11:25.

59. Acts 27:21–26.

live. The one for the many. After spending the winter in Malta, Julius commandeered another Alexandrian ship and set sail for Rome. When they arrived in Rome, Paul "was allowed to live by himself, with a soldier to guard him."[60]

Paul's shipwreck experience and house arrest in Rome fits with the New Testament pattern. Paul himself said, "We must go through many hardships to enter the kingdom of God."[61] From Rome he wrote, "Now I rejoice in what was suffered for you, and I fill up in my flesh what is still lacking in regard to Christ's afflictions, for the sake of his body, which is the church."[62]

Luke began his Gospel by alluding to Rome. "In those days a decree went out from Caesar Augustus that all the world should be enrolled."[63] And now, sixty-two or so years later, Paul is in Rome, the place where that decree was issued, but under house arrest, chained to a Roman soldier assigned to keep watch over him. Luke's final word in the Book of Acts is "unhindered" (ακωλύτως). Paul is subject to house arrest. He is chained to a Roman soldier and a victim of judicial foot-dragging. He is vulnerable to state-sponsored persecution and opposed by a hard-hearted, stiff-necked Jewish resistance, but none of these count as hindrances! From any worldly point of view these are all hindrances, but to Luke the means of the Spirit are up to the challenge. "Unhindered" is just the right word. This is a powerful, liberating word because it frees us up to rest in the will and work of the Spirit of Christ.

Followers of the Lamb

The apostle John described himself as our "brother and companion in the suffering and kingdom and patient endurance that are ours in Jesus."[64] This is a beautiful description of what brothers and sisters in Christ ought to be for one another. John expressed the bottom line for the followers of the Lamb with such clarity and humility. The simplicity of John's Spirit-inspired spiritual direction is set against the backdrop of evil's overwhelming power and complexity. Our defense is simple and straightforward. How should we live for Christ in an anti-Christ world? John tells us: "This calls

60. Acts 28:16.
61. Acts 14:22.
62. Col 1:24.
63. Luke 2:1.
64. Rev 1:9.

for patient endurance and faithfulness on the part of the saints."[65] John has nothing new to add. We have heard it all before. Keep God's commands and hold fast to the testimony about Jesus. Remain pure and undefiled. Follow the Lamb. Speak the truth.[66] Stay alert. Be ready at a moment's notice. It's what the saints have always done: prayer and obedience, worship and witness, purity and truth-telling. To be faithful requires wisdom and the ability to discern the true nature of evil. Confidence resides not in our own personal stamina or will power, but in God's faithfulness.

We take to heart the voice from heaven, which says, "Come out of her, my people, so that you will not share in her sins."[67] We know the difference between being in the world and of the world. "My prayer," said Jesus, "is not that you take them out of the world but that you protect them from the evil one. They are not of the world, even as I am not of it. Sanctify them by the truth; your word is truth. As you sent me into the world, I have sent them into the world."[68] We are not looking to God to make us successful in the great city, but we are looking to God to make us faithful to the end in the great city. Saints may infiltrate the structures and systems of the great city, but they will never feel at home there. "For here we do not have an enduring city, but we are looking for the city that is to come."[69]

---

65. Rev 13:10; 14:12.
66. Rev 12:17; 14:4–5.
67. Rev 18:4.
68. John 17:15–18.
69. Heb 13:14.

Bibliography

Allen, Roland. *Missionary Methods: St. Paul's Or Ours?* Grand Rapids: Eerdmans, 1962.

Althaus, Paul. *The Theology of Martin Luther*. Translated by Robert C. Shultz. Philadelphia: Fortress, 1966.

Atkins, Anne. *Split Image: Male and Female After God's Likeness*. Grand Rapids: Eerdmans, 1987.

Bailey, Kenneth E. "Women in the New Testament: A Middle Eastern Cultural View," *Theology Matters* (January/February 2000) 1–14.

Barna, George. *Marketing the Church: What They Never Taught You About Church Growth*. Colorado Springs: NavPress, 1988.

———. *User Friendly Churches*. Ventura, CA: Regal, 1991.

Barnes, M. Craig. *Searching for Home: Spirituality for Restless Souls*. Grand Rapids: Brazos, 2003.

Barnhouse, Donald Grey. *Acts*. Grand Rapids: Zondervan, 1979.

Barth, Karl. *Church Dogmatics*, vol. 1:1. Edited by G. W. Bromiley and T. F. Torrance. Edinburgh: T & T Clark, 1975.

———. *Dogmatics in Outline*. New York: Harper, 1959.

Barth, Markus. *Ephesians: Commentary on Chapters 4–6*. New York: Doubleday, 1974.

Barton, Ruth. "How I Changed My Mind About Women in Leadership." In *How I Changed My Mind About Women in Leadership: Compelling Stories from Prominent Evangelicals*. Edited by Alan F. Johnson, 35–48. Grand Rapids: Zondervan, 2010.

Beasley-Murray, G. R. *Baptism In the New Testament*. Grand Rapids: Eerdmans, 1962.

Belcher, Jim. *Deep Church: A Third Way Beyond Emerging and Traditional*. Downers Grove, IL: InterVarsity, 2009.

Belleville, Linda L. "Teaching and Usurping Authority: 1 Timothy 2:11–15." In *Discovering Biblical Equality*. Edited by Ronald W. Pierce and Rebecca Merrill Groothuis, 205–23. Downers Grove: IL: InterVarsity, 2004.

Bethge, Eberhard. *Dietrich Bonhoeffer: A Biography*. Minneapolis: Fortress, 2000.

Bilezikian, Gilbert. *Beyond Sex Roles: What the Bible Says About a Woman's Place in Church and Family*. Grand Rapids: Baker, 1986.

Blamires, Harry. *The Christian Mind*. London: SPCK, 1963.

Boom, Corrie ten, with John Sherrill an Elizabeth Sherrill. *The Hiding Place*. Grand Rapids: Chosen, 2006.

Bonhoeffer, Dietrich. *Spiritual Care*. Translated by Jay C. Rochelle. Minneapolis: Fortress, 1985.

———. *The Cost of Discipleship*. New York: MacMillan, 1963.

Brown, Peter. *The Body and Society: Men, Women, and Sexual Renunciation in Early Christianity*. New York: Columbia University Press, 1988.

Calvin, John. *Institutes of the Christian Religion*, vol. 1–2. Grand Rapids: Eerdmans, 1979.

Carson, Donald A. *Christ and Culture Revisited*. Grand Rapids: Eerdmans, 2008.

Chambers, Oswald. *So Send I You*. London: Marshall, Morgan, and Scott, 1930, 1964.

Chrysostom, John. "Homilies on the Gospel of Matthew: Homily LX," *Nicene And Post-Nicene Fathers*, vol. 10, first series. Edited by Philip Schaff, 372–75. Peabody, MA: Hendrickson, 1995.

————. "To Prove That No One Can Harm The Man Who Does Not Injure Himself," *Nicene and Post-Nicene Fathers*, vol. 9, first series. Edited by Philip Schaff, 267–84. Peabody, MA: Hendrickson, 1995.

Coates, R. J. "Extreme Unction." *Evangelical Dictionary of Theology*. Edited by Walter A. Elwell. Grand Rapids: Baker, 1984, 398.

Covington, Dennis. *Salvation on Sand Mountain*. New York: Addison-Wesley, 1995.

Douglas, J. D., editor. "The Lausanne Covenant." In *Let the Earth Hear His Voice: International Congress on Evangelization, Lausanne, Switzerland*, 2–9. Minneapolis: World Wide Publications, 1975.

Durham, John I. *Exodus: Word Biblical Commentary*. Waco, TX: Word, 1987.

Elliot, Elisabeth. *Let Me Be a Woman: Notes to My Daughter on the Meaning of Womanhood*. Wheaton, IL: Tyndale, 1976.

Edwards, James. "Earthquake in the Mainline," *Christianity Today* (Nov 14, 1994) 38–43.

Erickson, Millard J. *Christian Theology*, vol.2. Grand Rapids: Baker, 1984.

Fee, Gordon D. *God's Empowering Presence: The Holy Spirit in the Letters of Paul*. Peabody, MA: Hendrickson, 1994.

————. "The Priority of Spirit Gifting For Church Ministry." In *Discovering Biblical Equality*, Edited by Ronald W. Pierce and Rebecca Merrill Groothius, 241–54. Downers Grove, IL: InterVarsity, 2004.

Giles, Kevin. "The Subordination of Christ and The Subordination of Women." In *Discovering Biblical Equality*. Edited by Ronald W. Pierce and Rebecca Merrill Groothius, 334–52. Downers Grove, IL: InterVarsity, 2004.

Gillquist, Peter. "A Marathon We Are Meant to Win." *Christianity Today* (October, 1981) 22–23.

Goetz, David L. *Death by Suburb: How to Keep the Suburbs from Killing Your Soul*. San Francisco: Harper, 2006.

Green, Michael. *Evangelism in the Early Church*. Grand Rapids: Eerdmans, 1970.

Grenz, Stanley. "Biblical Priesthood and Women in Ministry." In *Discovering Biblical Equality*, Edited by Ronald W. Pierce and Rebecca Merrill Groothius, 272–86. Downers Grove, IL: InterVarsity, 2004.

Groothius, Rebecca. "Equal in Being, Unequal in Role: Exploring the Logic of Women's Subordination." In *Discovering Biblical Equality*, Edited by Ronald W. Pierce and Rebecca Merrill Groothius, 301–33. Downers Grove, IL: InterVarsity, 2004.

————. *Good News for Women: A Biblical Picture of Gender Equality*. Grand Rapids: Baker, 1997.

Harvey, Thomas Alan. *Acquainted with Grief: Wang Mingdao's Stand for the Persecuted Church in China*. Grand Rapids: Brazos, 2002.

Hauerwas, Stanley and William H. Willimon. *Resident Aliens*. Nashville: Abingdon, 1989.

Hawthorne, Gerald F. *Philippians: Word Biblical Commentary*, vol. 43. Waco, TX: Word, 1983.

Hess, Richard S. "Equality With or Without Innocence: Genesis 1–3." In *Discovering Biblical Equality*. Edited by Ronald W. Pierce and Rebecca Merrill Groothius, 79–95. Downers Grove, IL: InterVarsity, 2004.

Hinlicky, Sarah Hinlicky. "Talking to Generation X." *First Things* (February, 1999). http://www.firstthings.com/article/2008/12/002-talking-to-generation-x-30.

Holmes, Arthur F. *All Truth is God's Truth*. Grand Rapids: Eerdmans, 1977.

Horton, Michael S. "How the Kingdom Comes." *Christianity Today* (January 2006) 46.

———. "Seekers or Tourists?" *Modern Reformation*. (July/August, 2001) 14.

Howard, Thomas. "A Note from Antiquity on the Question of Women's Ordination." *Churchman* 92:4 (1978) 323.

Hunter, James Davison. *To Change The World: The Irony, Tragedy, & Possibility of Christianity in the Late Modern World*. New York: Oxford University Press, 2010.

Johnson, Alan F., editor. *How I Changed My Mind About Women in Leadership: Compelling Stories from Prominent Evangelicals*. Grand Rapids: Zondervan, 2010.

Kierkegaard, Søren. *The Present Age & Of The Difference Between A Genius and an Apostle*. New York: Harper & Row, 1962.

———. *Training in Christianity*. Translated by Walter Lowrie. Princeton, NJ: Princeton University Press, 1957.

Kreeft, Peter. *Jesus-Shock*. South Bend, IN: St. Augustine's Press, 2008.

Kreider, Alan. *The Change of Conversion and the Origin of Christendom*. Harrisburg, PA: Trinity Press International, 1999.

Krupp, Robert A. "Golden Tongue & Iron Will." *Christian History* 44 (1994) 6–11.

Labberton, Mark. *The Dangerous Act of Worship: Living God's Call to Justice*. Downers Grove, IL: InterVarsity, 2007.

Lewis, C. S. *God in the Dock: Essays on Theology and Ethics*. Grand Rapids: Eerdmans, 1970.

———. *The Four Loves*. New York: Harcourt Brace, 1960.

Liefeld, Walter L. "The Nature of Authority in the New Testament." In *Discovering Biblical Equality*. Edited by Ronald W. Pierce and Rebecca Merrill Groothius, 260–70. Downers Grove, IL: InterVarsity, 2004.

Lincoln, Andrew T. *Ephesians: Word Biblical Commentary*. Dallas, TX: Word, 1990.

Lubac, de Henri. *Catholicism: Christ and the Common Destiny of Man*. San Francisco: Ignatius, 1988.

Luther, Martin. "The Babylonian Captivity of the Church." *Three Treatises*, 113–260. Fortress, 1970.

MacDonald, Gordon. *Who Stole My Church? What to Do When the Church You Love Tries to Enter the 21st Century*. Nashville: Thomas Nelson, 2007.

McGrath, Alister E., editor. *The Christian Theology Reader*. Grand Rapids: Baker, 1997.

Nazianzen, Gregory. "The Last Farewell," Oration XLII. *Nicene And Post-Nicene Fathers*, vol. 7, second series. Edited by Philip Schaff, 385–95. Peabody, MA: Hendrickson, 1995.

Newbigin, Leslie, *The Gospel in a Pluralistic Society*. Grand Rapids: Eerdmans, 1989.

Niebuhr, H. Richard. *Christ and Culture*. New York: Harper, 1951.

———. *The Kingdom of God in America*. New York: Harper, 1953.

Olson, Roger E. *The Story of Christian Theology: Twenty Centuries of Tradition and Reform*. Downers Grove, IL: InterVarsity, 1999.

Orwell, George. "Politics and the English Language," 1946. Text source: Orwell Project by O. Dag. — 1999-2004 www.orwell.ru) 5.

Packer, J. I. "Let's Stop Making Women Presbyters." *Christianity Today* (February, 1991) 18–21.

Palmer, Parker J. *The Courage To Teach: Exploring The Inner Landscape of a Teacher's Life* San Francisco: Jossey-Bass, 1998.

Seaver, George. *David Livingstone: His Life and Letters*. New York: Harper & Brothers, 1957.

Scotti, R. A. *Basilica: The Splendor and the Scandal: Building St. Peter's*. New York: Viking, 2006.

Sittser, Gerald L. *A Grace Disguised: How the Soul Grows Through Loss*. Grand Rapids: Zondervan, 1996.

———. *Water from a Deep Well: Christian Spirituality From Early Martyrs to Modern Missionaries*. Downers Grove, IL: InterVarsity, 2007.

Snodgrass, Klyne. *Ephesians: The NIV Application Commentary*. Grand Rapids: Zondervan, 1996.

Spener, Philip Jacob. *Pia Desideria*. Philadelphia: Fortress, 1967.

Spurgeon, Charles Haddon. *The Metropolitan Tabrnacle Pulpit,* vol. 12. Pasadena, TX: Pilgrim, 1973.

Stackhouse, John Jr. "How to Produce An Egalitarian Man." In *How I Changed My Mind About Women in Leadership: Compelling Stories from Prominent Evangelicals*. Edited by Alan F. Johnson, 235–44. Grand Rapids: Zondervan, 2010.

Stedman, Ray. "Giving and Living." In *Discovery Publishing*, 1995. www.raystedman. org/new-testament/1-corinthians/giving-and-living

Steiner, George. *Errata: An Examined Life*. New Haven: Yale University Press, 1997.

———. *Real Presences*. Chicago: University of Chicago Press, 1991.

Stevens, Paul. "Breaking the Gender Impasse." *Christianity Today* (January 13, 1992) 235–44.

Stott, John R. W. *God's New Society: Ephesians*. Downers Grove, IL: InterVarsity, 1979.

———. *The Living Church: Convictions of a Lifelong Pastor*. Downers Grove, IL: InterVarsity, 2007.

———. *The Spirit, the Church, and the World: The Message of Acts*. Downers Grove, IL: InterVarsity, 1990.

Sullivan, Andrew. "When Not Seeing Is Believing." *Time* (October 9, 2006) 58–60.

Sumner, Sarah. "Bridging the Ephesians 5 Divide." *Christianity Today* (December, 2005) 59-61.

Suurmond, Jean-Jacques. "A Fresh Look at Spirit-Baptism and the Charisms." *Expository Times* 109 (January, 1998) 103–6.

Thielicke, Helmut. *The Waiting Father: Sermons on the Parables of Jesus*. Translated by John W. Doberstein. New York: Harper & Brothers, 1959.

Thiselton, Anthony C. *The First Epistle of Corinthians*. The New International Greek Testament Commentary. Grand Rapids: Eerdmans, 2000.

Towner, Philip H. *1–2 Timothy & Titus: The IVP New Testament Commentary Series*. Downers Grove, IL: InterVarsity, 1994.

Towns, Elmer L. *10 of Today's Most Innovative Churches*. Ventura, CA: Regal, 2990.

Wallace, R. S. "Sacrament." *Evangelical Dictionary of Theology*. Edited by Walter A. Elwell. Grand Rapids: Baker, 1984, 965.

Williamson, G. I. *The Westminster Confession of Faith*. Philadelphia: Presbyterian and Reformed, 1964.

Webber, Robert. *Exploring the Worship Spectrum*. Edited by Paul A. Basden. Grand Rapids: Zondervan, 2004.

Wendel, Francois. *Calvin: The Origins and Development of His Religious Thought*. New York: HarperCollins, 1963.

Wesley, John. "An Address to Clergy." In *The Works of the Rev. John Wesley*, vol. X, 480–500. London: Wesleyan-Methodist Book-Room, n.d..

———. "Letter on Preaching Christ," In *The Works of the Rev. John Wesley*, vol. XI, 486–92. London: Wesleyan-Methodist Book-Room, n.d..

Willimon, William H. *The Intrusive Word: Preaching to the Unbaptized*. Grand Rapids: Eerdmans, 1994.

White, R. E. O. *Christian Ethics*. Philadelphia: John Knox, 1981.

Wright, Christopher J. H. *The Mission of God: Unlocking the Bible's Grand Narrative*. Downers Grove, IL: InterVarsity, 2006.

Zwingli. "An Account of the Faith of Zwingli." In *On Providence and Other Essays*. Edited by Samuel Jackson and William John Hinke, 42–43. Durham, NC: Labyrinth, 1983.